Understanding Argument

The Journey from Consumer to Critic, Critic to Advocate

Second Edition

Paul Bingham
Korry Harvey
Steve Woods
Western Washington University

greatriver
TECHNOLOGIES

Contents

ACKNOWLEDGMENTS

The Authors would like to take this opportunity to thank the many students, mentors, and colleagues we have worked with through the years. Their invaluable guidance and feedback are the foundation upon which this work is laid. Although too numerous to name individually without unintentionally leaving someone out, we wanted to particularly thank the many wonderful debate coaches, partners and judges who have played a very direct role in shaping and forming our thoughts about argumentation and debate. The debate community has been very much like a family for us. And on that note, a very special thanks goes to our families for their patience and understanding. Each has been an unfailing source of support, without which this text surely would never have been completed. We owe them a tremendous debt of gratitude. We also appreciate the support we have received from Western Washington University and the Department of Communication. Particular thanks go out to the Western Debate Union and the ongoing excellence of the students and fellow coaches in inspiring and supporting our dreams. Finally, we are grateful to the good people at Great River Technologies and Kendall Hunt Publishing for the support they have offered in making this all possible.

INTRODUCTION

As a basic tool for solving problems and making difficult decisions, argumentation is a valuable communication skill. Unresolved problems can slowly eat away at a relationship, whether an interpersonal one between individuals or an international one between entire countries. Unfortunately, many people consider arguing to be impolite and negative, no matter the situation. They see conflict as something to be avoided at nearly any cost. However, it is important to understand that argument is inevitable. Even when there is good reason to avoid a conflict, sometimes it simply cannot be done. While conflict certainly can be confrontational and result in negative outcomes, there is also a great deal of potential value in the pointing out of different perspectives which could lead to better decision-making and greater understanding among people. It is not our intention to suggest in any way that people should argue with one another without purpose. Instead, it is our goal to encourage people to see argumentation as a tool that, when used properly, can help to manage and resolve conflicts rather than make them worse.

This text will help you become comfortable and competent in engaging in argument in the form of a debate. Debate requires people to bring their concerns and differences out into the open where they can be defined, discussed, and hopefully managed. Sometimes simply defining a problem or conflict in clear terms is enough to make its solution evident. If not, then the back and forth nature of organized argument can at least make it possible to make use of reasoned judgment in thoughtfully considering the available options and then selecting the one that seems best. But what exactly do we mean by *argumentation* and *debate*? While these are common terms, it is important to take a look at them in a specific way as we prepare to learn and put into practice our own argumentation and debate skills.

An **argument** is more than a mere disagreement between two parties. Often we think of the summary of differences between two people as an argument. However, the pointing out and listing of disagreements is simply the place where we identify an argument as existing, not an actual argument itself. Later in the text we will lay out the specific components of an argument in greater detail, but for now it is sufficient to note that an argument is composed of elements of support beyond a simple statement of opposition or contradiction. Further, simply making a controversial statement does not necessarily mean one has made a complete and explicit argument. Of course the complexity of argument varies greatly, but it is important as both a consumer and composer of argument that one understands the basic elements in order to understand the relative worth of a point of view.

It is also good to understand that not all arguments take place in the context of a debate. **Debate** tends to designate a formal and organized means to engage in advocacy, which in turn allows for the development and comparison of differing ideas. An informal argument between two friends may take on elements of a debate because of a sense of mutual respect. The two friends may like each other well enough and respect each other's opinions enough to let each other take turns making statements, or reminding each other to stay on "topic." In other cases, there may not be the framework of a personal relationship in place to moderate the persons involved in an argument, but rather a formal structure imposed by an agenda, parliamentary procedure, rules of operation, charter, or other means that serve to formalize the exchange of ideas, both adversarial and supportive. This text will largely focus on the specific form of academic debate that designates a topic to be discussed and the assignment of formal sides or positions for those participating. It is a learning tool, and in many ways a sort of "game" as well, though certainly an educational game, not solely recreational activity or for amusement.

A Good Argument is Well Constructed and Supported

Moving beyond simple disagreement requires a foundation in sound reasoning and the appropriate support for that foundation. In other words, good arguments should utilize a structure that helps the arguer to construct valid positions. There is a basic need in productive argumentation to bring forward good reasons to substantiate one's claims when they are an advocate for a particular position or point of view. There is an argumentative burden placed upon an advocate who is seeking to make a claim that their viewpoint is more beneficial than some other. This text will address some of the various models and elements that are used in this construction.

GOALS FOR THE READER

Although there are already several fine argumentation and debate texts out there, in writing this text we hope to address argumentation from more of a practical perspective than solely an academic or theoretical approach. In our experience, argumentation makes the most sense when we can see the application it has to our everyday lives. While recognizing that there is indeed an important purpose for the more highly specialized debate handbooks available, this effort is directed less toward the argument theorist or experienced academic debate student than toward a more general audience. In our combined experience of teaching argumentation and coaching debate for over four decades, we have witnessed a real need for an approach to argumentation, critical thinking, and debate that is accessible to those outside of a school's competitive debate team.

Everyone faces conflict and challenge in their lives. Everyone is subject to a myriad of political and social messages on a regular basis. Everyone is tasked with making difficult decisions. It is our hope that this text can assist the reader in understanding the intricacies of argumentation, and in so doing act as a guide along the journey from being simply a consumer of argument to becoming a critic of argument, and then acting as an advocate for those things they believe. Rather than passively being bombarded by arguments (via the media, religious institutions, the government, political campaigns, social movements, etc.), our intention is to help people develop the skills necessary to recognize when argument is coming at them, to critically assess the argument for its validity, and then to respond appropriately by either spreading the message or effectively confronting it. In a world that is changing as rapidly as ours currently is, such skills seem to be in great demand.

While debate can seem complex, and in some ways that is its value, there are also distinct benefits that participating in debate can help to develop. The method of debate is a unique chance to advance both basic and complex learning goals and often in an integrated fashion. Debating should add to your self confidence as well, as being experienced and comfortable in engaging in a difference of opinion can help to create more confidence in each subsequent encounter, both formal and informal.

Specifically, the goals of this text include the ability to understand the theory of argument as it relates to its construction and also its context. You should be able to know what specific elements make up an argument and how those parts influence the overall quality and validity of the whole. Your understanding of theory should also help you to understand how audience, time, and other elements of context can influence how an argument can be constructed. Which is the second specific goal: you should be able to construct an argument. After you have read this text, using research and your understanding of argument structure, you will be able to put together a position of advocacy in support of an idea. The third goal is based on getting practice in debate: the ability to present your arguments more effectively in a public setting. Often the hard part of speaking up in a public setting is lacking the knowledge or the ability to create a strategy for presentation that is engaging and persuasive. Once you have done the work to understand argument and build one for yourself, in many ways, the actual presentation part is easy.

This text will help you to create a framework or organizational structure for your ideas that is appropriate for the situation or context in which you need to present them. In some cases, you may have more time and ability to go into detail in presenting your position; in other cases, you may need to say less and create more of an impression in a shorter time. Part of that comes from being informed. It is easier to think of ways to support your argument, or even think about how to structure it, if you know some things about the issue. Familiarity with a topic requires additional research into both facts and ideas about your topic. And, once you have all of those elements in order, the meaning of "practice" is not only the practical application of theory, but also the concept of running through a presentation a few times before giving it, or engaging in organized discussions on topics in order to work on being able to extemporaneously discuss complex ideas more easily.

PLAN FOR THE TEXT

The organization of the text is fairly straightforward. Part I will offer a basic understanding of the foundations of argumentation, decision-making, and conflict management. Making an actual argument is a bit more complicated than simply expressing a controversial claim or assertion. A complete argument includes supporting the claim with evidence and/or reasoning as well as an explanation of the claim's significance and the denial of counterarguments. Likewise, there is more than just one way to reach a decision, and the many different types of conflicts we all face call for management techniques that are situational in nature. In other words, no two arguments or conflicts are exactly the same, and an appropriate response should reflect these differences.

In Part II of the text we begin to assess critically the validity of arguments. When critically evaluating an argument, we will test the language, the evidence, and the reasoning that is used to substantiate the claim in question. It should perhaps be noted here that, rather than delving into the complex world of formal logic, we will instead concern ourselves with the use of informal logic—basic reasoning and sound judgment. It has been said that "some people don't mean what they say, while others don't say what they mean." In this section of the text we will work on the skills that will help us to look beyond the simple words expressed in an argument to understand more genuinely the message being portrayed.

Part III will address the presentation of arguments in both spoken and written form, as well as the implications of nonverbal communication. Because so much of what we communicate with one another is never spoken, if we fail to recognize the nonverbal signs we may be missing the point.

Finally, Part IV will take a look at competitive debate in various formats. This chapter also will address the complicated skill of effectively writing in an argumentative form.

Although, as mentioned previously, this text is not primarily concerned with teaching formalized debate techniques and procedures, they do serve an important role in helping the student to understand argumentation theory. Many, perhaps even most, of those who read this text will never find themselves in a formalized, competitive debate setting. Nevertheless, the skills one can gain by practicing these skills in the relative safety and comfort of the classroom are easily applied to a wide variety of life experiences, including learning how to research a topic thoroughly, defend an important idea effectively, make your claims more persuasive, and gain confidence in speaking in front of a group of people. It is our intention to convince the reader that arguing constructively is neither as scary nor as difficult as one might think. Who knows, you might even find that you enjoy it.

PART I

ARGUMENTATION: WHAT IS IT?

CHAPTER 1

THE BASICS OF BUILDING ARGUMENTS

To repeat what others have said requires education; to challenge it requires brains.
Mary Pettibone Poole

Fear not those who argue but those who dodge.
Marie von Ebner-Eschenbach

To argue with a man who has renounced the use and authority of reason. . .is like administering medicine to the dead.
Thomas Paine

Think about situations when you may have been in an argument. Did the parties involved get angry as a result? Did the discussion end up improving understanding and leading to a better way of doing things? We may argue about little things: Which movie should we go see? Where should we eat dinner? What is the best way to get to school? We may argue about more important things: What is just treatment for those who have committed crimes? Who should our elected leaders be? How should tax money be spent? Arguments stem from a difference of opinion amongst people about the way things are or what course of events should take place. It is a perfectly normal way for humans to interact, and is often quite essential for positive outcomes for all, even those who may have entered the discussion with a different point of view than may end up being the final outcome. For example, you may have wanted to go to a fast food restaurant because you felt it would be a cheaper option and it was more recognizable to you, but were convinced that eating at a food truck serving homemade tamales was an OK idea, and you ended up spending less and eating better! The authors of your text firmly believe in the positive nature of argument as interaction and feel that it is easier to get a positive outcome by better understanding what argumentation is and how to do it.

The primary focus of this text is the analysis and construction of arguments. Of course, the presentation of argument will also be covered related to a specific form of argument, that of debating, but before we get to that stage it is important to understand what an argument is. In many popular understandings, argument is seen as a type of interpersonal conflict that involves anger and irrationality. People often think that arguments are things that should be avoided, or show a failure of communication on the part of people engaged in an argument. Unfortunately, this can be very true in many instances. But consider a world without argument. How would people register their disagreement with one another or advance competing ideas for what is "good" or "fair"? Perhaps what is important, then, is to think of argumentation as a tool. The next question becomes how to use that tool both civilly and effectively. The goal of an argument should not be just to win the argument, or to make one's point of view the dominant one, but to lead to better decision-making and understanding among the persons involved. As such, this text will teach an understanding of the elements and structure of an argument that can be used constructively.

To begin this understanding, conceptualizing an "argument" as a complex construction of reason and support for a claim (or overall advocacy in some cases) is critical. An argument is not the concluding idea, or the final action an advocate is trying to get across, but the supporting elements of fact and reason that lead to that conclusion or call to action. Often the failure of an argument, and the breakdown of reasoning that precipitates the popular view of an argument as an angered and irrational exchange, is due to the lack of reason or support for what is being said. People often express what they want or what they think, but not why.

To help you be able to think about arguments in a more complete and complex manner, and, ultimately, to understand better the arguments presented to you and to help you construct your own arguments more effectively, we will begin with a look at the structure of an argument. Later we will contextualize these constructions in specific ways that will allow you to practice and test your arguments through the use of debate in a variety of formats. Ultimately the goal is to help you engage arguments you encounter in meaningful and constructive ways no matter in which context they arise, informal or formal. While most often you will encounter arguments as a receiver of those messages that will require you to make decisions about what to accept or not accept, you will also want to learn how to be an effective producer of arguments capable of stating your ideas rationally and reasonably.

Box 1-1 BASIC ETYMOLOGY OF ARGUE AND ARGUMENT

The historical roots of the word argument provide an explanation to the multiple common usages of the word in Modern English. Tracing the long evolution of the word from Proto-Indo European (PIE) roots over the last 6,000 years shows how some of the different meanings and connotations of the word were incorporated over time. The root "Arg": meaning to shine; white; was often used in reference to silver. One of the uses of the root "Arg": brilliant, clear; was incorporated into Latin and used as a verb: to make clear, to demonstrate. The same base is used in the construction of several Latin words including: "Arguere" to make clear, demonstrate; and the related: "Argutare," to prattle, babble; and "Argutari" to babble foolishly, childishly. Several of the Latin based words were incorporated into Old French, and later adopted in English.

The modern word "argument," and the closely related verb "to argue," have both undergone an evolution and presently have multiple meanings.

PIE: Arg: "to shine; white"

PIE: Arg-u: "Brilliant; clear"

PIE/Latin: Argu-yo: "to make clear, demonstrate"

Latin: Arguere: "to make clear; prove, allege; demonstrate"

Latin: Argutare: "to prattle, babble, chatter"

Latin: Argutari: "babble foolishly, childishly"

To argue, a verb, is to engage in an exchange of ideas centered on a common subject matter. In the context of a debate, to argue is to present ideas in an effort to persuade. **Arguing,** outside of the academic world, usually has a negative connotation; while inside the academy the practice is a core activity. We believe the concept should be viewed in a non-normative way; arguing is neither good nor bad, it is simply a communication form that is commonly used by humans. While in the abstract *arguing* and *argument* are neutral terms, there are of course good and bad arguments. Heated, emotional, angry yelling matches are not good (arguments), nor are calm cool collected reasons why the Holocaust did not happen (an argument). Each kind of argument must be viewed in its own context before the basic "goodness" can be judged.

Although Box 1-1 above does not present a complete, formal etymology of the words, and the definitions provided are abbreviated, taking into consideration all of the avenues the words examined have meandered down reveals the complexities of their common usage. The pejorative meaning of root words in Latin clearly influences our understanding of argument as a squabble where people blather on. In the grander world outside of the classroom, it is unlikely that a revolution will occur concerning the way that the words *argument* and *argue* are understood. However, in class, your authors hope that people embrace the non-normative meanings of the words, and look to incorporate this new understanding into the way that they think about the terms in the larger world.

ACADEMIC UNDERSTANDING OF AN ARGUMENT

Intellectual interest in argument is easily traced to the ancients. The Western-based understanding and development of argument are tied directly to the golden age of Athens in ancient Greece. As Greek society gained power and wealth, a new class of scholars arose, freed from the labors of the material world and dedicated to understanding the metaphysical world. There is also an aspect of evolving forms of participatory democracy leading to an interest in the study of argument. As the people could have a say in how the power and resources were allocated in a democratic system, rather than the authoritative non-argumentative proclamations of kings or chieftains dictating what was done, members of the society could have influence on those decisions. The ability to argue was a way in which people could have the capacity to shape their own destinies through words rather than violence.[1]

---

[1] Admittedly, the Greek democratic project was not completely open to participation as there were still those left out of the ability to vote or participate in government, like women and slaves. But let this be a reminder that our abilities to participate, to in fact argue, are important parts of our civil life to be practiced in both the sense of learning how to do it, and then actually doing so.

Great thinkers of the time involved themselves in a project to understand argument from a perspective of truth. The concept of the "ideal" form of truth was an accepted way of thinking, and arguments were used to reveal that truth as closely as possible. Quite literally, **rhetoric**, or the strategic and thoughtful use of language, was seen as the hand-maiden to truth, the means by which it could be revealed after its discovery. Plato, Socrates, Aristotle, and others devoted themselves to knowledge acquisition and education of the youth. In fact, your participation today in learning "how to argue" is directly related to these ideas developed 2,000 years ago.

The development of inductive and deductive reasoning is often attributed to these Greek thinkers. The Greeks had understanding of how *pathos* (emotional appeals), *ethos* (the credibility of the speaker), and *logos* (logical or analytical appeals) contributed to the success of the speaker. As a main element of being persuasive, the Greeks evolved an understanding of argument in the abstract, applying their ideas on the formalization of good and bad arguments in the form of logical fallacies. Over one hundred different logical fallacies were identified and analyzed. "Good" and "bad" arguments became understood in this theoretical context, an absolutist perspective that left little room for a practical or functional understanding of an argument. If a statement lacked one or more parts, then it was not an argument. Arguments were viewed as tools used to uncover previously unknown truths. This overall perspective shaped the way that argument was addressed in the modern academic tradition, tied into the study of logic and housed in the philosophic realm in early universities. An argument would be dissected into its constituent parts and their interaction analyzed to determine the validity of a given argument. Individual arguments were good or bad based on their absolutist adherence to developed patterns. This absolutism stemmed from that accepted belief in an absolute, unchanging truth discussed earlier.

THE TOULMIN ARGUMENT MODEL

Argument was examined in this purely formal way until the twentieth century, when almost by chance a new model for defining an argument was developed by Stephen Toulmin in his 1958 work *The Uses of Argument*. Frustrated with the limitations and flaws of the traditional study of logic, Toulmin introduced a practical model for understanding what "an argument" is.

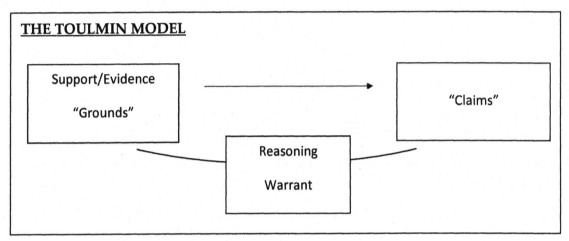

Figure 1-1 The Toulmin Model

Though met with some skepticism in his native Britain, Toulmin's work was widely adopted in the United States and currently serves as a primary model to understand and analyze argument in the field of rhetorical communication. Originally intended as a commentary on written argument, the model was adopted to analyze verbal argument as well. Focusing on practicality, the **Toulmin Model** provides a way of analyzing any given set of ideas that are presented as an argument. Unlike in the Greek tradition, a statement that lacks or under-develops one or more particular parts is still an argument, just one that is not particularly powerful. We will take a look at this model to understand a contemporary understanding of what an argument is. The elements that Toulmin identifies and then explains in terms of how they interact are all based on elements with which we already have great familiarity.

The idea that people make "claims" is something even those considering only bad arguments would readily recognize. The idea that people offer "evidence" or "grounds" to back up their claims is also something we may be familiar with, and even have actively employed as part of our normal day-to-day decision-making. It is the element of "warrant" that is a bit more abstract, and requires a specific definition to get at the meaning of Toulmin's model. Where the Greeks could rely on breakdowns of formal logic known as fallacies to warrant or disqualify an argument, Toulmin's understanding reflects that not everyone is going to share common assumptions about what counts as formal logic. They also may not agree on the known "truths" that would be upheld through the codification of fallacies. The key distinction is that Toulmin accepts a contingent or socially determined truth as an element of an argument rather than the Greek reliance on a homogenous cultural understanding of Truth. The distinction between little "t" truth and capital "T" Truth is intended. The "t"ruth is something that is socially constructed about things for which empirical evidence or logical analysis may not necessarily be the best means of resolution. For example, questions such as "are people naturally lazy or industrious?" lead to development of government policy based on appeals such as: "the number of people on welfare should be reduced because they are lazy and need an incentive to be independent." If you hold the ontological belief that people are by nature lazy then the argument makes sense. However, if you believe that many of the people on welfare are just caught in a tough situation through corporate down-sizing, jobs being sent overseas, or a downturn in the technology sector then it is not such a good argument (or reason for a claim).

THE CLAIM—THE ASSERTION

The basic premise that the advocate is asking his or her audience to accept is the **claim**; the essence of an argument. Claims can suggest information or a belief that the speaker is attempting to persuade others to hold, or a course of action that the advocate suggests should be followed. Claims are usually presented at the beginning of an argument and function like a topic sentence in a written paragraph. The claim is the umbrella that all other parts of the argument fit under and support. One way of thinking about it is that although the claim may be the first thing an arguer says, it is also the conclusion the arguer wishes the audience or an opponent to reach. Everything can be a claim: the sky is the limit, more money more problems, love is all we need, pizza should never be microwaved; almost any idea that is presented by an advocate can be a claim.

For our example let us follow the argumentative claim that "handguns make people safer."

THE GROUNDS—THE SUPPORT

Different argument texts use different words to describe the next feature of an argument in the Toulmin Model, but the principle is generally the same. The **grounds** (or evidence or data) are the information that is used to support the claim. The grounds attempt to answer the "why" question by representing the "because" part behind the claim. The premises used to justify the claim are included in the grounds. The grounds can be facts, figures, data, expert testimony, common observations—basically anything that helps to show why the claim in question is "true" or valid. The grounds are usually presented directly after the claim.

In our example of handguns and safety, the grounds may be that handguns protect people from home invasions. In this case we would expect some form of empirical data to be introduced. What is the basis for saying that handguns protect people from home invasions unless there is some form of factual support? Is the evidence that is offered an article from the local paper about a gun-toting Granny protecting herself from an attack, or is it an extensive and comprehensive examination of home invasion statistics? Advocates need to be careful that the grounds that they present are not simply a restatement of the claim—"handguns make people safer because people with guns are safer," in order to avoid circular reasoning, or the "Begging the Question" logical fallacy. There needs to be an answer to the question "why?"

THE WARRANT—THE LOCALE OF REASONING

Just because a fact that is used to support a claim is "true" does not necessarily make the overall claim true. The **warrant(s)** is (are) the principle(s) and/or provision(s) that show that the grounds provided are appropriate proof for the claim being presented. The warrant clarifies the assumption made about how the grounds support the claim and acts as a bridge between the two. Often this element is thought of as the "reasoning" for the connection between the evidence and the claim. In the handgun claim, the "gun-toting Granny" anecdote may well be true in the example given (in other words, the facts in that case are

16

accurate), but should one potentially isolated instance of an event be generalized to all home invasions? The statistical analysis may be more defendable as proof if in fact it can show that its results are more generalizable because of the total number of examples examined.

We might define **reasoning** as the capacity for logical, rational, and critical thought, or to use sound judgment in drawing inferences or conclusions. Accordingly, "to reason" is to argue or deliberate logically or with good sense. Before we can test the validity of reasoning processes, we must first understand some of the basic characteristics of some common reasoning types.

Reasoning By Analogy

The human brain tends to utilize patterns of association and similarity in its thinking processes. If a particular perception or idea fits reasonably well into an existing pattern, we are more likely to accept it as being valid. Working under this assumption, to **reason by analogy** is to make a comparison between two cases (these could be people, character traits, cars, cities, etc.) and to infer that what is true of one case is also true of the other. We will look more specifically at two different types of analogies. The first is a **figurative analogy**, which refers to a comparison between two or more items that are each of different types, classes, or categories. For instance, we might suggest that "children are like birds—they need the freedom to fly." Children are obviously not birds, but the analogy may prove helpful in illustrating a useful point that you are trying to make. Nor or are all people attacked like defenseless Grannies; most would believe themselves more capable, making the analogy even stronger—if a "Granny" can do it, I certainly can! But because figurative analogies compare items of different categories or types, they are typically useful for illustration purposes only. The second type of analogy, a **literal analogy**, is a comparison between two or more items of the same type or category, and therefore a literal analogy might be quite useful when used as proof for your claims. In fact, when faced with an aggressive and weapon-wielding attacker, you *are* as defenseless as a Granny and at a relative disadvantage to a motivated and seasoned attacker.

Causal Reasoning

Also referred to as "cause and effect," **causal reasoning** is used to indicate that a certain force (the cause) is directly responsible for something else (an effect). When presenting an argument, it is a good practice to attempt to demonstrate that a causal relationship is in operation. By showing the "links" between variables, you help the audience to better understand the connections behind your claims. It is important to make sure that you are going beyond mere coincidence, or correlation. Although difficult to do, establishing causation is highly persuasive to an audience. Not only does it give your argument a greater degree of credibility, but it also gives your audience a sense of security in that people like to feel as if they can somehow predict what will happen in the future, and causal evidence offers the closest thing to that. It is surprising how many people will accept the assertion of a causal relationship without question, even when the evidence is weak. Just how many examples of Grannies were examined? Are there any counter-examples that would show the presence of a gun in fact turned out to make the situation worse for the "defender" who produced it or had it in their residence?

Reasoning From Sign

To **reason from sign** is to infer a relationship or correlation between two variables, where the absence or presence of one variable indicates the absence or presence of the other. It assumes that the variables in question are reliable markers for one another. Signs can take several forms, including actual symbols, behaviors, symptoms, religious icons, social or political actions, and many others. One particular form of reasoning from sign is called **effect-to-cause reasoning**, such as when a criminal investigator looks at physical evidence signs (e.g., fingerprints, blood, and tissue samples) as an indicator of whether or not a particular individual was the perpetrator of a crime. Likewise, a doctor uses the symptoms of swollen glands, slight fever, and little red bumps on the arms and chest as a basis for diagnosing chicken pox. For our handgun example, it may be harder to conceive of someone applying this type of reasoning to this combination of evidence-to-claim. How good would be an argument that said that when guns are present it is a sign that a crime will not occur? Does that not also justify an interpretation of the signs to be that crimes occur because of the presence of guns?

Inductive Reasoning

Inductive reasoning, or induction, is the examination of a set of particulars (examples) in order to form a general conclusion. In other words, it is the assumption that what is true of the individual parts will also hold to be true of the whole. Also known as reasoning from example, inductive reasoning is the basis of the scientific method–the establishment of generalized theories based on limited observations. When used properly, inductive reasoning can help improve the ability to draw accurate conclusions and forecast the likely outcomes of future events, even in situations where there is limited data. This ability to make projections, whether economic forecasts, political prognostications, ecological ramifications, or others, means that inductive reasoning is a potentially powerful problem-solving tool. However, there are also dangers associated with inductive reasoning. Inaccurate conclusions can be drawn if observations are faulty or are based on too few or unrepresentative samples. Due to its speculative nature, if it is rushed along too hastily, the chance of error with inductive reasoning is high. This is directly relatable to our example of handguns. Is this too quick or too limited of a basis on which to make a judgment about guns and protection from crime? This is often referred to as a hasty generalization—and the way to avoid a hasty generalization is to ask, is the data introduced into the debate comprehensive and substantial enough to be considered reasonable for drawing general conclusions?

Deductive Reasoning

The relative opposite of inductive reasoning is **deductive reasoning,** or deduction, which refers to the application of a general principle to a specific instance. Deduction is the assumption that what is true of the whole will also hold to be true of the individual parts. Just as inductive reasoning has a basis in the scientific method, so too does deductive reasoning, only from the opposite direction. Whereas induction is used to establish general theories, deduction begins with a hypothesis or theory and assumes that this general scientific rule can be applied to all cases. As with inductive reasoning, deductive reasoning can be either valid or invalid depending on the situation in which it is applied. If, in fact, a comprehensive examination of all reported home invasion and gun-defended interaction is accounted for, one might be in a position to deduce about that relationship (even to the extent of knowing if Grannies are a strange anomaly for effectiveness, or equal, or less in effect).

With the Toulmin Model, these three concepts (claim, grounds, warrant) need to be present in order for an argument to be persuasive and provide sufficient proof. These elements are not always presented in order, are sometimes combined with one another, and often the different parts are presented as one string of ideas, leaving them undifferentiated from one another. Regardless of the order in which they are presented, it is important to develop and practice the skill of following and understanding an argument by looking for each of the three concepts and being able to analyze not only each one, but their interrelationship with one another.

Some additional, more detailed means of analyzing arguments are developed by Toulmin as a secondary set of concepts in the model. Although not required, they are often included in "good" arguments. In everyday application, arguments are typically offered in a vacuum, meaning that they are presented without an implicit engagement of any pre-existing discussion. The academic world is premised on building the total wealth of human knowledge with each idea and extension of the ideas that have already been developed. In academics, arguments are usually presented in the context of a larger discussion, with a recognition that they compete with previously held ideas. The second set of components in the Toulmin Model is particularly applicable to situations where the argument is being made in specific fields, where any given argument is presented within the context of an established dispute. The assumptions defense experts make about a certain state of affairs will change the way that they evaluate, or even understand, risks and the weighing of competing evidence about situations, compared to a group of political activists, or indigenous communities in the middle of a conflict. For our example, an association of law enforcement officers is likely to evaluate the argument on access to handguns differently than a jury hearing a case involving the gun-toting Granny. The concepts of backing, qualifier, and reservation are all useful in preemptively answering challenges to the arguments that are likely to emerge from the existing world of ideas. These components are used to strengthen an argument and to dismiss the common objections that the receiver of an argument is likely to hold.

BACKING

Not all warrants will supply enough reasoning and analysis for everyone to accept the claim as "true." **Backing** provides additional support, analysis, and credentials for the reasoning behind the warrant. The claim about the Granny could be constructed to show that even someone considered weak and likely physically challenged in some ways could still even the score with a far more dangerous attacker by having a gun. The grounds justify the claim (guns protect you), the warrant justifies the grounds (you *can* generalize in some ways about Grannies who are not like you), and the backing shows why the warrant is logical for the argument (the least likely to succeed at using a gun for defense still did). Backing can also function as further warranting if the original warrant is rejected by the recipient of the argument.

QUALIFIER

Rarely do actual arguments attempt to be universal "truths," and Toulmin developed his model out of frustration with the established methods of analyzing arguments that traditionally placed a premium on the universality of a potential argument. The **qualifier** in an argument explains when and how an argument is applicable, and recognizes the relative strength of a given claim. The limits of the claim or the degree to which it is "true" are identified by the qualifier(s) presented. From a practical perspective, the more realistic an argument is, the more persuasive it will be. Modifiers (usually, often, in this case, assuming, etc.) are frequently used when qualification of an argument is presented. Some qualifying statements for the handgun example might include: "When isolated and far from emergency responders…"; "If law enforcement support has been severely reduced…"; "In situations where you are highly vulnerable (temporarily, long-term based on societal standards, or by circumstance)…" Qualifiers are often presented after the claim, grounds, warrant(s), and backing are presented; but they can also be presented earlier on in order to establish the applicability of the claim.

RESERVATION

Also called "rebuttal" by some, the **reservation(s)** presented in an argument answer common objections to the claim.[2] Like qualification, reservations suggest that arguments are not universally true, but rather should be applied to the situations in which they reasonably fit. Advocates who present reservations to their arguments strengthen their credibility and deprive potential opponents of the ideas that would normally be used to counter the argument. In the case of our Granny gunner, the presenter might try to point out that the Granny had been attacked in the past, before she had a gun, or to show how she has been free of crime since the instance in question in order to establish a cause and effect relationship. The presenter might say, "as a response to an attack earlier, she chose to defend herself and, when the situation arose again, she came out with a positive rather than negative result." It even sets up the rebuttal that it is too late to realize you are at a disadvantage until you are in one; guns preemptively create balance in an aggressor-defender situation.

In both competitive debate and everyday argument, advocates generally do not wish to provide ammunition to their opponents. Thus, speakers rarely use the latter two parts of the Toulmin Model, with the hope that their opponents will not bring up the issues. In debate (either competitive or everyday debates) there is a back and forth to any given dispute, so advocates have an opportunity to qualify and refute in later presentations. Advocates generally try to present their arguments as strongly as possible, and then react to the objections raised by their opponents. So the actions of qualification and reservations will occur, but they do not necessarily need to be a formal part of an argument. However, in some circumstances, an advocate will want to be preemptive, and in those situations speakers will incorporate these left-out concepts when presenting their arguments.

---

[2] The text will use the word "rebuttal" to describe what happens when people respond to the arguments of others, and also as the name for a specific kind of speech in debate, so the use of "reservation" in this section is intended to avoid confusion.

APPLICATION OF THE TOULMIN MODEL

The basic understanding of the Toulmin Model as presented here may raise some questions about your experience of and expectations about argumentation. In some ways, Toulmin is saying that these formal structures and standards for arguments exist, yet acknowledges that there is an informal element to them. This idea once again speaks to the contingent element of public discussion and contemporary policy that makes the actual application of argument more relative than absolute. As you consider your own interactions with argumentation, both currently and in the future, in what ways will you be an expert or an outsider to the argument being addressed? The realm of politics brings together the opinions of experts (those giving congressional testimony, professionals in bureaucratic agencies, publicly recognized experts), and those of the public at large as moderated by representatives who have a variety of constituencies. There is a need to consider a balance between both the role of the expert and the amount of access that the public has in participating in making reasoned decisions about an issue. In what ways can you use your understanding of an argument to contribute to this community of ideas? How can your advocacy be made both "stronger" in construction and of greater "quality" for its representation, as well as better acknowledge other viewpoints and opinions?

As already described, the Toulmin Model is a leap forward in terms of understanding the arguments that people use in everyday life. Toulmin developed the model further in his latter works, as he witnessed his model being adopted in a wider context then he originally intended. The explanation of the model in this text is a simplistic summary; in more advanced applications, the model is further complicated with additional detail. Although the model is adopted for use in analyzing verbal arguments, your authors feel that the model's strengths lie in written argument, a subject to be covered later in this text. Although the Toulmin Model seeks to analyze any given argument, it can be redundant or inefficient in some ways.[3] Although the Toulmin Model is far

---

[3] Depending on the context of a given argument, it can be difficult to separate out the grounds, warrant, and backing. In many applications, the difference between qualification and reservation can also be hard to delineate.

more useful in the context of debate than the more formal traditions found in the academic study of logic, it is difficult to apply while also learning to debate.

COMMON ARGUMENT MODEL

In competitive debate, there are many arguments presented in support of, or in objection to, the topic for the debate. Debates are often decided on the differing degrees of relevance of the arguments advocates use when considering whether the topic should be supported or rejected. With the Toulmin Model, the overall import of a given argument is either implicit from the context of the argument, or embedded in all of the six different parts of the argument. In debate we want the importance of any given argument to be explicit, so that arguments can be evaluated in context of each other. Given the limitations of the Toulmin Model we have discussed, the difficulty of using a potentially redundant model in a time-sensitive activity, and the lack of overall significance, competitive debaters have modified the model to suit their more specific needs. There are several variations within debate-based argument models, with differences in terminology usually being the biggest difference. In this section we will present the next model as a hybrid of the best ideas within the competitive debate community, using the terms that are most widely accepted. The **Common Argument Model** is also called the **Complete Argument**, and we introduce both terms because each helps to show why the model is more practical. This model is helpful in almost any application where argument occurs; it is useful in the real world, and not just in competitive debate. There are three parts to this model: claim, warrant, and impact.

CLAIM

In the Common Argument Model, the claim is very similar to the Toulmin Model; it is the idea that the advocate would like the intended recipients to agree with or consider valid. The claim is the assertion that the speaker is attempting to prove. Claims should be clearly phrased so that all people who hear the argument know what the overall point is. When the argument is presented, the claim is typically the first part. Unlike the Toulmin Model, in the Common Model each part of an argument is more explicit. Claims should be clearly identifiable, and observers of the argument should not have any trouble identifying what the claim behind the argument is. Advocates do not need to literally label the claim in their speech, but they should construct the content of their argument so that the claim is readily apparent.

WARRANT

The purpose of the warrant in the common model is also fairly similar to that used in the Toulmin Model, to provide the rationale in support of the claim. The warrant contains two important elements. First, the warrant should provide evidence or data to support the claim; the proof. Second, the advocate should provide analysis and reasoning to connect the evidence to the claim and show how it supports the claim. Often it is the second part of the warrant that speakers lack in their presentation, so advocates should make sure that they are explaining why the evidence they provide validates the claim they are attempting to support. In the warrant, the Common Model essentially combines the grounds, warrant, and backing parts of the Toulmin Model. When presenting the warrant, the speaker should be clear with his or her rationale; often warrants are strings of ideas presented in combination to give complete support to the claim. Warrants in the Common Model are rarely single statements, but rather a chain of logic. Another way of thinking about the warrant is that it provides the "because" part of an argument in response to the "why?" question.

IMPACT

The final part of the Common Model is the impact. The **impact** explains why the argument matters if it is found to be "true"; it provides the significance of the assertion and its overall relevance to the dispute. In the Toulmin Model, the impact of the argument is not an explicit concept; rather, it is assumed to be self-evident. When there are many arguments in a given discussion, all with varying degrees of applicability, the most compelling arguments will answer the "so what?" question. Like the warrant, the impact is often a chain of ideas. Usually the impact will begin with a claim, and then expand on the ramifications or consequences of that claim being "true." Said another way, the impact of the argument is why the audience should care about it; in a way it is a measure of the importance of the argument. In the last form of debate explored in this text, impacts will become very important, and the concept will be explored further.

SUMMARY

The word *argument* often has a negative connotation in everyday use, but in reality the term is neither good nor bad; rather the context of an argument is what is important. The historical evolution of the word helps to explain why it carries multiple meanings. Arguments are simply exchanges of ideas on a given topic, and an argument comprises the individual ideas that are used to support a given understanding of a topic. Argument is a common part of everyday life, but the study of argument from this practical angle is relatively new. The Western tradition of analyzing argument is rooted in Greek society. For a long period of time, academics focused on what made for "true" arguments and used argument as a way to discover truth. In the middle of the twentieth century, Stephen Toulmin developed a more practical argument model designed to analyze any given argument, viewing an argument as a hypothesis to be tested, rather than a method of uncovering absolute truth. The Toulmin Model provided a way of understanding argument in a relative manner; in other words, arguments are "true" to varying degrees. The Toulmin Model helped to make analysis of argument more applicable to everyday life, and it is very useful in understanding what makes a given argument more or less persuasive. However, Toulmin's model is still a bit too complicated for easy use in the context of either competitive or interpersonal debate. The model made the analysis of everyday arguments easier from an academic perspective, but it is still a little too complex for general use. The Common Argument Model has been developed by competitive debaters over time, modifying Toulmin's model for a specific application. The Common Model is very versatile, and it can be applied to almost every argument that is commonly used in everyday life. The Common Model also adds the important element of impact, which allows us to compare and contrast the relative significance of competing claims.

CHAPTER 2

ARGUMENTATION AND THE FUNDAMENTAL PRINCIPLES OF ACADEMIC DEBATE

*It is **better to debate a question without** settling it than to settle a **question** without debating it.*

Joseph Joubert

AN OVERVIEW OF COMPETITIVE ACADEMIC DEBATE

Students at institutions of higher learning have been engaged in organized academic debate for well over a century. Currently thousands of institutions in the United States and across the globe engage with one another in academic debate competition. Debate is not just at the university level; secondary schools all over the world provide opportunities for their students to participate in debate, with some beginning as early as the sixth grade. Dozens of debate leagues exist, each with its own guidelines and practices. Millions of people across the globe are current or former participants in organized competitive debate, linked in a network loosely known as the debate community.

As debaters do tend to argue, and as the subject can elicit strong personal feelings, a "fair history" of competitive academic debate is nearly impossible. That said, here are a few historical notes, hopefully without controversy. The Oxford Debate Union, perhaps the world's most famous and influential debate society, began organized discussion and debate in 1823, at a time when university officials shunned free expression of political ideas.[4] The tradition of debate is only slightly younger in the United States, with a handful of debate organizations tracing their lineage to the mid-nineteenth century.[5] At the turn of the nineteenth century, and into the early twentieth century, the first intercollegiate debate tournaments were held, and competitive debate proliferated across the United Kingdom, Ireland, and the United States, and has since spread globally.

Although practices and formats have varied widely since the beginning, some common principles are foundational to the competitive activity. While this text aims to focus more on the general application of debate and argumentation, it is instructional to briefly examine some of these constructs. These principles are the most basic features that bind divergent debate formats and styles together even when they may differ significantly in actual practice. Although there is really never any universal consensus in the debate community, the similarities discussed here are widely practiced. The principles and logistics addressed in this section will form the backbone to the debate models discussed and practiced later in the book and in your course.

PRINCIPLES AND LOGISTICS

RELATION TO ARGUMENT THEORY

While the study of argument as a formal discipline as a part of the field of communication can be a complex matter, there is no need to be intimidated by

---

[4] http://www.oxford-union.org/about_us.
[5] For instance, Wake Forest 1854, http://groups.wfu.edu/debate/HistoryPages/AbbreviatedTimeline.html; Northwestern 1855, www.communication.northwestern.edu/learn/student_activities/debate/; Boston College 1868, http://www.bc.edu/schools/cas/communication/fulton/history.html.

the thought of participating in a debate. In many ways, the practical considerations of putting together your notes for a debate are more important than the theoretical questions of argument theory. This chapter will help take some of the ideas brought up in Chapter 1 and explain them in the context of issues and ideas you would talk about in a debate.

In our previous discussion of settings where an argument might take place we hypothesized a variety of situations and contexts. For both competitive and in-class debates you will participate in a format that has an exact question to be argued, as well as a speech order and time limits for the exchange that will be a part of an overall set of rules and expectations. Once you get familiar with those expectations, you can begin to construct your own set of arguments, which we will refer to as your "case," to support your role in the debate.

COMPETITION

In practice, organized academic debate may seem like the antithesis of dialogue, yet in some ways the intended outcome of a debate has certain similarities: a sharing of divergent ideas so that all have a better understanding of an issue at the end. The fundamental difference between organized academic debate and dialogue is competition—in organized academic debate, there are winners and losers.[6] However, it is not simply the ideas themselves that are judged in the competition, but also the way in which they are formulated and presented. Participants gain education by refining ideas so that they are made more competitive; participants also learn critical thinking and persuasion skills. Ideally, the competitive nature of the activity not only rewards those with more finely honed skills, it also encourages all participants to work hard in order to excel.

Competition in academic debate encourages the interaction and exploration of ideas and in the strategy necessary to win debate rounds. Participants in debates use the ideas within a preset topic to compete, with each idea becoming like a chess piece, with various strengths and utilities dependent on the nature of the given game. This eliminates some of the personalization that

---

[6] To be clear, what we are referring to here is what the "debate team" does. There are all sorts of organized debates, both competitive and noncompetitive, on college campuses featuring important academic and social issues. We are focusing here on competitive debate.

many arguments outside organized academic debates have. In this way, debaters are somewhat shielded—they are not necessarily using their own personal beliefs, but rather the arguments that were available to support a given side of a topic. When you lose, it is not that your personal beliefs are wrong, but rather that the other participants were better at using the available arguments (chess pieces) to support their side of the topic in question.

While competitive debate is often viewed as debate for the sake of debate, the hope is that both critical education and skills development will be significant outcomes beyond the mere winning and losing. The principles one learns from competitive debate should then be applied to the world. Your job is to learn to debate so that you can utilize the skills you gain to improve your life.

THE TOPIC[7]

A primary goal of all participating in organized academic debate is topic education, or the knowledge gained about an issue in the preparation for and participation in the debate. Education is what drives most people into debate, and the kind of in-depth knowledge that can be gained from having a debate on any subject is one of the most highly valued aspects of debate. Some debate formats use the same topic for an entire year, with the topic carefully crafted over months; others use a topic just once and switch to a new topic with every debate. The length of the topic's use, as well as the goals concerning topic education, shapes the wording and concentration of a given topic.[8]

The starting point for any debate is the question that will be addressed in the debate. That **question** usually takes the form of a statement that implies an advocacy relating to a specific action or belief that is to be addressed. It is also referred to as the "resolution" because it often explicitly or implicitly asks that the participants actively take up, or be resolved, to the positions that they are

---

[7] Also known as "The Resolution," "The Motion," or "The Question Before the House."

[8] In High School Policy Debate, where one topic is debated for an entire year, the topic broadly covers an issue that can be viewed in a vast number of ways. The 2011–2012 topic was "Resolved: The United States federal government should substantially increase its exploration and/or development of space beyond the Earth's mesosphere." In College Parliamentary Debate, where a new topic is used every round, a topic may be very specific. For example, consider this topic from the 2009 NPDA National Tournament, "The U.S. Federal Government should enact into law the Employee Free Choice Act of 2009." Topics covering ethical or philosophical concerns are common in some debate formats, as for example, "When in conflict, security should be valued over liberty."

representing. A topic often identifies a specific actor or agent that is to be the focus of the advocate.

The topic to be debated should be balanced, with ample room available for argument from all sides. Participants should feel free to approach the topic from a variety of angles and should attempt to provide rationale supporting their side. Although there may be a popular bias on one side of a topic, there should still be rational and substantial arguments available on the contrarian side.[9] A balanced approach is necessary for an entertaining and intellectually stimulating debate, and is vital for in-depth education.

Topics often leave room for multiple interpretations; to prevent stagnation, unnecessary repetition, and potential boredom, there are often several legitimate ways of understanding a topic. This increases intellectual freedom and allows participants to explore in a myriad of ways their understanding of any issue. Flexibility in interpretation also allows people who feel strongly about one side of a topic to be creative in challenging their currently held assumption. Someone who feels strongly about the right for same-sex couples to marry may feel uncomfortable arguing against a topic like "The government should allow gay people to legally marry." However, they could creatively approach the "Against" side of the topic by arguing that the government should not be involved with marriage in any manner, for either same- or opposite-sex couples, and that the decision is a private choice between consenting adults and their church, if they chose to incorporate religion into their lives.

For example, consider the following as a topic:

Resolved: The United States Federal Government should end its embargo of Cuba

It identifies a specific action in the lifting of the embargo, which would require a change of policy from the one that exists now. It also identifies the agent that is the appropriate body to be able to remove the embargo. Even though we are not

---

[9] For example, "Cold-blooded murder for fun is justified," is probably not a two-sided topic, whereas "Violence is a justified response to political oppression" provides ground for each side to base its arguments.

a part of the federal government, we can still discuss the merits or costs of taking such an action. Since the U.S. government initiated the embargo, only it could remove the action. It is also quite possible in this example that all of the good reasons or benefits for removing the embargo may benefit Cuba more than the United States in the end result, so even if the federal government is the agent, it need not always be the key benefactor of the action advocated.

One thing our example also points out is that topics often ask for a change from the way things are now. The conceptualization of the current system in debate is often referred to as the "status quo." Debate will often use terms from Latin, owing to its roots in the Roman rhetorical and legal canon, and in this case the term means simply the state of affairs that currently exist.

Sometimes a topic may pose a question of a more philosophical nature, such as:

Resolved: Security should be a priority over privacy

In this example, there is no specific agent identified, nor a policy that can be compared to the way things are now. Such questions are often the root of a philosophical discussion that may still include examples that stem from the real world. And certainly, the end result of asking such a question would be to help resolve some issue of real-world concern. So, while the question itself is philosophical and abstract, the supporting elements like evidence and logical reasoning have to draw from the concrete. Even the abstract question would require reasoning that identifies specific outcomes from favoring one side of the proposed dichotomy over the other.

The reason that debate requires concrete proof or rationale stems from a point of advocacy regarding the supporting of a topic. In advocacy, just being able to claim that something is "good" is not adequate support; it is typically not enough to convince an audience. Mere assertion of the conclusion of a point of view does not serve to support a reason to prefer that state of belief over some other. It takes us back to the idea of building a "case" for your point of view. Remember, the construction of an argument in theory does include some assertion or claim about some preferred state of affairs. Consider the earlier example of a topic about Cuba and that a likely claim to be made by someone favoring the topic would be that lifting the embargo is good. But that claim by itself is not enough. In the basic form of an argument, there is an accompanying set of facts or evidence and a connecting rationale why that proof is a good support for the claim made. Relative to the question about Cuba, some economic evidence may support a reason to interact with Cuba rather than isolate them. The resulting increase in trade could be a significant boost for both countries. The underlying warrant or reasoning which connects that evidence to the claim is to point out that good economies outweigh other aspects of relations with another country, thus increased trade is better than the current political gains we get by embargoing them.

PARTICIPANTS

There are generally two sides to a competitive academic debate; different formats use different names for each side and for each speaker. Formats range from one-on-one competition,[10] to eight participants from four different institutions arguing the two sides of a given topic,[11] and everything in between. In all of these formats, each of the participants may have different titles indicating his or her side and duty, but for the sake of simplicity this text will use the terms *For* and *Against*.[12] Simply put, the **For** side tries to prove that the topic is valid while the **Against** side tries to deny that effort. When participants come together and have a debate, each individual match is referred to as a **round**. Most tournaments feature at least four or five rounds, followed by some sort of elimination process that eventually recognizes a tournament champion.

The Affirmative or "For" Side

The same components of argument in theory also exist in applied debate, but in a way that allows you to build those arguments from materials available by researching the issue you are going to be addressing. Academic debate allows for a way to examine the complex parts of an argument in a structured manner

---

[10] Some examples of one-on-one debate formats: Lincoln-Douglas Debate, Individual Parliamentary Debate, SPAR Debate.

[11] British Parliamentary (BP) or World-style debate: two teams, both made up of two people, are on each side of the topic, with each individual team assigned either an "opening" or "closing" role for its side of the topic.

[12] We could also use "Affirmative vs. Negative," "Proposition vs. Opposition," "Government vs. Opposition," "Proponent vs. Opponent," etc.

so that you can better understand complicated issues in the real world. So, to continue looking at those parts, we will focus in on the usual starting point of an academic debate, the Affirmative or Proposition side of the question. In debate the need to have all of the parts of an argument present is conceptualized as the **burden of proof**. In a case where there will be a decision about a question, it is typically required that the side that begins the debate take a position of advocacy in the form of challenging some current assumption about the way things should be. Going back to its ancient rhetorical roots, the construct of *prima facie* is a Latin term meaning "at first glance," and relates to the fulfillment of one's duties as an advocate to present a complete enough level of proof to stand alone or be taken on face value when presented in a forum to make decisions on such things. For our purposes, simply understanding that an advocate has an obligation to prove sufficient support of their position can get us started. Rather than arguing about "burden of proof" as an actual term used in the debate, the components of that burden are more often the focus of the types of things a debate will be about, or more specifically, what the Affirmative team might be saying in their first speech. Some traditional approaches to academic debate have identified these common elements of the burden of proof as the "stock issues."

The first of these specific elements of the burden of proof, or stock issues, is to establish that currently there is some "harm" or problem in the system that needs to be addressed. To go back to the example from Cuba, one might argue that people in Cuba are at best unfairly disadvantaged and at worst actually oppressed by the lack of commerce and technical and scientific expertise from the West because of the U.S.-enforced embargo. The advocate may also want to point out that American businesses lose a lot of money from not being able to trade with a nation that is a mere 90 miles away. Along with identifying harm, there is also an expectation to be able to prove that the harm in question is a significant one—that the problem identified is something of such scope or importance that re-thinking the way we are doing things is worth it.

The next step in building a case is to show that you can do more than merely identify or complain about a problem, but that you can also offer a way to resolve it. In traditional practice, this element of the case is referred to as **solvency**. While in general we can understand how new markets might mean more trade, does that mean it is true for the United States and Cuba? Those in favor of ending the embargo would have to identify the exact points where positive exchange not only *could* occur but actually *would* occur if there were no embargo. Rather than just believing good things would happen, being able to identify what those things are and by what mechanisms or actions they come to be is a critical way to extend the "evidence" related to the harm to the reasoning process or "warrant" for why it supports the claim of lifting the embargo being a good thing.

While we have been referring to the term **case** so far as a conceptual organizing term, it is also used to refer to an organized set of ideas related to the debate that will be used by those participating. In presenting that case, the debaters present a series of contentions to build their case for the topic. Sometimes the convention of the debate may be to even explicitly refer to that organizing structure as part of the oral presentation of the debate itself. A speaker may refer to their first contention as a means to identify the substantive elements of their presentation that represent the ordered and structured means by which they will be supporting their advocacy.

One elements that helps further establish a case is not only to identify the harm that is being addressed, but also to identify the action or behavior that forms the basis of the way things would be made better by the advocate's proposed solution. In other words, there should be some rationale for why the agent of action identified in the topic, or the logical extrapolation of the appropriate agent, is fully capable of resolving the harms. The concept which allow debaters to project the likelihood of their ideas working to solve harms is the ability to utilize *fiat* to overcome whatever it is in the *status quo* that is currently preventing the solution from happening. Rather than being a special power or gaming trick to do the impossible, *fiat* is the process by which we imagine what the world would look like if the proposed solution were to be put into place so that the merits can be debated. Rather than arguing about the political feasibility of actual implementation, the use of *fiat* allows the debaters to focus upon a world where the solution is in place and then to deliberate whether the action would work or not based on its actual merits, not current socio-political dynamics. Otherwise, debates would quickly get bogged down in discussions about which political party or representative(s) would block the vote, or other political concerns, rather than an evaluation of the merits of the proposal.

Sometimes there is an expectation that the debaters which take the Affirmative side of the topic be bound to the expectations or particular terms contained in the specific topic itself. This is expressed as **topicality** in the stock issues view of debate mentioned earlier. While it is usually not a specific point identified in one's case, it is often implicit in the way that the advocate frames their case. The Affirmative will typically point to some practice in the status quo as being the basis for their harm and suggest that these harms will continue unless the change suggested in the topic is adopted. In some situations of competitive academic debate an Affirmative proponent may try to avoid taking the advocacy embraced in a topic because it is deemed to be rather difficult to defend. However, because the fundamental purpose of an academic debate with a formal topic is to determine whether or not the ideas of the topic should be affirmed, it is a reasonable requirement that the Affirmative side defend the notion of the topic. So topicality in that context is a means of keeping the Affirmative side in the debate tied to the role assigned by the topic regardless of its perceived merits. Most often classroom debates are more clearly role playing and practice exercise than competitive experience, making concerns about the gaming uses of topicality largely irrelevant to the debates.

The Negative or "Against" side

The structure and expectations for contentions and presentations in specific debates are outlined in later chapters. So, while there is more detail to be learned later about what goes into the Affirmative side of the debate, we will move on at this point to the other side of the debate, referred to as the **Negative** or Opposition. In some ways, while the Affirmative is the logical starting point to look at debate, it can seem that they have the easy job because, by starting the debate, they are to build the best case they can and know the whole time exactly how they will do it. Often, as the Negative, you may never be totally certain what the specific advocacy of the Affirmative team will be until you hear them.

In educational debates it is to the benefit of both the Affirmative and Negative to cooperate to some extent to identify the main issues in common and to disclose in a general sense the direction of advocacy or strategy that will be utilized. The educational merits of preparation in advance far outweigh the competitive advantage of trying to nullify or make irrelevant what the other side has worked to prepare. There is also some precedent in the legal system where the prosecution and defense must comply with full disclosure practices related to evidence and witnesses in advance. Cooperation also gives one a chance to know what is coming and to be able to build up a response in advance.

On both sides of the debate, you will have to do more than simply present your side of the issue; you must also defend your argument against the attacks of the other side. The ability to go beyond one's initial position to account for the ideas of the other team and still be able to support your case is a critical factor in persuasion. So, while educational debates can make being the Negative a bit more manageable, there are some other things about being opposed to the topic that start to even the scale of fairness in the debate.

One of the key tenets of the Negative is the concept of **presumption**. In its most basic form it is the common idea that "if it ain't broke, don't fix it." As the topic is typically framed as a change from the status quo, the Negative always has the baseline of the way things are now to compare to the way things might be if things are changed for the worse. It takes advantage of the known always being a more favorable quantity than the unknown or change from the way things are. Presumption also means that, while the Affirmative must be an advocate, the Negative may only have to prove the Affirmative wrong, rather than offer their own way of looking at things, because by default if we do not choose the Affirmative the worst thing that happens is things remain the way they are now. That is not to say that the Negative can simply be passive. Just as the Affirmative has the burden of proof, the Negative has the **burden of rejoinder**, or the requirement to refute the arguments presented by the Affirmative with their own proof and reasoning. This concept can also be seen as **refutation**, but it is appropriate to think of refutation as both the larger level strategy as well as any individual response to a point of your opponent. In some cases the Negative may go beyond the burden of rejoinder in their response and present arguments to develop independent reasons why the Affirmative may be a bad idea. As we go into more detail on the Negative we will begin with elements of the burden of rejoinder as they relate to the stock issues of harm and solvency.

One clear refutation strategy is to address directly the elements of the Affirmative's **contentions**, or main points and structure. They may have set up a structure that identifies a harm and then explains how they would solve it and how that would work. To the extent that the contentions are in some ways argument constructions, rather than having to beat all the elements of the argument, by breaking a link in the chain of reasoning, the Negative may be able to show why the Affirmative falls short of their advocacy. Some elements of this direct refutation relate to some of the stock issues we discussed in relation to the Affirmative.

First, we will consider the issue of harms. While logically addressing this makes sense, remember that, while it may be the "evidence" or "fact" part of the argument that you are pointing out is in error, doing so may mean having to address or minimize some aspects of the world that require extreme sensitivity. Our Cuba example can serve here as well. In addressing the suffering related to the embargo, a point about a lack of medical care or access to medicine for many people may be forwarded. Rather than simply saying, "well, that is too bad, but that is what you get for living in communism," a more nuanced critique points out that Cuba is actually a destination for medical tourism to many Europeans, so care at the top end of the spectrum is quite good. It can also be pointed out that Cuba offered to send 500 doctors to assist in the wake of Hurricane Katrina. So, rather than disregarding the pain or suffering of others, you can point out that this suffering is a structural problem of the Cuban system that openness will not solve, or that the assumptions about Cuba's poor and backward health care are wrong and they have plenty of services available. Again, while these strategies of denial and minimization can be appropriate and revealing in terms of the strength of the argument, a debater always has to remember that, in some cases, refusing to recognize the existence of harm can show moral blindness or reveal an acceptance or denial of that state of affairs. That is where not having to deny all parts of the Affirmatives argument can serve the Negative. It may not hurt to concede or agree that some harm is occurring.

The second stock issue, solvency, offers a variety of ways to question and challenge the position taken by the Affirmative. There may be a variety of reasons why some approach, strategy, or action may not work. For the issue of Cuba the solvency may not occur because, even if trade is opened up, the government of Cuba could still manipulate interaction with the United States in such a way as to minimize any positive social and political effects. Also trade with the United States may compound Cuba's economic problems by returning them to their former status as the Sugar Bowl of the United States, growing cane for export instead of more sustainable local food projects. Trade may also exacerbate the development of the most exploitive forms of economic interaction, such as tourism and service industries, along with cultural clashes regarding more access to Western entertainment and media. Along with the policies themselves not working, they may have no effect as the embargo is kind of a joke, it is pretty permeable by those who care, and irrelevant to plenty of nations. It may be possible to point to little to no likelihood for Cuba to want to trade. Our example of Cuba is pretty direct in that having the U. S. embargo as the subject means that the United States is the correct agent to be able to solve the problem. In other cases, you could argue that the specified agent or actor is not the right one to try to address the issue. For example, some might argue that the federal government should not make education policy because it is too far removed from the individual context of any given school district. Thus, education policy should be left to the states, and any federal initiative would not solve the issues in education because there is no one-size-fits-all approach that could work.

There are more arguments the Negative can advance beyond the refutation of the contentions of the case of the Affirmative, but this examination of the parts in relation to the argument model reveals the core root argument theory utilized in academic debate and how it serves to reinforce the skills of both constructing arguments and consuming the arguments one encounters. Some of those other argument options will be discussed in the context of some of the assignments and debates in class.

Specific Competitive Debating Logistics

In addition to the institutions/schools debating against one another, an outside party from a neutral institution/school evaluates the debate. Again, different formats have different practices, but all have one or more evaluators who make a judgment on the outcome of the debate—deciding who wins and who loses. There may be one or more evaluators for each round, some of whom may be highly familiar with the activity, but others may not be. Occasionally public competitive debates are held with the entirety of the audience serving as judges, representing potentially hundreds or even thousands of votes. How the evaluation should be made and by whom are two questions that often divide different debate formats and leagues. When adopting competitive debate for the classroom, the winning and losing is often relegated to the backseat of the debate or is not determined at all. Judging is critical in competition, but for the sake of learning, judging often makes people unnecessarily uncomfortable.

Participants are usually assigned in some random manner to be on the For or the Against side of the topic to be debated; although debaters may wind up supporting what they personally believe, this is not a requirement of debate. Rather, participants are to develop their side of the topic as completely as they can, without regard to their personal politics.[13] Generally the goal is to maximize academic freedom and exploration on a topic, not to advance preconceived personal beliefs. Participants will gain a better understanding of their beliefs through role-playing and testing all aspects of a given topic. Debaters present their given side, not what they personally believe. In almost all formats of competitive debate, participants switch sides from round to round, and must thus be familiar with both sides of any given topic.

PREPARATION

How participants prepare for debates is one of the most revealing features that distinguishes different debate formats from one another. In formats where the same topic is debated for a preset period of time (a month, a term or semester, a

---

[13] This assumption is challenged in two different aspects. First, academic and ethical responsibilities provide a constraint on argument selection for debaters to consider (i.e., lying is not acceptable). Second, some leagues may restrict arguments in order to conform to educational goals (particularly in high school leagues), as well as to respect religious beliefs.

year) the topic is announced publicly, allowing participants to spend a great deal of time researching fairly specific elements of the topic. Other formats focus on limited-preparation debate, allowing only a brief amount of preparation time, with new topics for every single debate round. Topics in these formats can be either centrally announced, written and presented to the competitors in each individual debate, or posted on the Internet. Participants in limited-preparation debate focus on more generally preparing for a wide variety of potential topics. Almost all debate formats encourage a good understanding of current events, with specific research needs dictated by the norms of the particular league where participants compete.

DISTINGUISHED FROM OTHER FORMS OF DEBATE

SPECIALIZED LANGUAGE

All professions and communication groups to some extent have a specialized jargon, or vocabulary, but competitive academic debate is rife with it.[14] Jargon arises when concepts that are used often in a debate gain a shorthand reference that is commonly understood by most in the community. As some debate formats are conducted at a rapid rate, and the ideas that are expressed become complicated, the highly technical language of debate can get quite sophisticated. The theoretical issues associated with how and why debate works is a place where jargon has allowed competitive debaters to develop highly advanced argumentative structures and explanations. It often takes years to learn some of the more complex ideas, and because it is debate, there are never any really firm answers—just more debate. For this text we will try to keep the jargon to a minimum. We have tried to simplify our explanations of debate theory and to use logical names for specific concepts. Although the jargon can be invaluable in understanding how a debate works, the ideas and terms do reflect real-world concepts, so being careful while using debate jargon outside of a formal debate is not a bad idea.

---

[14] Examples include: counterplans, permutations, internal links, topicality, conditionality, fiat, etc.

POLITICAL DEBATES

Although many arguments in our everyday lives may share aspects of organized academic debate, or even appear in some ways to be the same, it is important to point out some of the differences. Political debates share many similarities with academic debate, but the two activities are different from one another in a couple of important ways. The winner of a political debate is now more likely to get into office and the loser less likely. In competitive academic debate, all you lose is a debate round. In other words, what is at stake is quite different across the various applications of debate. Sound bites and media clips often dominate political debates, particularly those in the United States, whereas competitive debate assumes the speech will be considered only in its entirety. In political debates, the common understanding of the obligations for each participant in the debate is less clear and poorly understood.

PUBLIC DEBATES

Academic debates and public debates are held as events by a myriad of different institutions. These events are often organized with principles and desires similar to those of competitive debate. Topics and formats can vary even more widely than in competitive organized debate, but sponsors seek to provide an organized exploration of an idea or set of ideas, with the hope that information will be exchanged and ideas refined. Again the expected outcome is divergent between the different activities. The participants of academic and public debates are usually experts in their fields, hoping to add to and spread general human knowledge. Competitive debaters are trying to win debate rounds, while learning about topics they may know little about. In most competitive debate formats, the competitors switch sides with every round. In public debates, many speakers will only ever argue on one side of the topic.

INFORMAL/INTERPERSONAL DEBATES

The debates that you get into with your friends and family are a little different from formal debating. Although your friendly arguments will often have an implicit format—either you take turns talking, or you talk over one-another, rarely does another friend time your speeches. When you engage in argument in the real world, the stakes are often higher; you try to persuade people to agree with you for significant reasons. Maybe it is a political action or belief that you wish to spread, or your need to convince the boss that you deserve a raise; perhaps you have behaved badly and need to find a way to reconcile. All of these occasions for logical persuasion are far more significant than winning cheap plastic trophies in debate competition.

IN-CLASS DEBATES

You will be debating many times in class, both formally—in front of the class and evaluated by your instructor, and informally—practicing the theories and techniques explored in this text with your peers. Debate is extremely simple to participate in—just be willing to present your ideas in response to those presented by others; and yet extremely difficult to master—there are so many potential arguments in any given debate that just keeping track of them can be dizzying. Selecting the right arguments can be hard, and debate can be very frustrating. Your mouth and brain are often in conflict, especially when you are under pressure. When presenting their ideas in a debate in front of others, people may feel exposed or vulnerable, making them nervous. Competitive debate is not for all people. Although your authors welcome and encourage all to give competitive debate a try, we realize that some people just do not care for it. To reconcile the educational benefits of debate with the emotional drawbacks, the evaluation of in-class debates will be based upon effort and participation rather than competitive outcomes.

SUMMARY

Competitive academic debate has tremendous educational benefits, and it has been a fun and stimulating extracurricular or co-curricular activity for millions of people across the globe. The way that it is practiced has evolved over time, and some of its application has become incredibly complex—laden with esoteric jargon and highly specialized argument forms and individual speaker responsibilities. However, there are some common features of competitive formats that can be used in the classroom to introduce students to debate in order to develop the skills that participants take from the activity. It is important to note that competitive debate has both similarities and significant differences from the kind of debate and argument that you see in everyday life.

Debate teaches valuable information about the world. Equally important, it teaches people how to organize and process information, how to evaluate high-quality logic, and how to persuade people to agree with presented ideas. There are many great examples of people who participated in debate and then went on to make massive changes in the world, including some very well-known people: JFK, Richard Nixon, Malcolm X, Karl Rove, and others. When you think about it, this is a fairly interesting group of people — adored by their followers while hated by their enemies, each left a very clear mark on the country. Though their politics were wildly divergent, all were very successful at advancing their ideas and persuading people to agree with them. Many successful politicians, business and community leaders, and lots of lawyers have competitive debate experience.

The intent here is to show that competitive debate, coupled with an inquisitive mind, can help anyone learn to approach everyday problems, both large and small, from a rational perspective, and to see how individual action and persuasion can make a difference. No debate is ever perfect, and the ideas presented in this text often take people years to fully understand. It is important to remain positive and inquisitive. There is no need to worry about trying to be perfect; just concentrate on how you can improve. Preparation will pay off, so be prepared to devote some time to getting ready. Most importantly, have fun while you are doing a debate. A debate should be a safe space to try out ideas and to experiment with presenting them. Take advantage of the opportunity to practice new ideas and learn new skills.

PART II

ARGUMENTATION: WHY WE DO IT

CHAPTER 3

IN DEFENSE OF DEBATE

The idea that argumentation and debate are educational in nature is one of the primary reasons to do them. By being practiced in both constructing and listening to arguments, you will be a better decision maker and more purposeful citizen in an open and democratic society. A well-educated person will not just be aware of the various issues in contemporary society, but will also become an active participant in those issues. The Internet and the rapid advance of new information technologies almost guarantee that access will no longer be an obstacle relating to information. The main issue will be the ability to utilize critical thinking in the context of that information. Good reasoning is more than the collection of ideas; it is the ability to analyze, give context to, and weigh competing views.

ARGUMENTATION IN THE DEVELOPMENT OF ACADEMICS

The idea of a discourse that develops differing points of view on an issue in a structured and reasoned manner is in many ways the core of classical Western education. While the very foundation of public speaking models to this day, the work of Greek, and later Roman, thinkers is more often associated with the development of the philosophical framework for the ideas that created democratic systems and legal structures. One of the fundamental purposes of many of the most learned of these thinkers was to prepare people to plead their cases in front of legislative or legal forums where their very words could change the course of public policy or law. This preparation was based on understanding sound reasoning, often presented in the form of dialogues that were structured investigations into ideas that developed differing viewpoints and advocacies as a means to practice critical thinking.

Beyond being at the conceptual center of academic endeavor, the practice in academe is to use these methods to continue its work. Differences of viewpoint in the academy are resolved through research and engagement in ongoing exchanges about differences in theory or findings. How did the dinosaurs die? Your answer may depend on when you went to school and learned about it, as the consensus of scientific opinion on the matter has shifted significantly in the past 30 years. Is global climate change actually occurring? Such questions are often more about the ability of those conducting research to use their scientific findings to establish the reliability of their theories than anything else.

For our purposes, we will use debate as an actual educational practice or method. Just as a writing or composition class has a five-paragraph essay designed around particular writing traits, debate has a format and certain expectations as to how to present an argument in a classroom or public setting. By participating in in-class debates, you will work on your skills in conceptualizing, researching, public presentation, critical thinking, and listening. Being able to synthesize all of those skills toward a specific public speaking outcome is a process that will start with simple elements at first, and then add toward more complex formats. Of course, while thinking about it in a class context may make debate seem as though it is just another assignment, the ability to have active class time involved in debates will actually be fun and a great way to meet and interact with classmates. Many colleges and universities actually have teams or clubs that get together for intercollegiate debate competitions, so it must have some element of reward and enjoyment related to participating!

GENERAL BENEFITS OF ARGUMENTATION

DEVELOPMENT OF SKILLS

There are many good reasons for including argumentation and debate as part of your experience in higher education. Employers will look for practical skills in their employees. Those applicants who can demonstrate an ability to think on their feet, express complex ideas verbally, and be able to not just identify problems, but also solve them will be in the highest demand. These are real and recognizable skills that employers notice. Even in other classes, you will notice how these skills are transferable—they will help you think critically about your assignments and papers, organize them in a reasoned form, and present them in a more persuasive fashion.

In addition to employment opportunities, experience with argumentation and debate can be useful for those considering post-graduate education. For those considering law school, a number of deans and law professors cite debate as an important preparation for the rigors of legal study and practice[15]. Those considering graduate education in a variety of disciplines will find that debate knowledge can provide a critical foundation for preparation in almost any discipline.

---

[15] "Law School Deans' and Professors' Statement of Support for Urban Debate." National Association for Urban Debate Leagues. http://www.urbandebate.org/pdf/statement.pdf

CONFLICT MANAGEMENT

Differences of opinion are quite natural and normal among humans. Indeed, our ability to reason and think critically about any number of issues is one of the primary characteristics that set humans apart from other animals. Unfortunately, the intensity of those differences can sometimes lead to negative consequences for all parties involved. The ability to voice one's thoughts can often reveal conflict, but it is critically important to understand that it is this very ability that can be the means for resolving that conflict as well. When handled properly, conflict does not have to result in a negative outcome, but can in fact produce positive results. Take, for instance, cooperative situations like a design team, or a group of kitchen workers—the ability to discuss differing ideas and opinions for what may be the best way to do something or how to improve some aspect of an outcome is definitely a conflict of ideas, but not necessarily a conflict of relationships or goals. Conflict, like money, power, or technology, becomes either positive or negative depending on the way it is managed, not because of some innate quality or characteristic.

BUILDING YOUR OWN ADVOCACY

While this text takes a short-term focus on theory and practice in the form of debate, the point of doing those things now is so that you can use your voice on matters that impact your life. Those can be simple things like cooperating with a neighbor about a common issue of concern, or influencing education policies that impact your family, or even political matters relating to allocation of services or resources. The ability to present a relevant, coherent, and supported position can influence the outcome of these decisions. Your ability to do those things also means that as you evaluate ballot measures, political candidates, or even financial choices, your application of critical thinking toward others' arguments is a way to make sure that in even those things that you are not able to be directly involved in, you can at least understand and choose positions on the issues in a meaningful way.

Being an Advocate is a Responsibility of Citizenship

Ultimately, the goal of being able to reason and argue well is for the benefit of one's society. Being able to speak out and to do so in a way that brings forward meaningful contributions to public discourse is a way to be supportive of actions that are transparent and fair. Doing so in a civil and respectful manner is a means by which argument and conflict can be used in a constructive and positive way to reflect upon the various methods for resolving our societal challenges in the most optimal fashion. In a diverse world of culture and ideas, being able to bring forward your own opinions and encountering those of others means that you are going to have to create and consume ideas in a dynamic environment. In many ways this is an obligation of members of any society—to be vocal and participatory in their views regarding what is in the best interests of their community.

CHAPTER 4

DELIBERATION AND DECISION-MAKING METHODS

It is in your moments of decision that your destiny is shaped.
Anthony Robbins

We human beings are a problem-solving species. When faced with problems or difficult choices, people come up with a vast number of ways to single out their preferences. In this chapter, we will address some of the various methods, models, and techniques that can be utilized in reaching a decision, whether as an individual or as a group. Some methods are better than others, and we will discuss several that we do not necessarily recommend but are nevertheless included for educational purposes.

WHAT IS DECISION-MAKING

It is perhaps useful to begin by simply defining what decision-making is. We define **decision-making** as the act or process of reaching a judgment or conclusion. There are a number of different decision-making methods and techniques. Some are based on chance, others on reason, while yet others are determined by long-standing cultural traditions. Before moving into the types of decision-making that this text is primarily concerned with, we will first examine a few other varieties so as to make clear that decisions can and are made in a variety of ways. It is also important to understand that argument and decision-making take place on many different levels. Decisions can be made on the individual, family, neighborhood, community, regional, national, international, and global scales.

Intrapersonal decisions are those decisions that take place internally or without the involvement of another person, whereas **interpersonal** decisions are those that are made with at least one or more other person involved in the process. While an interpersonal argument can technically be defined as argumentative communication between two or more people, it often takes on the common meaning of the more emotionally laden informal arguments between two friends, partners, siblings, etc.[16] As such, perhaps it would be helpful to differentiate between the type of argument we typically refer to as a "fight" or "quarrel" between two individuals, and the more rhetorical sense of an argument wherein we advance a claim, supported by facts and reasoning, in an effort to convince another person of the validity of our perspectives and ideas.[17] While many of the ideas of this text are arguably applicable to either variety, our primary concern here is with those arguments and decision-making practices of the rhetorical sense, rather than simply a quarrel between two friends.

---

[16] Refer to Chapter 1 for a more detailed discussion of this distinction.
[17] O'Keefe, Daniel. "Two Concepts of Argument," *Journal of the American Forensics Association*, 13: Winter, 1977.

TYPES OF DECISION-MAKING

UNCONTROLLED OR RANDOM DECISION-MAKING

Some decision-making methods involve little or no reasoning but are rather left up to mere chance. These techniques might include the tossing of a coin, the drawing of lots or names from a hat, the roll of the dice, playing rock/paper/scissors, or even the magic answer ball where a person asks a question then shakes the ink-filled ball and waits for the object inside to rise to the top with the answer. While these methods are certainly quick and decisive, they may not be entirely appropriate for a number of situations. For instance, if someone were to ask you to marry them, would you trust leaving your answer up to the whims of the magic answer ball? Imagine the person of your dreams being sent packing simply because the ball happens to turn up a negative response. Due to the uncontrolled and random nature of these techniques, they are appropriate only for those decision-making situations where the result is not really that important to anyone impacted by the outcome, such as a group of friends deciding which movie they will attend when all the choices are relatively equal in desirability.

MYSTICAL OR SPIRITUAL DECISION-MAKING

Sometimes when people are faced with making a particularly difficult decision, they may choose to turn to some form of spiritual guidance for assistance. Such practices might include things like prayer, superstitions, spiritual counseling, psychic reading, tarot cards, ritual, and numerous others. Because these particular methods are rather personal issues of faith, with each individual choosing according to his or her own relative belief systems, we will not go into any level of detail on this technique beyond mentioning it as a possible approach in the decision-making process.

CULTURALLY SPECIFIC DECISION-MAKING

It is helpful to understand that just as there is great diversity amongst cultures, so too is there an accompanying variety in the decision-making techniques that are practiced in those cultures. While some societies openly embrace the free expression of conflicting views and perspectives, others will go to great lengths in order to avoid even the slightest appearance of dissention within the community. For example, Western nations often tend to be rather individualistic in their basic outlook while many Asian and African nations have a propensity to be more communitarian in nature. Furthermore, several Western nations utilize English common law to some extent or another, while many Muslim nations follow *Sharia* (Islamic law) to greater or lesser degrees, and yet still others maintain traditional customary norms of decision-making that are hundreds or perhaps even thousands of years old. Here we will offer just a few interesting examples to show the great assortment of problem-solving methods used around the world.

Just off the coast of Papua New Guinea lies an archipelagic group called the Trobriand Islands. For some time, the various Trobriand villages would engage in limited warfare with one another over any number of different disputes. Unfortunately, with such small populations, the loss of even one or two people in combat could seriously hamper the village's development. Each person lost in battle meant one less person to hunt and gather food, to build shelter, and to help watch after and raise the children. As a result of these hardships, the Trobriand Islanders decided they needed to find a way to settle their disputes in a less destructive manner. Well, like with much of the world, the Trobriand Islands had been colonized by the British, and along with other elements of British culture had come the game of cricket. In a rather ingenious move, the Trobriand Islanders adopted a modified version of cricket as a substitute for their own traditional warfare.[18] Unlike the standard game, however, in Trobriand cricket each village could have as many players on their team as were available to play, and it became standard practice for the home team (or village) to be honored by always winning. The home team, however, was also responsible for hosting the visitors to a great feast and celebration. In this way, both sides were winners and no one suffered irreparable damage.

---

[18] *Trobriand Cricket*. Dir. Gary Kildea and Jerry Leach. Ronin Films, 1979.

In several West African cultures, people rely at times on an individual known as a *griot* to mediate some of their disputes.[19] The *griot* is both a wandering musician and an oral historian or storyteller (similar to bards in Greek mythology, such as Homer). Each *griot* is highly familiar with the histories of both local families and of the culture at large. When two families have a dispute with one another, they may choose to pay the local *griot* for his or her services. In this situation, each family will share their side of the story with the *griot,* who will then retreat into isolation for some period of time (perhaps a day or so) to contemplate the matter. Upon returning, the *griot* will perform a song for the families. This song will include a little bit of the local history, some background about each of the families involved, and interspersed within this song will be the *griot's* verdict, in verse form. After sharing the song, the *griot* will vacate the area, leaving the families to interpret the song in order to determine the *griot's* judgment.

As a final example of culturally specific problem-solving methods, consider the throat-singers of the Inuit people (people whom we often inaccurately refer to as "Eskimo"). When two individuals experience a disagreement with one another, they may choose to determine the outcome of the quarrel with a friendly throat-singing contest.[20] Although some males have recently begun taking up the tradition, it is usually women who will engage in this unique vocal competition with one another. The two will stand face-to-face, mere inches apart, and proceed to sing long, elaborate, vocal rhythms practically into one another's mouths, using the other singer's mouth and nasal cavity as a sort of resonance chamber. The first singer who either loses her breath or breaks the rhythmic pattern and becomes no longer able to continue the vocal challenge essentially loses the contest. Would it not be rather interesting to see two people in a large American city, following a minor fender bender, proceed to the nearest available sidewalk and engage in a public throat-singing duel!

In our own culture, we too have commonly preferred methods of settling disputes. Americans like to think of themselves as living in a "nation of laws,"

---

[19] Hoffman, Barbara G. *Griots at War: Conflict, Conciliation, and Caste in Mande,* Bloomington and Indianapolis: Indiana University Press, 2000.
[20] Wood, Nicholas. "Face to Face," *Sacred Hoop,* Issue 30, 2000.

so when someone is facing an irreconcilable difference with an opposing party, Americans commonly resort to litigation. In other words, we sue, making America the most litigious society in the world.[21]

COERCION AS A DECISION-MAKING PRACTICE

Sometimes coercion is employed to elicit a preferred decision-making outcome. **Coercion** is defined as the use of physical force or even simply to threaten the use of such force. For instance, we could tell you that you had better come to class or we will have a couple of our big thug buddies break your legs. You very well may choose to come to class based on such a threat, but it would obviously be a choice made out of fear rather than one based on the academic merits of attending class.

Coercion is often used at both ends of the decision-making spectrum–from an interpersonal quarrel to international relations. An abusive spouse or parent uses threats (or, even more tragically, actual force) to control and intimidate the behavior of other family members. Likewise, one nation can threaten another with something as serious as all-out military invasion or as symbolic as recalling an ambassador, or something in between like economic sanctions, in order to elicit a desired response. We have seen this happen quite notably in America's foreign policy toward nations of the Middle East. Prior to the Iraq War, the United States demanded that Saddam Hussein give up his WMDs (weapons of mass destruction) or face military invasion. This threat was followed up with an actual invasion. Similarly, the United States has repeatedly threatened the Islamic Republic of Iran with intensified economic sanctions, a naval blockade, as well as possible military strikes if it does not disband what the United States believes to be a covert nuclear weapons program. To be sure, it is certainly not only the United States that uses coercion in international affairs,[22] but it should

---

[21] Baye, Michael. "Comparative Analysis of Litigation Systems: An Auction-theoretic Approach," *Economic Journal*, July, 2005.

[22] The oil embargo of the 1970s is a good example of the Middle Eastern nations, through OPEC, using their oil wealth to coerce the United States. Russia has also used both military threats and actual force as well as the denial of vital energy resources to coerce Eastern European nations on numerous occasions. North Korea's provocative missile tests over Japanese air space are another example.

be noted that a nation (or even an individual for that matter) typically needs to hold a certain degree of power or influence relative to others before it can be in a position to make its threats seem credible to others.

REASONED DELIBERATION AND DECISION-MAKING

The types of decision-making methods and techniques explored up to this point tend to lack the significant use of reasoned judgment in their calculations. We will now turn our attention to types of decision-making processes that are more deliberative in procedure. **Deliberation** entails the careful and thorough consideration of competing arguments. This includes the contrasting and weighing of relative risks against one another according to the proportional magnitude or size, timeframe, and probability or likelihood of each. A deliberative process also typically involves consultation with others in order to more fully consider and explore the numerous perspectives and interpretations of evidence brought forward to support competing positions. Finally, deliberation is very intentional. In other words, it is undertaken with clear purpose and is marked by fully conscious behavior. It is done in a thoughtful manner, as if to try to avoid error. This approach to decision-making is based more firmly in reasoned judgment than the others mentioned above. Problems and proposed solutions should be thoroughly thrashed out until an appropriate resolution is found. A good decision-making process relies heavily on problem-solving, in-depth questioning, critical assessment, and the vigorous challenging of common norms and assumptions. We will now take a closer comparative look at three variants of this more contemplative manner of decision-making: debate, dialogue, and deliberation.

DEBATE

While we will be going into much greater detail about debate in other parts of the book, it is useful for the purpose of comparing decision-making models to offer a brief overview at this point. A **debate**, at least in the more formal sense intended here, could be described as a form of argument that has strict rules of conduct, follows a structured format, and uses sophisticated arguing techniques.[23] Ideally, a formal or "academic" debate should have a topic that offers a fair **division of ground**; in other words, there should be at least two reasonably balanced opposing sides to the topic with plausibly defensible arguments on either side of the question. The side that has been assigned to agree with the topic is alternately called the proponent, the advocate, the Affirmative, or quite simply the For side, while the side that will be disagreeing with the topic might be called the opposition, the Negative, or simply the Against side.

Debate is different than either discussion or dialogue in that it is much more competitive and adversarial in nature. Just as in a court of law, where one cannot be found both guilty and innocent, in a formal debate there are clear winners and losers, with an unambiguous goal of coming to a decision which excludes one side or their position on the topic. In this way, academic debate follows an adversarial or judicial model.

DISCUSSION

Discussion is perhaps the most common way in which people tend to communicate argumentatively in their everyday lives. It is much less formal than an organized debate. During discussion we present our thoughts and ideas and everyone analyzes and dissects them from their own particular points of view. While ideally everyone involved is allowed to participate and share their perspectives, like debate, the basic purpose of discussion is still "to win" (see Figure 4-1) or to make sure that your point of view is the one that is ultimately favored. Although less structured and with fewer rigid rules of conduct than a debate (see Figure 4-2), in a discussion each participant still wants to prove that he or she is right and the most knowledgeable on the subject. There is, however, greater room for compromise than exists in a debate; for example, in discussion different people's ideas can ultimately be combined into a single final solution. During a discussion, each participant will assess the relative strengths and weaknesses of each other's claims in an effort to find agreement. With everyone trying to "win the argument," however, sometimes no one's mind is changed and no decision can be reached. If this happens, we end up either in a stalemate,

---

[23] For a more thorough discussion of formal debate and its guidelines, refer to Part IV.

having additional follow–up discussions, resorting to a simple vote in order to determine the majority's preferences, or a group leader will use his or her authority to decide for everyone.

As opposed to the process involved in the simple majority rule voting procedures discussed below, respectful discussions allow everyone, even those who may not be as verbally active as others, to express openly their ideas, concerns, and opinions for consideration by the group. Members of the group get a chance to learn from other participants' perspectives and thinking, to empathize with their experiences and backgrounds, and perhaps even change their own attitudes about certain issues as they become aware of new ideas and points of view. Furthermore, as in a debate, they can challenge those assumptions and solutions that they find to be faulty, obsolete, or unethical. However, they are generally more free to explore and adopt the more dynamic kinds of solutions–such as radical reformations, compromises, bargains, integrative solutions, etc., that are often overlooked when an argument gets polarized or restrained by rigid voting procedures or are simply incompatible with the much more strict rules of a formal debate.

DIALOGUE

Unlike either debate or discussion, **dialogue** is more of an open-ended exploration of ideas, with very few rules (see Figure 4-2). In a dialogue no one is really trying to "win"; rather, the goal of the participants is to try to learn from one another and develop new approaches and perspectives, such as during a brainstorming exercise. During dialogue everyone works together, contributing toward a cooperative exchange of ideas. In the dialogue approach, the whole is considered greater than the sum of the parts; therefore more is achieved from the dialogue as each person's ideas are added to the last. This is very unlike debate (or discussion, to a certain extent), where the losing side's arguments are necessarily rejected as a part of the process. Participants are expected to set aside their individual assumptions and preconceived notions in order to be more open to fully exploring new concepts and approaches (see Figure 4-3). It is a free flow of ideas, with all contributions treated as relatively equal in importance. There are three basic elements to dialogue:

- **Participants should suspend their assumptions**. Suspending one's assumptions is not an easy task, since they are often so deep-seated in our subconscious that we generally do not even know that they are assumptions. Instead, we take them for granted as our own personal version of the truth. However, dialogue comes to a grinding halt when someone digs in their heels and becomes determined to show everyone that their way is *the* way. When working within a dialogue framework, assumptions need to be suspended in order to be open enough to accept truth whenever and wherever it happens to be revealed.

- **Group members must be thought of as equals**. When interacting as equals, group members tend to feel less vulnerable to attack and can avoid the need to be defensive of their thoughts. Ideally, this makes everyone less likely to either want to dominate the discussion or alternatively to resist saying anything at all out of fear of being ridiculed. Again, this is much easier said than done; many people feel the need to defend their opinions constantly and assertively, as well as the urge to attack the ideas of others. While this kind of reaction is fairly normal human behavior, its presence quickly negates the virtues of dialogue (see Figure 4-4). Unfortunately, it takes only one or two individuals behaving in this manner to basically ruin the dialogue for everyone else.

- **There is often a facilitator**. A good facilitator can help encourage open-mindedness through the suspension of individual assumptions and judgments, or at least to recognize and identify them when they appear. They also function to make sure that each participant's contributions are being treated equally. The facilitator plays an important role in encouraging everyone's participation and keeping the dialogue moving smoothly along whenever it might slow or stall. As a group becomes better skilled at dialogue and more familiar with one another, the need for a formal facilitator becomes reduced.

COMPARISON OF THE DELIBERATIVE MODELS

It is unlikely that anyone is so open-minded as to be able to avoid completely engaging in moments of debate while in a lengthy discussion or dialogue. Likewise, few are so close-minded that they will not at least listen to some of the ideas of others. Dialogue sometimes behaves more like a discussion, and occasionally debates result in opposing sides having a friendly, cooperative discussion, finding that they have much in common. The lines between these methods are sometimes blurry and it can be difficult to make sharp distinctions. Each technique may even at some point be used as a tool within the larger framework of one of the other methods. Nevertheless it is still educational to compare and contrast them. We have provided some visual comparisons that include the additional category of a **quarrel** (a hostile dispute or altercation between two or more people; a fight) so as to offer a more complete continuum for contrast.

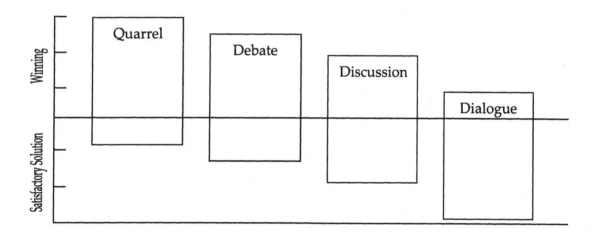

Figure 4-1 Emphasis on Winning Versus Finding a Satisfactory Solution

Figure 4-1 exhibits the extent to which each of the various methods emphasizes "winning" as a primary goal of the communicative exchange, as opposed to the goal of discovering a more mutually satisfactory solution to a problem. Of the four different methods addressed, it is only dialogue that does not identify winning as a rather significant goal vis-à-vis finding a more communal solution to a problem. Figure 4-2 depicts the relative absence or

63

presence of formally written rules. Unlike the other charts comparing the models in this section, which show a somewhat more gradual change from one method to the next and a relatively steady shift between the extremes, this chart shows debate to be somewhat unusual when compared to the other methods in that it maintains a significant set of written rules by which it is governed. While there may be unwritten rules and codes of conduct for the others, formal debate operates under a much more extensive set of codified rules and procedures, as will more clearly be seen in Part IV.

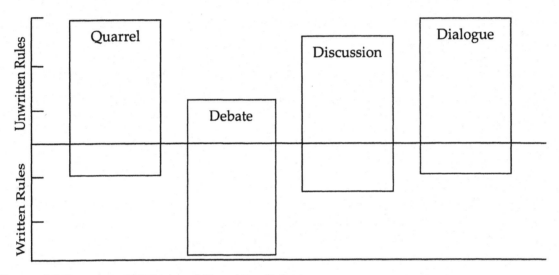

Figure 4-2 Presence of Written and Unwritten Rules

Figure 4-3 demonstrates the degree of open-mindedness typically displayed by participants of each method. As noted above, dialogue requires a significant degree of open-mindedness in order to meet its objectives of nonjudgmental inclusion and equity; whereas the sometimes-strong emotions and obvious defensiveness typical of a quarrel represent the opposite extreme.

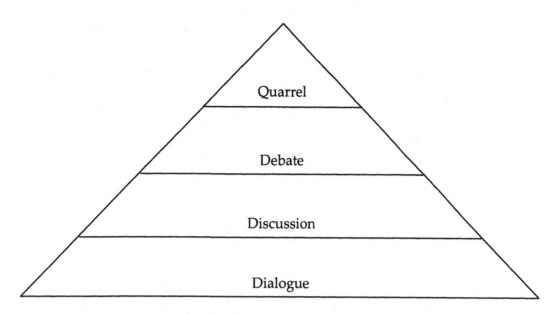

Figure 4-3 Extent of Open-mindedness

Along fairly similar lines, Figure 4-4 illustrates the degree of interpersonal hostility and aggression associated with each of the different techniques, with dialogue and a quarrel again representing the extremes. Finally, in keeping the general pattern of the two previous forms, Figure 4-5 shows the relative levels of both emotionality and rationality which characterize each of the methods.

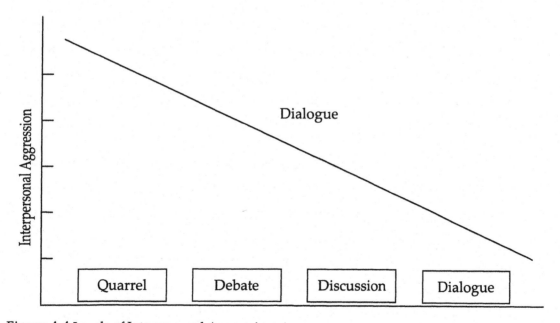

Figure 4-4 Levels of Interpersonal Aggression

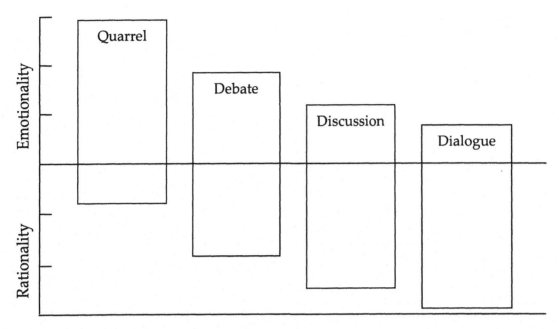

Figure 4-5 Levels of Emotionality and Rationality

THE FINAL STEP—CULMINATING PROCEDURES

The decision-making methods discussed thus far might be considered the *processes* we utilize prior to the reaching of a conclusion, in which we attempt to persuade others that our ideas are the most valid.[24] Now we will consider the *procedural* nature of the final, culminating act of determining an outcome to the process. In its simplest and broadest form, we might refer to this concluding step as the *verdict,* despite the fact that some of these procedures do not necessarily embody what we commonly assume that term to mean. In other words, this culminating procedure might be considered the last step in finalizing the decision-making process.

Debate, discussion, and, sometimes, even dialogue (although to a much lesser degree), all conclude with some sort of culminating step which determines an outcome or directs an action to be taken. For instance, while a debate can be thought of as the competing persuasive appeals offered by two or more individuals holding firm positions, it takes place *prior to* a third party's verdict or vote. In the same way, discussion could be considered a less regimented and

---

[24] To a certain degree, even within the dialogue framework, we are often sharing ideas that we believe to be valid.

somewhat more cooperative manner by which people exchange perspectives, but again it occurs *prior to* a settlement by means of either a vote or group consensus. Even dialogue is a process that takes place *prior to* some kind of final result or outcome, however informal it may be. We will look at three particular types of culminating procedures: hierarchical conclusions, majority rule, and consensus.

HIERARCHICAL CONCLUSIONS

Some decision-making processes culminate with a **hierarchal** conclusion or verdict, meaning that there is a "top-down" decision made by an authority figure with the power to dictate an outcome. This procedure could be as benign as the judge of a competitive intercollegiate debate competition who has been empowered by the schools involved to decide a winner of the match, or as malevolent as the dictator of a country imposing an edict on his or her subjects. The chart below (Figure 4-6) indicates the basic structure of some of these hierarchal types of culminating procedures as well as several of the benefits and challenges associated with them.

Figure 4-6 Hierarchy—"Top-Down" Authoritative Decision Structure

Autocratic (single-person rule)   **Consultative (single-person rule with advisors)**

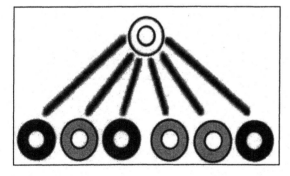   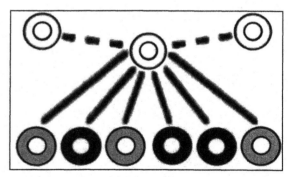

Benefits   *Challenges*

- o   It is fast—it is good for crises, emergencies, conflict situations, etc.
- o   Clear responsibility and accountability
- o   Explicit structure

- o   Fosters coercive and domineering behavior
- o   Encourages competition and pandering
- o   Undemocratic/unrepresentative
- o   Many views go unheard
- o   Subordinates may not understand the decision and may lack commitment to carry out decisions.

MAJORITY RULE—THE COUNTING OF PREFERENCES

People will often mistakenly suggest simple majority rule through voting as a reasonably democratic method of decision-making. It is fairly quick, offers a distinct winner, and it is a process most people are very familiar with. Simple **majority rule voting,** however, might be more aptly defined as a procedure for tallying preferences as opposed to an actual decision-making process.[25] Rather, voting is a procedure that takes place after debate or discussion has ended. Voting is often criticized as a lazy technique because, rather than encouraging the same level of careful consideration that makes up some of the other available options, it simply "counts the beans." Indeed, sometimes a vote is suggested precisely to avoid engaging in the difficult work of a lengthy discussion or complicated debate.

MAJORITY RULE VOTING AND INTENSITY OF PREFERENCE

Except under rather limited circumstances—for example, situations when there are only a few possible options to consider—it may prove somewhat difficult for a group to reach a conclusion that is fair and equitable for all parties simply by counting the preferences of a group of people. Even in situations with only a few options, simple majority rule voting fails to consider the intensity of preferences each individual might feel. Because each person has only one vote, and the side that tallies even a slim majority ultimately wins, this process is unable to account for the distinct possibility that some people might feel very strongly opposed to a decision while a slight majority are only mildly in favor. Take, for example, a small town voting to elect a new mayor, where there are three candidates: a Democrat, a Republican, and a Libertarian. Let us assume that the town is slightly more Republican than anything else. It might be the case that this slight majority only mildly supports the Republican candidate, whereas the somewhat smaller number of Democratic voters are strongly opposed to the Republican candidate. Let us further assume that neither the Republican nor the Democratic voters are strongly opposed to the Libertarian candidate. In such a situation, it might make the most sense for each side to compromise on the Libertarian candidate, thus finding a solution that all the voters might find least reasonably

---

[25] Janis, Irving. *Groupthink*, Boston: Houghton-Mifflin, 1982.

acceptable. Otherwise, the Republicans voters will be mildly satisfied, while the Democratic voters will be noticeably distressed, and the Libertarian voters might feel disenfranchised. A simple majority rule voting procedure lacks the flexibility to account for such variables.

MAJORITY RULE VOTING AND THE INTERESTS OF OTHERS

Majority rule voting not only has a limited ability to protect the rights and interests of the minority, as we can see with the example above, but it also fails to consider the interests of future generations, those prevented from participating in the voting process by procedural or economic restrictions, or any other party either prohibited from or choosing not to vote.[26] By failing to protect the interests of those not voting in the majority, such simple voting procedures may result in an inequitable distribution of consequences. Majority rule voting necessarily means that the minority will not get what they want, and if the majority's preference is one that scrupulously disregards those interests or concerns, the minority may become disillusioned and choose to leave the group or perhaps even consider some kind of retaliation.

MAJORITY RULE VOTING AND POLARIZATION

Perhaps voting can therefore produce satisfying results only if there is near-unanimity of opinion or if everyone in the group is extremely tolerant. If enough people are genuinely committed to starkly different proposals or if there is significant competition for power within the group, the process will often bog down, factionalize, or possibly even slide into coercive manipulation. Knowing that there will be a final winner-take-all vote at the end of the process can tend to polarize the discussion by motivating people to deceptively argue for a more extreme position so that they can later "compromise" back to their actual intentions or goals.[27] Thus, majority rule voting without prior deliberation appears to be rather limited by its inability to explore in any considerable depth

---

[26] Fisher, Roger and William Ury. *Getting to Yes: Negotiating Agreement Without Giving In*, New York: Penguin Books, 1981.

[27] For further discussion of the pros and cons of compromise, see Chapter 3.

the complete range of concerns and available options in a genuine, non-adversarial, and cooperative manner.

Figure 4-7 Majority Rule Voting

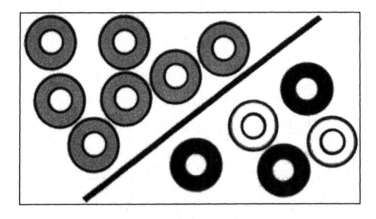

Benefits	Challenges
o Most people are experienced with it.	o It encourages competition and manipulation.
o It provides an easy and obvious structure to follow.	o It polarizes the group; losers often have no commitment to the decision.
o It works with any size group.	o Decisions contain bad parts of the winning proposal, but lack good parts of the losing one.
o It creates a distinct winner.	o It is simplistic; it does not accurately represent group opinion when more than 2 or 3 choices are involved.
o It is generally fast.	

BENEFITS OF MAJORITY RULE VOTING

Of course, despite the many shortcomings raised here, majority rule voting need not be completely eliminated from effective argumentative proceedings. A process that includes the elements of a good discussion can still meaningfully end with a simple vote. In fact, an exceptionally good voting process may be largely indistinguishable from other forms of decision-making until the final step of actually indicating the direction of one's vote, so long as special care is taken to deemphasize the significance and finality of the vote itself and instead focus on the process that leads up to vote.

CONFUSION OVER CONSENSUS

Some people believe consensus is an idealistic scheme where every problem always ends up with a good, simple solution that mysteriously incorporates everyone's ideas and satisfies everyone's concerns. Others see consensus as a diabolical plot designed to create the illusion of democratic participation while a select few control the true outcome. While each of these extreme versions tends to be a bit unrealistic, the value and effectiveness of consensus as a procedure varies widely depending on how well it is executed by those involved. In some situations consensus works quite wonderfully, while in others it is a disaster. In any case, there seems to be a good deal of confusion and ignorance about what consensus actually is, how it should theoretically work, and when it should most appropriately be used. In this section, we will outline the basic practice of consensus and try to dispel some of the common myths surrounding it.

CONSENSUS IS CONSENT, NOT UNANIMITY

Many people mistakenly consider consensus as simply an extended voting procedure in which everyone involved must eventually cast their votes in the exact same way.[28] However, such complete **unanimity** rarely occurs in groups with more than just a couple of members. Figure 4-8 displays some of the benefits and challenges of unanimity. Groups of more than a couple members trying to reach this kind of accord are likely to end up becoming extremely frustrated. In such a situation, decisions are either never reached, leading to the stagnation and possible demise of the group, or some member(s) of the group may resort to coercive measures in order to dominate the rest. At times it will be a majority that dominates, at others a minority, and sometimes even a single individual. Regardless of the numbers involved, such a coercive and hierarchal approach is not consensus (see Figure 4-6). Rather, **consensus** is a procedure for determining what is best for the group as a whole. Under the consensus framework, the group's final decision is rarely the first preference of any individual member, and many may not even like the final result. It is, however, a decision to which they all consent, not because they are in complete agreement

---

[28] Gastil, John. *Democracy in Small Groups*, Philadelphia: New Society Publishers, 1993.

with one another's positions, but because they know that it is the best option for the group (See Figure 4-9)

Figure 4-8 Unanimity—Complete Agreement

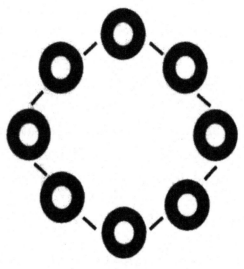

Benefits	*Challenges*
o Great when it occurs because everyone is satisfied	o Extremely difficult to achieve with more than a few people
o High level of commitment to the decision	o Can lead to coercive efforts to manipulate
	o Frustration can result in stagnation and possible disbanding of the group

CONSENSUS IS A COOPERATIVE PROCESS

Consensus is a procedural tool for people who want to work together honestly in a good faith manner in order to find solutions that offer the greatest advantages for the entire group at large. It is not a method that can be used effectively by people who are not willing to work cooperatively. As such, the consensus process should probably be avoided by any group with people who attempt to dominate or control others or who make efforts to maintain their own positions of privilege at the expense of others. Consensus encourages everyone within a group to actively participate and work collaboratively in order to reach mutually beneficial outcomes. At its core, the consensus process is an egalitarian and participatory endeavor. Rather than abdicating authority to a leader, the consensus framework puts the decision-making power directly in the hands of the group's individual members, thus modeling democratic governance.

Figure 4-9 Consensus—Cooperative Search for a Mutual Decision

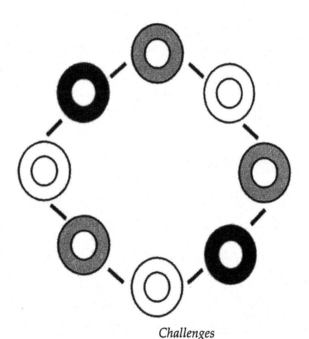

Benefits	Challenges
o Encourages cooperation by reaching a decision which all can accept	o Usually takes more time
o Synthesizes all ideas into one	o Sometimes frustrating
o Brings conflicts into the open, minimizing efforts to manipulate	o Requires good listening skills
	o Requires cooperation and mutual concern
o Minority opinions and concerns are heard and considered	o One person can block a decision by "stonewalling"

CONSENSUS—EASIER SAID THAN DONE

While consensus clearly holds numerous advantages as an outcome-based procedure, there are several challenges to be considered as well. First of all, consensus is a difficult and complicated procedure that is unfamiliar to most people. As mentioned earlier, there are many misconceptions about what consensus is, and if there are participants who hold any them the likelihood of reaching actual consensus is rather slim. An effective consensus procedure needs either a large portion of the decision-making group to be somewhat familiar with the concept or a few very capable leaders with a solid grasp of the method to guide everyone else through it.

Even assuming that nearly everyone in a group is familiar with the consensus process, it is far from a guaranteed success. Not only can consensus take a long time to reach, making it inappropriate for time-sensitive matters, but sometimes consensus is simply unattainable. The assumption that the presence of so-called "facts" will quell disagreement fails to take into account either those who will disagree over the meaning of the facts, or those who would disregard them altogether.

THE DOWNSIDE OF CONSENSUS

In certain circumstances, truly oppositional interests might exist which should not be simply glossed over for the sake of producing a superficial illusion of harmony. Some may later regret the compromises they made and either withdraw from the group or undermine its work. Moreover, while the occasional compromise can be an effective and useful tool in addressing differences of opinion, some things are better left uncompromised. The account of King Solomon proposing that a child be cut in half to settle a quarrel between two women claiming to be the child's mother offers a clear illustration of this point—some people are willing to go too far in settling a question. And, as has been mentioned previously in this chapter and will be addressed again in the next, knowing that compromise will be a formal part of the process can motivate some participants to begin with exaggerated positions.

Finally, if a group is struggling to reach consensus and frustration with the process begins to settle in, both direct and indirect pressure may come into play with individuals or groups attempting to push others into conformity with their position. Not only does this negate the true objectives of consensus, but it also creates a manipulative atmosphere wherein the most assertive and competitive participants will be motivated to take advantage of their more accommodating colleagues.

SUMMARY

Any group or set of individuals faced with the need to make a difficult decision should carefully consider the style or method they will use and then devote the necessary amount of time and energy for learning the nuances of that process, developing the new skills involved, and addressing the challenges of each. For instance, learning and practicing the skills, behaviors, and procedures involved with the above decision-making processes and procedures may require a level of effort beyond that to which people are usually accustomed. A certain amount of time should also be occasionally spent assessing the continued usefulness of the method chosen so that the process can be steadily improved. Finally, it is important to remember that no single method is best or most appropriate for all situations. Because the problems we face as individuals and as a society are of a wide variety of shapes, sizes, and colors, so too should the decision-making methods applied to them be of a diverse and circumstantial nature.

CHAPTER 5

COPING WITH CONFLICT

Leadership has a harder job to do than just choose sides. It must bring sides together.
Jesse Jackson

The greatest threat to freedom is the absence of criticism.
Wole Soyinka

There is practically no limit to the number of interactions wherein an appreciation for the complex dynamics of conflict management is not only useful, but even necessary for effective and meaningful participation in communication. This is particularly true when confronting issues of a controversial nature in which conflict is likely to arise. The purpose of this chapter is to identify the role that conflict management plays in the conduct of positive and constructive communication about potentially divisive issues.

Although there are no easy answers, we will attempt to clarify some of the complexities of conflict management through an investigation of various conflict management styles that may help to overcome the most difficult barriers to civil discourse when appropriately applied in a situational manner. The objective here is to work toward the goal of becoming more aware of the contextual use of these differing styles in an effort toward resolving differences in a positive and cooperative, rather than confrontational, manner. Moreover, an effort will be made to show that conflict is not necessarily limited to being solely a negative communication attribute, but rather that it can actually serve a positive role when managed effectively.

CONFLICT

WHAT IS CONFLICT?

Conflict exists whenever incompatible activities or agendas occur.[29] An activity or agenda that is incompatible with another is one that prevents, blocks, or somehow interferes with the occurrence or effectiveness of another. Individual and group objectives (these could be either need-based or based purely on desire) are not always consistent and parallel with one another, and sometimes they are even in direct opposition. Conflict typically arises because someone's objectives are not being met. A conflict can be as small and simple as an interpersonal disagreement over whose turn it is to do the dishes, or as large and complex as international warfare over some scarce resource. It can originate internally within a single person (**intrapersonal**), externally between two or more people (**interpersonal**), within a single group (**intragroup**), or between two or more groups (**intergroup**).

THE INEVITABILITY OF CONFLICT

Conflict, both between individuals and among groups, is largely inevitable. We live in a world full of diverse people who have a wide variety of beliefs, values, customs, opinions, needs, and desires. When seemingly contradictory objectives come into contact with each other, some form of conflict is ultimately to be expected. There are many different sources of conflict, including resource competition, poor communication skills, either real or perceived injustices, disparities in social and/or economic status, moral dissimilarity, and numerous others. Tensions often surface when individuals disagree over issues about

---

[29] Deutsch, Morton. *The Resolution of Conflict: Constructive and Destructive Processes*, New Haven, CT: Yale University Press, 1973.

which they are passionate. There is certainly nothing wrong with people genuinely caring deeply about something. However, the sometimes-difficult challenge lies in how to effectively manage the conflict that often arises when these caring people are at odds with one another.

Additionally, conflict may actually be a more natural state for some than for others—their family experience may have been confrontational in nature, they may lack the skills to prevent conflict, they may be under frequent or intense stress, they may find confrontation to be exciting, conflict might be used as a form of distraction from other issues, etc. While most people tend to avoid conflict when possible, others, those who might have experienced one or more of the conditions just mentioned, may actually find some form of comfort through the familiarity of the pursuit of conflict.

ATTEMPTS TO MINIMIZE CONFLICT

Although conflict is largely inevitable, this does not mean we cannot attempt to minimize its occurrence—especially the "negative" kind of conflict. There are some strategies that may help prevent conflict from happening in the first place, or at least diminish its severity. By dealing with the "little issues" before they become big ones, a more harmonious academic, workplace, or family environment can be nurtured. Emphasizing group- or organization-wide goals can both improve efficiency and encourage people to work together, rather than creating adversaries by pitting groups and individuals against each other. Further, when stable, well-structured tasks are provided, all parties can more clearly see what their various roles are. These efforts reduce the likelihood of disagreements because everyone's responsibilities are clearly communicated, thus avoiding uncertainty and misperceptions, while encouraging accountability. Finally, efforts to share rather than compete for resources can help to limit some conflicts by avoiding win-lose relationships.

Although there are some measures we can take to limit the likelihood of conflict, it is unlikely that it can be prevented completely—there are just too many factors that encourage conflict to be able to control them all. Let us also not forget that conflict can actually be a very valuable process if handled skillfully. Properly managed conflict can function as a healthy response to a wide variety of difficult challenges and may even serve to strengthen embattled relationships rather than further damaging them. However, if conflict is handled poorly, a bad situation can most definitely be made worse.

THE CONSEQUENCES OF CONFLICT

All conflict has consequences, and these consequences can be either negative or positive. We will begin by addressing some of the negative consequences, with which most people are already somewhat familiar. We will limit our discussion here to those negative consequences of conflict that fall short of physical violence, for that level of confrontation should rightfully be seen by all as an undesirable outcome to be avoided in every instance.

NEGATIVE CONSEQUENCES

Some of the negative outcomes of conflict might actually follow what initially appear to be positive consequences. For instance, **group cohesion** refers to a common response to conflict wherein external threats cause a group to set aside their internal differences and become more cooperative. This is a phenomenon that often occurs in times of national crisis when an external threat creates a "common enemy" that unites people in a protective struggle. For instance, in the days and weeks following the attacks of 9/11, it was quite common to hear comments such as, "We are no longer either Democrats or Republicans; we are all Americans." In the workplace, a division or department might experience a greater sense of urgency and focus when faced with an external challenge. In an effort to deal with the conflict, the department members may spend less time idly and work harder to accomplish their tasks. However, such an increased level of effort may not last forever. **Burnout** occurs when an individual is overworked, and may actually result in a net decrease of productivity in the long run. It is also quite possible for hard feelings to develop if the increased level of effort does not accomplish group goals. Grudges may be established that can create intergroup bitterness and possibly prevent effective communication in the future.

Sometimes a conflict, particularly one viewed as a crisis with the need for an immediate response, might give rise to **autocratic leadership**. In this instance, a strong, decisive leader is thought to be more capable of responding to a difficult situation than relying on the slow and perhaps less-qualified response of democratic participation. In some cases this may be quite true, such as with a terrible accident involving the spill of potentially lethal chemicals; in such an instance it would likely be a better approach to trust the person who announces that he or she has years of training in the Marines dealing with chemical weapon attacks rather than taking the time to have a democratic discussion, making sure everyone receives equal opportunity to express himself or herself fully before a final vote about how best to respond to the impending doom. However, such dire events are rare; it is more likely that someone will attempt to create the impression that a situation is worse than it really is in order to gain a greater degree of power over others. Such changes in leadership roles may result in hurt feelings or misperceptions about intentions, which ultimately make communication and conflict management more difficult.

Finally, conflict situations quite commonly create both interpersonal and intergroup hostility. In the adversarial atmosphere of conflict, a rival group or individual is typically regarded as "the enemy." Our emotions get the best of us, and virtually every reason available for disliking them suddenly becomes an unquestionably valid one. Our perceptions become distorted to the point that we negatively stereotype others. We begin to overemphasize our own positive qualities and efforts while deemphasizing those of our adversary. Unfortunately, this irrational loathing tends to linger on even after the initial conflict is long resolved, blocking the opportunity for future cooperation.

POSITIVE ATTRIBUTES OF CONFLICT

While recognizing the many unpleasant elements of conflict, it is also important to emphasize the positive contributions that conflict makes to effective communication and deliberative decision-making. Although many people automatically consider conflict and confrontation as something entirely obstructive and to be avoided at all cost, this is not always the case. It should be understood that disagreement over controversial issues is not only to be expected, but is often a very healthy thing when handled appropriately. We all have different points of view, experiences, perspectives, and beliefs. That is part of what makes the world not only interesting, but also functional. If we all saw everything exactly the same way, not only would life be a little boring, but we might even have a difficult time solving the many problems that we face as a society. Just imagine if no one had ever decided to speak up and say that he or she thought slavery was inappropriate and should be abolished, or that a woman's right to vote should be recognized equally with a man's. When practiced in a meaningful manner, difference of opinion and disagreement have often been the vehicle of societal change and the cause of innovation and progress throughout history. In a thoughtful and progressive society, conflict is neither ignored nor covered up, but rather is actually encouraged.

We would do well to question many of the commonly held assumptions that abound about conflict. Despite its widely perceived negative connotation, disagreement can actually serve a rather constructive function in communication. It is important to understand that conflict typically arises when an individual or group views the current conditions, or the status quo, as either inadequate or even destructive. When someone becomes sufficiently dissatisfied with the way things are, he or she becomes increasingly willing to speak out and take actions with the hope of being able to influence the situation in such a way as to arrive at an improved set of circumstances. Thus, conflict and disagreement could rightly be viewed as a reflection of a diverse, healthy, and properly functioning society. A society that lacks such diversity of thought is in danger not only of continually repeating the same mistakes over and over, but also of being unable to adapt to changing conditions and to meet new challenges. In this perspective, conflict can be viewed as a process that we put ourselves through in order to make things better, rather than something unpleasant to be feared or avoided.

Even in our interpersonal relationships, conflict can serve positive functions when thoughtfully approached. By assessing disagreement from a somewhat neutral and objective perspective, we allow ourselves to become more able to recognize and address the presence of fundamental differences. This recognition is the first step toward resolving those differences in mutually beneficial ways. As a result, the act of respectfully acknowledging differences of thought can help us to build even stronger and ultimately more meaningful relationships. As Mary Follett put it

We must be ever on our guard that we do not confuse differences and antagonisms, that diversity does not arouse hostility. Suppose a friend says something with which I do not agree. . . . Our relations become slightly strained, we change the subject as soon as possible, etc. But suppose we were really civilized beings, then we should think: "How interesting this is, this idea has evidently a much larger content than I realized; if my friend and I can unify this material we shall separate with a much larger idea than either of us had before." If my friend and I are always trying to find the things upon which we agree, what is the use of our meeting? Because the consciousness of agreement makes us happy? It is a shallow happiness, felt only by people too superficial or too shut-up or too vain to feel that richer joy which comes from having taken part in an act of creation—created a new idea by the uniting of differences.[30]

Disagreement does not necessarily have to be of an adversarial nature; there is no good reason why a well-managed conflict cannot be positive and mutually respectful. Skills can be acquired and developed that can help to facilitate productive communication even when conflict is present. Through skillfully navigating the various conflicts we may find ourselves in, we are presented with opportunities to be creative and even self-defining. Indeed, when conflict is recognized early and positively embraced, it can help create learning conversations that build trust, shared learning, better outcomes, and improved relationships. When conflict situations are skillfully managed and successfully resolved to the satisfaction of those involved, they can have very powerful implications, including newfound levels of awareness and personal confidence. In this respect, past successes in finding creative solutions to conflict serve to further promote future successes, thus creating a win-win cycle. If absolutely nothing else, *conflict encourages us to do things differently than we traditionally have in hopes of improving our own lives and those of the people around us.*

The issue should not be whether conflict occurs, as we have already established that conflict is largely inevitable, but rather how we respond to conflict situations. Additional desirable outcomes of constructively managed conflict include[31]:

- higher quality decision-making through the use of critical thinking skills and creative problem solving

- increased motivation to take action

- greater satisfaction with achievements

- healthier cognitive and social development by being better able to deal with stressful situations

---

[30] Follett, Mary. *The New State,* New York: Longmans, Green and Company, 1926, p. 40–41.
[31] Johnson, David W., and Roger T. Johnson. *Teaching Students to be Peacemakers* (3rd ed.), Edina, MN: Interaction Book Company, 1995.

- increased ability to cope with unforeseen adversities

- more stable and higher quality relationships with friends, co-workers, and family members

- a greater sense of caring, commitment, respect, and cohesiveness

Whether a conflict will ultimately serve a positive or a negative role will be determined largely by our ability to understand the nature of the conflict and the skillful application of various situationally appropriate conflict management techniques. In order for us to develop a more thorough understanding of the complexities of conflict, the following section will address the many different forms which conflict can take.

UNDERSTANDING CONFLICT TYPOLOGY

THE NATURE OF CONFLICT

The nature of a conflict situation takes several different forms.[32] **Goal-oriented conflict** occurs when one group or individual desires a different set of outcomes than another. This is a conflict of interests, where a clash may arise over whose goals are to be prioritized and pursued. Goal-oriented conflicts may occur over substantive issues such as money, natural resources, time, or some other commodity. They might also occur over more intangible issues, such as justice, equality, fairness, or respect. Goal-oriented conflicts may be over real or simply perceived incompatibility of interests, but in either case the parties involved typically believe that in order to meet their own interests, the interests of the other party must be sacrificed.

Cognitive conflict transpires when one group or individual holds opinions and beliefs that are inconsistent with those of another. This is the type of conflict that we often see in the case of debates over political or religious issues, where opposing groups hold competing values. **Values** are beliefs that people use to give meaning to their lives, and they are used to explain what different people see as "good" and "bad," or "right" and "wrong." Cognitive conflict results from differences in what we have been taught and in our accumulated life experiences. Although having differing value systems does not

---

[32] Cloke, Kenneth, and Joan Goldsmith. *Understanding the Culture and Context of Conflict: Resolving Conflicts at Work*, San Francisco, CA: Jossey-Bass, 2001.

mean that people cannot live together in harmony, sometimes one person or group attempts to force one set of values upon another. In other instances, one person or group may claim to follow an exclusive value system that does not allow for divergent beliefs. In either case, a dispute of some form or other is more than likely to follow, because most people place a rather high priority on their own values and beliefs.

Behavioral conflict is that type of conflict in which one group or individual does or says something that may be deemed unacceptable or objectionable by another. For example, when a pair of students consistently interrupts the class with their chatting, it is the behavior of the students, as opposed to some moral or political difference, that creates a conflict with the instructor and their classmates. Behavioral conflicts might also occur when there are differences in performance and reward expectations, where different groups are evaluated and rewarded according to different standards. At a restaurant, for instance, the wait staff is theoretically evaluated according to speed and friendliness of service, whereas the kitchen staff is more likely to be judged according to accuracy of preparation. However, when the kitchen staff consistently undercooks meat dishes, it is the wait staff who inevitably bear the negative consequences in the form of reduced tips. Such a situation is quite likely to create conflict among the workers.

Some additional types of conflict might include data conflicts, judicial ambiguities, and status inconsistencies. **Data conflicts** occur when people lack the necessary information to make accurate decisions. This may be because someone is withholding vital information, or when people disagree on the most important data, have competing data, or have differing interpretations of the same data. A **judicial ambiguity** is a conflict that emerges when it is unclear exactly where responsibility for an issue or a certain action lies, such as the power to hire or fire personnel. **Status inconsistencies** are based on relative degrees of authority and power, and they may result in conflict under such situations as a manager who takes extra time off and regularly arrives to work late, when others are not allowed to do so.

OVERT AND COVERT CONFLICT

In addition to these different types, conflict may be expressed in either overt or covert forms.[33] **Covert conflict** occurs when individuals express their differences or opposition only indirectly. The subtle underlying nature of this form of conflict makes it very difficult to effectively resolve divergent positions. After all, how can one be expected to resolve a conflict he or she is not even sure is there? **Overt conflict**, on the other hand, exists when individuals openly and directly express their disagreements with one another. This more straightforward manner of communication is typically more helpful in effectively addressing conflict situations. When opposition to an idea, a proposal, or a behavior is withheld or only covertly expressed, it often leads to misperceptions as well as feelings of being ignored or disrespected, which likely set the stage for even more deeply rooted conflict in the future.

TRUE AND FALSE CONFLICT

The ability to successfully distinguish between true conflicts and false conflicts is also essential and a necessary prerequisite for maintaining effective communication while navigating a conflict.[34] A **true conflict** is something that would tend to escalate and result in greater negative consequences if it is not resolved. **False conflicts**, on the other hand, are differences that for the most part are substantively irrelevant to maintaining a healthy personal relationship or work environment. For example, parents ignoring their teenage child's drug problem because they disagree on the most appropriate method of intervention would be a true conflict. Without intervention, the child's addiction will only continue to worsen and the consequences become more serious. Disagreeing about which restaurant to visit for dinner, however, would be a false conflict. The couple's relationship is not dependent upon, nor truly harmed by, their differing dining preferences.

Once we recognize that conflict can appear in numerous different shapes, sizes, and forms, it becomes clear that it is highly beneficial to address conflicts situationally, or on a case-by-case basis, rather than assuming that all conflicts are the same, and applying a one-size-fits-all approach. Such an inflexible and universal attitude toward conflict often sets the stage for failure. As the saying goes, "choose your battles wisely."

---

[33] Wood, Julia T. *Communication Mosaics: An Introduction to the Field of Communication*, Belmont, CA: Wadsworth, 2006.

[34] Moore, Ronnie. "Communicating Through Conflict," *The American Salesman*, 52, 2007, pp. 18–21.

CONFLICT RESPONSE

Although choosing one's battles and establishing open lines of communication are the initial steps in managing conflict effectively, understanding the basic components that differentiate the various conflict management responses is also crucial.

ACTIVE AND INACTIVE RESPONSES

Some conflict responses tend to be active in nature and scope, whereas others rely more upon inactive behavior. Communication theorist Julia Wood has identified what she sees as the four primary conflict responses: exit, neglect, loyalty, and voice.[35]

Psychologists sometimes classify our instinctual reactions to conflict in one of two categories: fight or flight. Falling in the second category, the **exit response** entails either a physical or psychological withdrawal from a conflict situation. Although this is an active response to confrontation that may indeed offer some limited but needed relief in the immediate face of rising tension, it is often ultimately an ineffective strategy in that it basically leaves the source of tension unsettled. Furthermore, the exit response can sometimes even become a destructive one because it can allow unresolved latent pressure to build up into a potentially more explosive outburst at a later time.

The **neglect response** involves a basic denial of conflict. It is an inactive response form that simply ignores whatever the problem may be in the hope that it will somehow go away on its own. While that may occasionally happen—indeed, there may be times when simply ignoring a problem is even the best option available, most conflicts do not usually disappear of their own accord. This response mechanism risks a similar result to that of the exit strategy discussed earlier—rather than resolving conflict it may only serve to escalate tensions to a greater level of animosity.

Although passive in nature, the **loyalty response** can be constructive in certain situations. This response involves the continued maintenance of a personal or professional relationship, despite the presence of challenging differences. Similar to the neglect response just mentioned, the loyalty response carries an element of hope that the problem will somehow eventually fix itself. Although this kind of submissive response typically sustains the relationship for

---

[35] Wood, Julia T. *Communication Mosaics.*

a period of time, and thus provides the option of perhaps addressing the tensions at some later point, failure to address the tensions may actually end up causing even more harm to the relationship than the original conflict.

The final conflict response identified by Wood is called a **voice response**. This happens when an individual directly challenges the issue at hand by openly vocalizing his or her feelings. The voice response is both active and also potentially constructive. While there are obvious and undeniable risks associated with directly confronting a conflict situation, this might be considered the most effective conflict response of the four, in that it at least opens the door to engaging the conflict situation through communication as opposed to letting the conflict fester and possibly intensify.

CONFLICT MANAGEMENT STYLES

Although everyone has the ability to vary his or her response to a conflict, depending upon the demands of a particular situation, it is also true that most people have developed preferred ways of dealing with conflict in general. These preferences coalesce over time to become an individual's **dominant conflict management style**. Sometimes this preferred style works quite well, but at other times it does not. When the situation happens to favor an individual's preferred style of conflict management, the dispute is likely to be resolved without too much difficulty. Unfortunately, one's preferred style will not be ideally suited to all conflict situations, and it is quite likely that other parties involved in the disagreement may have very different preferences when it comes to resolving disputes. Either of these possibilities could make finding a satisfactory solution somewhat difficult. Even people who share a similar conflict management style can have trouble working together, depending on the nature of the particular conflict. Understanding that particular conflict situations call for particular conflict responses, and learning to identify your own conflict management preferences can be very helpful in understanding why things are going well or not so well.

One widely used method for understanding divergent conflict management styles was developed in the 1970s by communication theorists

Kenneth Thomas and Ralph Kilmann.[36] In very simple terms, their model uses a questionnaire to determine an individual's typical response patterns to various types of conflict situations,[37] then groups these tendencies into five different categorical styles: Competing, Collaborating, Compromising, Accommodating, and Avoiding. As Figure 5-1 shows, all five of these styles are a blend of two basic personality preferences—a preference for being assertive (or its opposite, being unassertive) and a preference for being cooperative (or its opposite, being uncooperative). Being **assertive** might be defined as the extent to which an individual attempts to achieve his or her own personal goals and interests, whereas being **cooperative** refers to the degree to which an individual attempts to satisfy the concerns of others.

An individual's dominant conflict management style is then identified as the style with the highest score on the questionnaire. Each of the five conflict management styles can be seen as having its own individual strengths and weaknesses, and each is best suited for particular conflict situations. Understanding how each of the different response styles functions in unique conflict scenarios can offer a great deal of insight in guiding our efforts to more productively resolve disputes by approaching a conflict situationally. Here we take a look at each of the conflict management styles identified by Thomas and Kilmann, followed by some recommendations for the type of conflict scenario under which each might be most usefully employed.

---

[36] Thomas, Kenneth W. and Ralph Kilmann. *Thomas-Kilmann Conflict MODE Instrument,*

[37] It should be noted that the Thomas-Kilmann method has been criticized for lacking cultural flexibility. Its questionnaire assumes that all users have similar backgrounds, but this is not the case. As discussed in Chapter 2, many cultures have very distinct and rather unique methods for responding to conflict. However, the model does offer a fairly good general understanding of different conflict management styles.

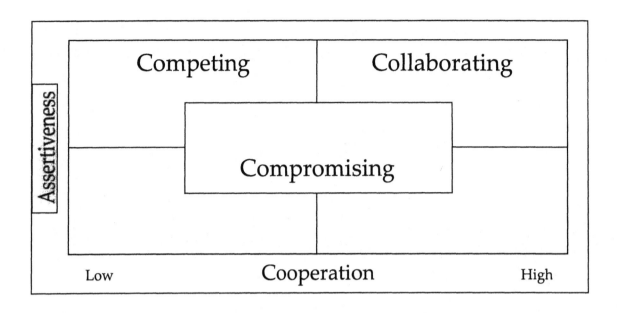

Figure 5-1 Thomas-Kilmann Conflict Management Styles

COMPETING—HIGHLY ASSERTIVE AND UNCOOPERATIVE

If someone's dominant conflict style is **competing**, then it is the differences between individual people that are seen as the central and most important issue in the conflict. A person who prefers the competing style is highly assertive, taking a firm stand in disagreements. The person tends to take up rather distinct and polarized positions, seeing certain perspectives as being "right," and viewing other positions as "wrong." Those choosing a competing style often operate from a position of relative power, typically drawn from an authoritative status or rank, wealth, expertise, or some other qualification or privilege. They tend to see the exploitation of their influence and possibly even the manipulation of others as acceptable tools for achieving a desired outcome. This approach sees conflict as an adversarial competition that will be won by the person demonstrating a combination of the higher level of competence or ability and the greater degree of assertiveness. This style places primary importance on the achievement of personal goals to the exclusion of concerns for the relationship between the conflicting parties, and it can create feelings of ill will and resentment if used inappropriately.

COLLABORATING—ASSERTIVE AND COOPERATIVE

If the dominant style is **collaborating**, then conflict itself is seen as being neither good nor bad in and of itself, but is seen rather as merely a symptom of the underlying tension in a relationship that should be treated accordingly. It is a fundamental assumption of this approach that if differences between individuals and/or groups can be properly interpreted and responded to, they can not only be resolved but also might even serve to strengthen relationships rather than damage them. An emphasis on collaboration suggests a certain degree of faith in each party and the assumption that working through differences will lead to creative and effective win-win solutions that everyone involved can support. Although people who tend to use a collaborative style can be highly assertive, this style differs from the competing approach in that it is also highly cooperative, viewing the interests and concerns of all parties as being important. Collaborative people embrace attempts to find solutions that integrate as many interests and perspectives as possible.

COMPROMISING—MILDLY ASSERTIVE AND COOPERATIVE

The **compromising** conflict style holds the view that differences between people should be resolved in a manner that prioritizes the common good rather than individual advancement. In this respect, it might be said that with this approach each party needs to "give a little and take a little" in order to reach the most generally positive outcome. With everyone in the disagreement expected to give a little, a compromise can often help to soften the potentially negative implications of conflict. The consequences of losing are made more tolerable because the relative gains of any opposing party are similarly limited. Through negotiation, both ends are basically played against the middle in an attempt to reach some form of common ground that will please everyone involved to greater or lesser degrees. Although it is obviously unrealistic to think that everyone will be completely satisfied, the compromising style sees the facilitation of adversarial win-lose relationships as obstructive and counterproductive. Instead, efforts are made to split the difference between divergent opinions, thus creating moderate win-win solutions that at least partially satisfy everyone. There is always the risk, however, that people may initially exaggerate or inflate their stated position so that they may later appear to be compromising, when in reality they are simply pursuing an undisclosed agenda. If this is the case, the compromise solution may be sufficiently weakened to the point that it fails to illicit serious commitment from others and thus blunts its effectiveness.

ACCOMMODATING—UNASSERTIVE AND HIGHLY COOPERATIVE

A person's willingness to meet the needs of others even at the expense of his or her own individual interests is indicative of the **accommodating** style of conflict management. A person displaying an accommodating pattern of conflict management tends to object to the negative consequences that differences between people might have on their relationships, and may reflect a psychological need for acceptance by others. Such people generally believe that self-sacrifice and placing the importance of a continued relationship above their own personal needs or goals is necessary for resolving differences of opinion. From the accommodating point of view, therefore, it may be better to just completely ignore differences rather than risk open confrontation by being overly sensitive or assertive. A preference for the accommodating style of management leads people to be highly cooperative. However, because personal objectives tend to be set aside in deference to the wishes of others, the cost of this management style easily lends itself to exploitation and can become personally damaging in the long term.

AVOIDING—UNASSERTIVE AND UNCOOPERATIVE

A tendency toward avoiding conflict could be the result of either denial—simply refusing to acknowledge that conflict exists in the first place, or suppression—while not fully denying its presence, a person downplays a conflict's importance and goes to extra effort in order to steer clear of it whenever possible. Those showing a preference for an **avoiding** style often lack strong opinions, typically delegate decision-making authority, readily accept majority rule, and quickly defer to others who are more assertive or whom they may see as more competent. They will do everything they possibly can to keep from hurting others' feelings, even if it requires going well out of their way and creating inconveniences for themselves. If someone's dominant management style is avoidance, it is quite possible that the person may have had some previous bad experiences with conflict. Alternatively, this preference might result from someone's assumption that "nice people don't fight." Those who lean toward this management style generally do not recognize the potentially positive attributes of conflict and seek to evade it in its entirety. As we will see later, there are scenarios when even an avoidance approach to conflict is quite appropriate. However, in most situations this is a largely ineffective method for resolving disagreements and can sometimes even result in making conflicts worse by allowing them to reach unmanageable proportions before they are dealt with more directly.

SITUATIONAL APPLICATION OF EACH STYLE

As previously mentioned, each of these styles might be seen as the most appropriate way to respond in particular circumstances. Once you have a better understanding of the different styles, you should be better able to identify which one (or perhaps a combination) will serve you the best under varying conflict conditions. Rather than a one-size-fits-all strategy to conflict management, you will be better prepared to address disagreements and confrontations in a much more appropriate and contextual case-by-case manner. Figure 5-2 offers a somewhat simplistic view of the primary goals and intentions for each of the conflict styles.

Primary Goal of each Conflict Management Style

- Competing—to win. *"My way or the highway."*
- Collaborating—to find a win-win solution. *"Two heads are better than one."*
- Compromising—to find middle ground. *"Let's make a deal."*
- Accommodating—to yield. *"It would be my pleasure."*
- Avoiding—to delay. *"I'll think about it tomorrow."*

Figure 5-2 Conflict Management Style Goals

APPROPRIATE SITUATIONS FOR THE COMPETING STYLE

- when quick and decisive action is necessary, such as during a crisis or emergency

- when your goals are important enough to you that you dare not risk letting them be ignored or neglected

- when an unpopular or difficult course of action must be followed

- when you are sure that you are right about an issue that is vital to your own or your group's wellbeing

- to protect yourself against those who might take advantage of noncompetitive behavior

APPROPRIATE SITUATIONS FOR THE COLLABORATING STYLE

- to find an integrative solution when multiple interests are too important to be compromised

- when the objective is to learn from others rather than simply to win

- to combine different perspectives for the best possible solution

- to gain the commitment and support of others for a decision by incorporating their needs

APPROPRIATE SITUATIONS FOR THE COMPROMISING STYLE

- when individual needs or goals are not as important as the maintaining of a relationship

- when opponents are equally committed to mutually exclusive goals

- to achieve temporary resolution to complex or time-sensitive issues

- to increase the likelihood of cooperation between parties by evenly distributing the negative implications of giving up certain interests

- when collaboration or competition has failed to achieve resolution

APPROPRIATE SITUATIONS FOR THE ACCOMMODATING STYLE

- when you realize that you are wrong; to allow a better position to be heard, to learn from others, and to show that you are reasonable

- when the conflict is much more important to the other person; by satisfying the needs of others you not only maintain cooperative relationships, but also build up goodwill for later when an issue is more important to you

- when avoiding damage to a relationship is especially important

- to assist the learning and development of others by allowing them to learn from their own mistakes; such as with a child

APPROPRIATE SITUATIONS FOR THE AVOIDING STYLE

- when the disagreement is trivial compared to maintaining a positive relationship

- when you have little or no chance of meeting your needs

- when the potential risks of confrontation outweigh the potential benefits to be gained

- to relieve levels of tension, allowing people to cool down and regain their composure

- when gathering additional perspectives is more important than reaching an immediate conclusion

Everyone has the ability to change his or her dominant style and overall response method. Although we will all have particular response styles that come more naturally to us than others, if a person genuinely desires to have a more constructive approach to conflict management, change is entirely possible. With some discipline and practice, a person can change or improve his or her conflict management skills to better provide a response that is appropriate to each individual conflict.

NEGATIVE STRATEGIES FOR CONTROLLING CONFLICT

Just as there are effective and contextually appropriate conflict management strategies, such as those previously outlined, there are also several ineffective and/or inappropriate strategies for handling conflict situations. **Administrative orbiting** occurs when a problem is acknowledged as existing, but no serious action is taken. A common example might be when a group of concerned citizens brings the government's attention to a problem that might be difficult or inconvenient to solve. In such cases, the government often tells the citizens that "more information is needed" and that the problem is "being studied." In reality, this is often a way to placate the concerned citizens without actually taking any meaningful action to resolve the problem.

Sometimes a government, corporation, or relatively powerful individual attempts to use bureaucratic methods to steer the outcome of a conflict in their own favor. They may set up procedures for addressing a grievance that are so time-consuming, complicated, expensive, or risky, that the procedures wear down the opponent in the conflict. Also known as **due process inaction**, it is an effort to force the less powerful party to give up prematurely. For instance, when a powerful corporation is sued by parents over a defective product that has harmed one of their children, the corporation has far greater legal resources at its disposal; it can set a team of attorneys in action and throw all kinds of forms and procedure at the parents, who are unlikely to have been able to afford more than a single attorney. The corporation knows that if they can just draw the process out long enough, the suing family is likely to eventually settle out of court (and thus out of the media spotlight) for a much smaller amount.

A prime example of this type of negative conflict management behavior involves the Exxon *Valdez* oil spill. In 1989, the oil tanker ran aground and spilled over 10 million gallons of oil into Alaska's Prince William Sound. Despite the fact that lawsuits were quickly filed on behalf of nearly 40,000 interested parties, approximately 32,000 of those claims remain unsettled.[38] An initial ruling in 1996 ordered Exxon to pay over $5 billion in damages. However, following extensive legal maneuvering, which resulted in the case taking another fourteen years to finally make it all the way to the U.S. Supreme Court, Exxon's liability was eventually capped at just $500 million[39]—a lot of money, to be sure, but substantially less than the original amount. The cost of the cleanup alone was nearly $3 billion, to say nothing of the lost income from seriously degraded fisheries and the negative impact on tourism.

Finally, when faced with potentially damaging or embarrassing opposition, rather than dealing with the problem directly, some may choose to resort to **character assassination**—an attempt to discredit someone's credibility or reputation. In this kind of "smear campaign," there may be less effort spent on countering an opponent's claims than on simply trying to make the opponent look bad. A powerful party, such as a government or corporation, may try this strategy to silence or discredit someone they see as a troublemaker.[40] However,

---

[38] Williams, Carol J. "Exxon Must Pay $480 Million in Interest over Valdez Oil Tanker Spill," June 16, 2009. http://articles.latimes.com/2009/jun/16/business/fi-exxon-valdez16, *Los Angeles Times*, retrieved July 6, 2009.

[39] Wakabayashi, Daisuke. "Exxon Agrees to Pay Out 75 Percent of Valdez Damages," August 27, 2008. http://www.reuters.com/article/topNews/idUKN2641081120080827, Thomson Reuters, retrieved July 6, 2009.

[40] For significant examples of character assassination, look at how the Bush Administration treated either Richard Clark (the prominent counterterrorism expert who said the government failed in its efforts to protect the public on 9/11), or Joe Wilson (the former ambassador whose wife was identified as an undercover CIA operative in retaliation when he challenged the evidence used to justify the invasion of Iraq). To be sure, it is not just the Bush Administration that has done such things, but these are particularly strong examples.

it is not just powerful groups or individuals who attempt to smear the reputations of people who confront them—how many of us know someone who has intentionally spread false rumors about someone whom he or she sees as a potential threat to his or her romantic interests? Unfortunately, this type of behavior is not only unethical, but also may actually serve to make the conflict worse rather than better, or create altogether new conflicts.

SUMMARY

We have taken a look in this chapter at a number of methods and strategies for effectively (and ineffectively) managing conflict. The success of these methods depends largely upon the attitudes of those trying to employ them and their willingness to acknowledge the positive attributes of a well-managed conflict. To use conflict constructively for mutual rather than individual benefit requires certain skills, to be sure, but perhaps more importantly it requires a healthy respect for the right of individuals to disagree with one another. Little is gained from attempts to manage conflict if the negative connotations of disagreement as being unpleasant and embarrassing, or simply a chance to take advantage of others, are allowed to persist. Those who are either unaware of or unwilling to accept the positive potential of conflict will either become frustrated and distressed in the face of conflict, or they will attempt to stifle potential controversy before it can be openly addressed. Such efforts to suppress disagreement may initially seem to preserve harmony and accord in a group or community, but they may eventually make conflicts even more difficult to handle, once they inevitably erupt. Or worse, the pressure to disallow conflict may push those in positions of power to attempt to force conformity to a limited number of beliefs or perspectives, which ultimately risks the well-being of a society. We should be ever mindful not to equate differences of opinion with antagonism or hostility. As the saying goes, sometimes we must simply "agree to disagree." Conflict and disagreement are vital parts of both individual and societal progress, and efforts to resolve the many challenges we face will be made much easier once we accept that disagreement is both a normal and valuable feature of life.

PART III

ARGUMENTATION: HOW WE DO IT

CHAPTER 6

EFFECTIVE LISTENING

"I've never learned anything while I was talking"
George Bernard Shaw

"My wife says I never listen. At least that's what I think she said."
Anonymous husbands everywhere

"We hear only half of what is said to us, understand only half of that, believe only half of that, and remember only half of that."
Kathy Walker

Most people already generally accept the basic notion that the practice of effective and meaningful communication is a fundamental element in the development of positive and respectful relationships with others. However, many fail to recognize that in order to be more successful in such efforts, people should endeavor to become more effective listeners. Communication is critical to any healthy relationship, and being a good listener is at the very foundation of good communication. Establishing truly healthy, respectful, and mutually advantageous relationships requires that people learn not only to express themselves effectively but also that they listen attentively to the expression of others. If you fail to listen effectively to what other people say, how can you possibly address their concerns or meet their needs? Unfortunately, when most people communicate they tend to focus primarily on the expressing of their own thoughts, ideas, and perspectives, while spending little effort on actually listening to what others have to say. People who fail to be good listeners often neglect to fully take others' interests into account, largely because they simply do not even know what they are, and soon find their relationships suffering as a result. After all, no one likes to spend much time with someone who never listens to them.

We will begin this chapter with a look at the importance of listening, both for communication in general and argumentation in particular, followed by a somewhat more comprehensive look at what effective and meaningful listening actually entails, and finally we will address various methods and techniques by which the development of good listening skills and habits can be further enhanced.

THE SIGNIFICANCE OF LISTENING

Although we do not often think about it directly, it seems reasonable to assume that most people spend greater than fifty percent of their time in communication engaged in listening rather than talking. It is likely that, in a typical conversation between two different people, the actual talking is usually divided somewhat roughly in half between the two participants.[41] It might also be expected that when a third person enters the conversation, the amount of time each individual spends talking would become further divided, roughly into thirds, and so on as the discussion continues to expand and include more participants. It only stands to reason that the more people there are involved in any given conversation, the more time each person will spend listening to others rather than talking themselves. A wide body of research exists to substantiate the notion that this balance operates in roughly the pattern we have described (see Figure 6-1).

---

[41] Obviously this is not always the case. Some people tend to be dominant in conversation while others are more timid. There are times when you may be the predominant communicator as well as times when you hardly say a word.

	Distribution of Communication Time			
Study	Demographic	Reading	Writing	Speaking	Listening
Rankin, 1930	Varied	15%	11%	32%	42%
Brieter, 1971	Homemakers	10%	7%	35%	48%
Weinrauch & Swanda, 1975	Business personnel	19%	23%	26%	33%
Barker, et al., 1980	US college students	17%	14%	16%	53%
U.S. Dept. of Labor, 1991	Government Managers	13.3%	8.4%	23%	55%
Bohlken, 1999	US college students	13%	12%	22%	53%

Figure 6-1 Research on Distribution of Communication Activity[42]

These numbers would seem to indicate that listening is a rather significant part of communication, yet we typically spend a disproportionate amount of time in communication classes working on the development of improved presentation skills and by comparison devote relatively little time and energy to developing our listening skills. This is unfortunate not only because we actually spend a greater amount of time listening than talking, but also because listening is such a vital part of truly comprehending communication and understanding what a conversation is about. To be sure, speaking well is a crucial component of effective communication. So, too, is listening well. Studies have estimated that

---

[42] It is interesting to note that two different studies show the percentage of time spent listening by college students to be over fifty percent and amongst the highest, yet their time spent speaking is significantly lower than the other demographic categories evaluated. For further detail, see http://www.listen.org/index.php?option=com_content&view=article&id=103:-time-spent-listening-and-communicating&catid=43:listening-facts&Itemid=74.

we learn over seventy percent of what we know from listening to others, yet we remember only about a quarter of what we hear. Apparently there is a great deal to be gained through the improvement of our listening practices.

Communication as a Two-Way Exchange

It is important for us to understand that communication is a process that involves a two-way exchange. Not only must an idea or thought be expressed in some fashion, but it must also be received. If reception does not occur, then communication has not occurred either. In other words, a person can talk and talk and talk, but if no one is listening, or even listening but not understanding, then communication has not actually taken place. In this respect, communication is perhaps a little more complicated than most people tend to think.

As Figure 6-2 shows, a conversation between even just two people is quite complex, with each participant involved in a number of activities that create a cycle of communicative exchange. Before actually speaking, a person begins with an intention—the idea they want to get across to the listener; encodes their speech—figures out exactly what they want to say and how they wish to say it; and then actually expresses their idea. Meanwhile, the listener is observing the speaker for clues about their thoughts and general demeanor. This includes the decoding of the speaker's message—an attempt to understand the actual words which have been said; interpreting the message—reading between the lines to decipher the speaker's rhetorical choices and determine their purpose; and concluding with offering their own response. When the listener responds, he or she will then do the same things the speaker was doing originally—creating an intention, encoding their message and then actually delivering it; while the original speaker becomes the listener and takes up all of the practices that correspond to that role. This process continues on and on in a repetitive pattern with each person taking turns either speaking or listening to the other.

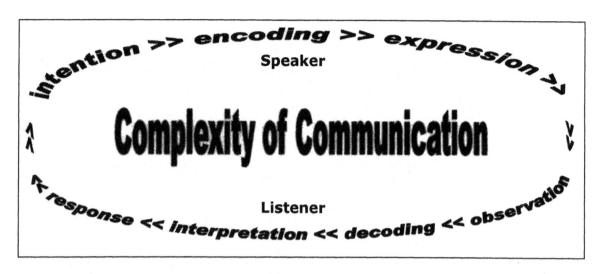

Figure 6-2 The Cyclical Complexity of Communication

The Significance of Listening in Argumentation

To begin, being an attentive listener is a good practice because it is simply a respectful and courteous thing to do. Establishing a civil atmosphere even for a debate encourages everyone involved to be a little less defensive and therefore a little less aggressive as well. After all, it should be the person or side with the best arguments that wins a debate, rather than the most interpersonally aggressive participant. Perhaps a general guideline to follow in this regard is that if you want others to listen to your arguments, then you also need to be willing to listen to theirs. It has been our experience that when this guideline is followed, most people are generally willing to at least hear one another out in a reciprocal manner.

Furthermore, if the goal in an argument or debate is indeed to "win," would it not make sense that in order to effectively disprove an opponent's arguments you would first have to actually listen to them? If you do not understand what an opponent has argued in the first place, how can you possibly deny their claims? Therefore, effective listening obviously plays a rather vital role in the comprehending of competing positions. In formalized academic debate, competitors use a highly stylized form of "listening" wherein they create an extensive written record of the other side's arguments in a practice known as "flowing," which will be addressed in greater detail in other parts of the text.

Listening Is Not the Same as Agreeing

Beyond these basic observations, it is also highly important for us to understand that listening should not be considered as being the same thing as agreeing. One need not agree with another person in order to simply listen to them. Not only is it quite possible to respectfully pay attention to someone's position or perspective despite not agreeing with it, but also, with respect to argumentation, it only makes good sense. Beyond being polite, listening closely to someone with whom we disagree offers us insight into his or her motivations and beliefs. A wise advocate *wants* to know why his or her opponents hold the positions that they do because this knowledge and understanding provides guidance for the best ways with which to try to persuade them that they should see things in a different way. In other words, if you really want to change the way someone thinks about something, you have to know what they actually think in the first place, and the only way to know this is to listen carefully to them. And who knows, you may even learn something that might cause you to look more carefully at your own beliefs. It is never a bad idea to critically reflect upon and even challenge our own assumptions.

UNDERSTANDING LISTENING

Most people tend to think that there is nothing complicated or difficult about listening. The truth, however, is that listening is not as simple as it may seem. In order to gain a more thorough understanding, we should take a closer look at what listening actually is.

Listening vs. Hearing

To begin, we should clear up a common misconception by making it clear that listening is not the same thing as hearing. Properly understood, **hearing** is a passive process—a physiological function which is the product of some action which creates sound waves which then cause vibrations to move the little hairs and bones in your ears, resulting in a signal being sent to your brain that some sound has occurred. You do not exercise a lot of direct control over hearing; it just happens. On the other hand, **listening** is an active, psychological process that requires focus and concentration in order to comprehend the sounds that

106

have been heard. While hearing might involve the old saying, "in one ear and out the other," listening involves the absorption of the meaning of words and statements and leads to the actual understanding of ideas. Listening requires concentration, which is the focusing of your thoughts on a particular issue. Generally speaking, one can hear without necessarily listening, but not the other way around.

Factors that Affect Listening

As mentioned above, listening is not as simple as it seems. Not only are some people poor speakers and certain subjects more boring than others, making listening more difficult in either instance, but there are also a number of factors that tend to make people poor listeners in general.

Selective Exposure. Psychologists tell us that people tend to seek out that discourse with which they agree and avoid that with which they do not, thus selectively exposing ourselves to ideas. It is far more comforting to believe that we are correct in our thinking than the alternative. We may therefore try to avoid exposing ourselves to those messages that might be contrary to our currently accepted belief system. While this behavior may be somewhat reassuring, it nevertheless prevents opportunities for us to learn from having heard new ideas and perspectives that challenge our own pre-conceived notions.

Distortion. Occasionally we find ourselves unexpectedly being exposed to messages with which we disagree whether we had intended to hear them or not. This might happen in general conversation, a classroom setting, or maybe a work environment, where we are suddenly presented with an idea or opinion that makes us uncomfortable when we might not have been expecting it. Under these potentially stressful conditions, a mental defense mechanism called distortion sometimes kicks in automatically. The human mind has developed a way of protecting us by altering unpleasant messages either into something more acceptable and in line with our own belief system, or, alternatively, something outlandish that is then easier for us to reject. Something in your subconscious mind just sort of twists the words around. Have you ever heard the saying, "You only hear what you want to hear"? That's distortion.

Intrapersonal Argument. Another common reaction to controversial messages, or simply a statement with which we personally disagree, is to anticipate the conclusion or goal of the message before actually hearing it in full and to begin a discussion of the issue inside our own heads. We think we know where the conversation is going so we stop listening to the other person and listen only to our own internal thoughts. This is a fairly common occurrence, but what if we are wrong in our assumption? What if the speaker is not headed toward the conclusion we thought was coming? If we stop listening and concern ourselves with only our own internal thoughts, we may miss the point entirely, or the speaker may become offended if they feel we are not giving them our full attention. Additionally, in certain argumentative settings, such as a formal academic debate, we might be a bit embarrassed if we make an inaccurate guess as to the speaker's intended conclusion.

External Distraction. Our focus becomes easily shifted away from a conversation when there are loud noises or other attention-grabbing events taking place nearby. For instance, we have probably all experienced how difficult it is to hold a small study group session when someone is playing loud music or watching television in the next room. However, external distractions are not limited to just loud noises—if you have to attend class or go to work on a nice warm, sunny day, you might end up spending as much time staring longingly out the window at the blue sky as you spend paying attention to the day's lesson. External distractions are anything that draws our focus away from the primary matter at hand.

Internal Distraction. As with the previous listening challenge, this factor involves people becoming distracted and having their attention drift to matters other than the conversation at hand, only in this case it is due to internal matters. If anyone has ever made the decision to go to school or work when feeling a little ill, they know just how difficult it can be to concentrate on either a boring lecture or a customer's requests. Instead, their attention focuses on whatever it is that is making them not feel well. Likewise, if someone has recently had an unpleasant argument with a friend or family member, or any other potentially traumatic experience, their emotions are liable to get the best of them, causing them to become distracted, rather than paying close attention to whomever they are talking with at the moment.

Some additional behaviors or reactions on the part of the listener that can have potentially negative consequences for effective communication include the following:

Stealing the spotlight—when the listener consistently interrupts in order to share their own similar experiences. This may make the speaker feel unheard and unappreciated.

Asking questions prematurely—rather than having to settle your own curiosity immediately, give the speaker a chance to provide a little more information that may answer your question. If they do not, wait until there is an appropriate break to ask your question.

Giving too much advice—rather than actually seeking your counsel, the speaker may simply want to express him or herself and be heard. Offering an abundance of consolation, such as repeatedly telling them that "everything is going to be okay" and that they are going to be "just fine," may not be as helpful as you think. Sometimes a person is simply seeking an open ear rather than a psychological evaluation.

DEVELOPMENT OF LISTENING SKILLS

We will now take a look at some particular listening skills. The development of these practices and behaviors can help people to become more effective listeners, and therefore better overall communicators. These skills are: nonverbal communication, active listening, and neutrality.

Nonverbal Communication

Nonverbal communication, including such behaviors as nodding, facial expressions, eye contact, gestures, and posture, helps give a speaker signals that you are paying attention to him or her without interrupting. These nonverbal signs, also referred to as body language, can communicate interest and respect for the speaker, which may make them comfortable in sharing their thoughts more openly.[43] It is also helpful to understand nonverbal signals as a speaker in order to gauge an audience's reception of your own messages. There are nonverbal behaviors which convey attentiveness and interest as well as those that show inattention and disinterest. The following chart may help to illustrate:

Attentiveness & Interest	Inattention & Disinterest
Making eye contact	Shoulder shrugging
Smiling	Looking away from the speaker
Nodding your head	Crossing your arms and/or legs
Sitting up straight	Sitting slouched over
Leaning toward speaker	Rolling your eyes
Uncrossing your legs and arms	Tapping your fingers

Figure 6-3 Nonverbal Signs of Interest

Active Listening

Active listening is a method of responding to others that elicits additional information and emotions from a speaker. The more you know about the person with whom you are speaking, the more information you have upon which to base your interpretations of what he or she is actually saying. In the following section we will take a closer look at the development of three important types of active listening skills, including the asking of open-ended questions; reflecting upon what the speaker is saying, thinking, or feeling; and summarizing the speaker's intent.

Open-ended Questions

Open-ended questions are the kind of questions that require more of an answer than a simple "yes" or "no." This type of question intentionally encourages expanded conversation, inviting the speaker to further elaborate and say more about an issue than they already have. This allows for a more in-depth and detailed exploration of the subject at hand rather than a simple and surface-level

---

[43] Body language will be discussed much more extensively in the next chapter.

examination. Open-ended questions will often begin with such phrases as "please explain," or "could you describe." The following examples of the same basic question being asked in both an open- and closed-ended manner should help to illustrate this concept:

Closed: Are you feeling bad today?
Open: How are you feeling today?

Closed: Do you think s/he likes me?
Open: How do you think s/he feels about me?

Closed: I think it's okay for gay couples to legally marry, don't you?
Open: What do you think about gay marriage?

Reflection

A powerful and important component of active listening is reflection — sometimes also referred to as paraphrasing. **Reflection** is a process whereby listeners check to make sure that they are understanding the speaker correctly, as well as letting the speaker know that they are paying attention. The listener can reflect by occasionally paraphrasing what the speaker has said into his or her own words, but without adding anything that was not there to begin with. The listener can also summarize from time to time what he or she thinks the speaker is feeling or thinking.[44] Clarifying the speaker's intentions in this manner can help a listener avoid making incorrect assumptions based on misinterpretations or preconceived notions, as well as offering the speaker an opportunity to possibly recalibrate what they have said if they perceive that they may have presented an idea or thought in a manner that did not accurately demonstrate how they truly feel. Finally, these reflection techniques can help to somewhat slow down the pace of the conversation, which can not only help improve comprehension but might even help to avoid emotional confrontation by keeping the conversation more pleasant.

---

[44] It should be noted that this type of occasional response to a speaker may not be possible in all instances, such as formal academic debate, when each speaker is given a certain amount of uninterrupted time. Some debate formats, however, might allow for this practice.

Neutrality

A certain degree of trust is vitally important in creating meaningful communication.[45] Trust allows another person to open up and more genuinely share their thoughts and perspectives. Moralizing, or being judgmental, may result in a hostile reaction from the speaker. In order to create trusting interactions, people need to learn how to maintain neutrality when another person is speaking. If a listener expresses his or her own opinion too strongly in an oppositional or confrontational manner, it may serve to make the speaker nervous and unwilling to share his or her thoughts any further. Therefore it is important to try to set your personal emotions, beliefs, and fears aside in order to keep them from interfering with your ability to listen actively. We have to accept that a speaker may say something that offends our personal value system. Rather than getting upset, try setting the judgment aside and continue to listen. Remember, as mentioned earlier in this chapter, simply listening to someone does not mean that you have to agree with what they are saying. In order to keep the lines of communication open, the listener needs to convey objectivity by using neutral language whenever possible—even when they may be passionate about a particular subject. Here are some examples of remaining neutral when someone is speaking about a controversial issue:

Speaker: Do you think abortion is acceptable?

Listener: Well, I have my own ideas, but I wonder what you think. What's your opinion?
OR

Listener: I think it's a very personal subject. What feels right to you?
OR

Listener: Since it's different for everyone, I'm interested in what you think.

SUMMARY

The importance of listening in communication is something well worth considering. Good listeners are often some of the best speakers and advocates because they have taken the time to find out what truly interests and concerns

---

[45] This is perhaps less true for formal, competitive debating than for other forms of communication.

people. If you understand what is important to people then you will better understand how to meet their needs or persuade them with your ideas. While effective listening is more complicated than most assume, with practice and effort everyone can improve his or her listening behavior.

CHAPTER 7

CRITICAL ASSESSMENT: TESTING THE VALIDITY OF DATA

*Truth is a river that is always splitting up into arms that reunite. Islanded between the arms the
inhabitants argue for a lifetime as to which is the main river.*

Cyril Connolly

Whether in social conversations, in classroom discussions, in business meetings, or even in the privacy of our own homes, we often find ourselves in the position of having made an assertion that once made must now be explained, supported, or even defended against attack. How many times have you made a statement to which the simple words *prove it* are the only response you receive from your listeners? On occasions such as these, a thorough working knowledge of the various elements and materials you can make use of in more completely developing and substantiating your position will be of real value. Entering into an argumentative situation without sufficient evidentiary support is similar to driving down a long, lonely Texas highway without much fuel in the tank—you are not likely to get very far. In this chapter we will examine a number of different options available to you for offering support to validate your claims. We will discuss not only different categories of evidence and reasoning, but also various tests that can be applied to them in order to determine their relative levels of veracity.

PROOF

WHAT QUALIFIES AS PROOF?

Considering the common response of the general listener mentioned previously, what do the words *prove it* actually mean? In other words, what exactly is proof? As discussed in Chapter 1, we prove our arguments by offering evidence and/or reasoning to establish the warrant behind our claims. However, one could quite reasonably argue that when a listener says *prove it*, rather than asking for a detailed factual defense of your statement, he or she may more likely simply mean *convince me*. Although this might seem like a rather simple distinction, it is nevertheless an important one because it suggests that the word "proof" has at least two different meanings, and they might be somewhat dissimilar from one another. First, it could mean, as previously alluded, that proof refers to the establishment of a claim's validity through the use of evidence and/or reasoning. In this sense, **proof** serves as the objective demonstration of factual truth, regardless of an audience's acceptance, wherein a claim could be hypothetically analyzed in an impartial way through the calculated assessment of evidence and the logical testing of patterns of reasoning. In this sense we have a fairly technical definition of proof, such as one might find in a textbook about argumentation theory.

The second interpretation, however, is much less technical. It assumes that, unlike the previous definition, not only is **proof** directed toward an audience but that it is also dependent upon that audience, because it is the audience's acceptance or rejection that serves as the critical factor in determining the claim's actual validity. In this sense, proof is not necessarily based upon a clinically objective verification, but rather on the much more subjective consideration of persuading an audience in terms of their beliefs or behaviors.

116

This interpretation is equally valid and thus might appear in the very same textbook.

ARISTOTLE'S LEVELS OF PROOF

If we were concerned solely with formal logic, we would limit our discussion to the first definition. However, because argumentation occurs between human beings who are not only logical but also emotive, we must concern ourselves with a dualistic approach to proof if we intend to be effective advocates. In this regard, we might ultimately define **proof** in the Aristotelian manner as anything that generates acceptance in the mind of the audience.[46] Aristotle identified three levels of proof, each with relatively equal validity as far as significance in persuading an audience. They are:

- **Logos**: logical proof. Coming from the ancient Greek for "explanation of the cosmos," logos refers to the rational and analytical support offered for a claim, such as statistics, scientific data, definitions, etc. We might refer to logos as "the cold hard facts."

- **Pathos**: emotional proof. Coming from the ancient Greek for "suffering," pathos is the use of your audience's emotions, such as sympathy, fear, or romance, in an effort to motivate their beliefs and/or behaviors. We might refer to pathos as "tugging on the heart strings," such as the telling of a sad story.

- **Ethos**: ethical proof. Coming from the ancient Greek meaning "of good character," ethos refers to the level of credibility you have with your audience. In other words, how believable are you? It is important to note that ethos does not necessarily refer to the ethical value of the arguments you use; rather it is an indication of how ethical your audience thinks you are.

Having established the varying elements and nuances of what might reasonably be considered as proof for our arguments, let us now take a look at some of the different kinds of support that can be used to prove your claims. Although it is difficult, even perhaps somewhat problematic, to try to separate

---

[46] Aristotle. *The Art of Rhetoric,* Translated by H. C. Lawson-Tancred, London: Penguin Books, 1991.

the three levels of proof mentioned here,[47] the following section will deal primarily with those logos-centered elements of an argument. This is because, in its most basic and rudimentary form, **evidence** refers to the more substantive and analytical elements of an argument that serve as the foundational building blocks from which we construct our claims.

EVIDENCE

It is important to examine your assertions carefully and as objectively as possible. You will need to back them up with as many statistics, facts, quotes, and examples as possible. As you begin doing this, consider the support that you already have for your claim, as well as the support that you might be lacking, and then begin doing your research with the intention of filling in the missing gaps in the development of your position or idea. It should be noted at this point that this chapter is concerned with the raw materials of research (the actual facts and data that provide evidence and proof), not so much with the research and evidence-gathering process itself. Before considering the evidence-gathering process, it seems only logical to first address the evidence itself so that you will know what you are looking for as you conduct your research.

To begin, the evidence that you might use to support your claims will fall largely into two broad categories: factual evidence and authoritative evidence. **Factual evidence** refers to those more objective forms of data, such as empirically observed facts, formal definitions, and statistical figures, whereas **authoritative evidence** refers to someone offering a qualified judgment or interpretation of that data. Take, for example, the legal profession, where people are trained to make every attempt to separate the facts from opinions, so that the prosecuting attorney in a trial might be heard asking a witness on the stand for "just the facts, please." Or consider the witnessing of a barroom fight, where there is a significant difference between reporting the basic facts as you saw them and making a judgment about who you believe was responsible for starting the fight in the first place. In other words, factual evidence consists primarily of the raw

---

[47] For example, the offering of either logos- or pathos-based arguments can help to advance a speaker's credibility or ethos, whereas a speaker's favorable ethos can make his or her logos- and pathos-based arguments seem more convincing to an audience. The line dividing these three types of proof is therefore less distinct than it might initially appear.

data itself, whereas authoritative evidence is someone's interpretation of or opinion about that set of data. In this respect, authoritative evidence might be best understood as applying meaning or significance to the information and data that have been gathered. Both serve an important role in the validating of argumentative claims.

STATISTICS

Statistics could be defined quite simply as the numerical expression of knowledge. They serve to add some quantitative impact to your claims by offering the facts, figures, and data that back your argument with substance. This is rather important in argumentation and debate, as many decisions are based on an assessment of the relative risks, the costs versus the benefits, the pros versus the cons, or the advantages versus the disadvantages, of any number of competing positions and proposals. In contemplating their judgment or conclusion, an audience will need to be able to compare and contrast the fundamental aspects of these competing claims against one another with as much accuracy as possible. This will include comparing the weight or significance, the magnitude or size, and the probability of the various options competing against one another.

Quantifiable statistics are among the best ways to help your audience make this comparative determination because they are largely free from emotional considerations and are therefore often judged to be more objective and factual than other forms of evidence. For instance, if a concerned group of parents were attempting to persuade the local school board that a particular reading program should be adopted by the schools in their area, their chances of success would be greatly enhanced if they were prepared to offer some data indicating that other school districts that had used the program had seen their students' test scores improve by a certain percentage. Numbers often speak to an audience, particularly to policymakers, in ways that other types of arguments do not, by appealing to the perceived need for rational, analytical judgment. Offering statistical data allows your audience to feel as if they are basing their decisions on something more than just simply taking your word for it. It gives your audience a greater sense of certainty in your clams.

DEFINITIONS

It only stands to reason that it is always important to be sure that your audience knows what you are talking about. If there are words or phrases in your presentation that are perhaps uncommon or highly technical, it might be useful to offer a definition for your listeners. **Definitions** are statements of meaning or significance, and there are times when even some commonly used words need a bit of clarification, because many words have more than one meaning or are used in a variety of different ways depending on the context. For example if you are trying to convince an audience that television is too violent, you may need to explain exactly what you mean by "violent": does it involve killing of any sort, or are you using "violent" to mean just when it seems gratuitous? What about fistfights or gun battles where no one is injured? Because there are many different possible interpretations of what it means to be violent, the speaker would need to be carefully clarify his or her terms.

Words can be defined in different ways. You might choose to define a word by quoting from a dictionary or a textbook, or you might choose to define it in more general terms by explaining what the word means to you personally. In this regard, there are two basic kinds of definitions: denotative and connotative. A **denotative** definition refers to the objective, literal definition of a word, such as one might find in a dictionary or other reference book. A **connotative** definition, on the other hand, refers to the more subjective or commonly used interpretation of a word.[48]

EXAMPLES

One of the most basic ways to substantiate your claims is to provide examples that support them, thus indicating that the circumstances associated with your claim are not unusual, but are instead rather similar to other existing circumstances. Technically speaking, an **example** is a specific instance or

---

[48] For example, when looked up in a dictionary, the word "hot" might be defined as being of very high temperature. However, when a group of friends sees a flashy sports car drive by and someone says it is "hot," they do not mean that the car is of high temperature. Further, someone could refer to the car as "hot" if they think it might be a stolen vehicle. The point is that a lot of words have many meanings, some of which may be based on common usage rather than on dictionary definitions.

anecdote that lends credibility to your claim. There are three fundamental types of examples: *brief, extended,* and *hypothetical.* A brief example is a simple and very specific instance, perhaps only a sentence or two, and you might use several of them together in order to support a claim. An extended example is a longer illustration or story that adds greater depth and detail to your claim than a simple or brief example. You may need only one or two extended examples in order to prove your point. A hypothetical example can be either brief or extended, as far as length is concerned, but it involves instances of a purely fictional nature.

TESTIMONY

Providing **testimony** to defend your claims is the process of quoting or paraphrasing the words of another person or group. As with statistics, offering testimony that supports your claims demonstrates to the audience that your arguments are not based solely on your own limited opinion or perspective, but rather are supported by others as well. Giving credit to your sources also displays your intellectual integrity, as well as demonstrating that you have undertaken serious research before reaching your conclusions. Each documented reference will improve the level of your credibility with the audience. There are three general types of testimony that we will concern ourselves with here: **expert testimony**—from someone with extensive training or education in a particular area; **peer testimony**—from someone similar to you or your audience; and **reluctant testimony**—testimony from a source that might normally be expected to support the opposing side[49].

PERSONAL OBSERVATION AND INTERVIEWS

Obviously much of the research you gather might be in the form of written sources or data that have already been compiled by someone else, but do not be too quick to overlook the option of gathering your own evidence through careful personal observation or interviews with knowledgeable people on your campus

---

[49] Reluctant testimony might involve a courtroom witness who, while under oath, offers incriminating evidence against a defendant even though he or she might wish for the defendant to be found innocent. It is often regarded as powerful testimony because, if the witness were lying, he or she would probably lie in the other direction in order to protect the defendant.

and in your community. This type of first-hand evidence may end up having more immediate impact with your audience than the opinion of some distantly removed authority figure or faceless scientific study, and it may be equally valid if your efforts have been thorough. Gathering your own facts and making your own statistical evaluations can be both an enjoyable and a rewarding endeavor. Such research not only brings you into contact with new and interesting people you would not have been likely to meet otherwise, but it also holds the potential to offer much deeper learning opportunities than simply reciting the facts gathered by others.

ADDITIONAL CONSIDERATIONS

As you build up the supporting evidence for your claims, you might consider gathering more data than you would reasonably be able to use in the limited amount of time you have available. You can then prioritize and select those details that most clearly and thoroughly illustrate your points. You will also want to be as specific and precise as possible. For instance, although stating that "light travels really, really fast" is undeniably true, it is also neither very interesting nor very enlightening. Stating that "scientists have determined the speed of light to be approximately 190 thousand miles per second" is an improvement, but better still might be to take it a step further and state something like this: "The sun is over 90 million miles from the earth. A traveler moving at sixty miles per hour would take over 10,000 years to reach it, whereas light travels that same distance in only eight minutes!"[50]

THE TESTING OF EVIDENCE

Of course, it is not sufficient to simply gather together a body of evidence in order to determine a claim's validity. A claim is only as good as the support offered to back it up. Therefore, we must also critically analyze and thoroughly challenge the quality and validity of the evidence itself. In this section we will offer a number of pertinent questions to be used in determining the value of the evidence that has been gathered. These questions can also be used to refute the

---

[50] Mermin, N. David. *It's About Time: Understanding Einstein's Relativity,* Princeton: Princeton University Press, 2005.

veracity of other people's claims in an argumentative setting, such as a debate or discussion.

TESTING STATISTICAL OR FACTUAL EVIDENCE

Statistical or factual evidence is often presented as being so factually based that it may seem as if it is beyond reproach and can be neither questioned nor doubted. This is far from the case. There are a number of factors that might cause statistical evidence to be invalid, or at least more invalid than it may have initially appeared.

Timeliness. A study that was designed to track unemployment trends within the service industry that was completed over ten years ago is likely to have little if any contemporary relevance, unless of course it were being used solely for historical comparisons. The service industry, like most of the economy and even the greater society, has changed so dramatically in the past two decades that the results of numerous studies become outdated almost as soon as they are completed. It is important, then, to determine when the research in question was conducted in order to accurately assess the continued relevance of its conclusions.

Source. The source of a statistical survey or scientific study can sometimes affect the investigation's conclusions. For instance, if an opponent in a debate offered statistical evidence indicating that the development of potential natural gas and oil reserves in Alaska's Arctic National Wildlife Refuge (ANWR) would result in the creation of hundreds of thousands of new jobs, such a piece of evidence would probably be very persuasive to an audience. However, what if you were able to demonstrate to the audience that the source of these employment figures was actually a lobbying group for the powerful oil industry?[51] Might this little revelation not change the audience's perception of the integrity of the numbers offered? What about statistics concerning the allegedly rampant criminal behavior of minorities, which were gathered by a white supremacist group? Or perhaps information concerning the safety of a new prescription drug that was compiled by the drug's own manufacturer?

---

[51] Waller, Douglas. "Some Shaky Figures on ANWR Drilling," *Time*, Aug. 13, 2001.

Though there is certainly not a direct correlation between the source of a scientific study and the neutrality of its conclusions, the source of statistical evidence should still most certainly be a contributing factor as we formulate our judgments about its overall validity.

Purpose. Statistical studies are done for particular reasons, and the underlying motivations behind them can sometimes influence their results. When a tobacco company undertakes a study of the relationship between the consumption of their product and the danger to a person's health, it is not difficult to guess the motive behind the effort. Because the intention of a study sometimes influences its outcome, we might rightly view the results with a healthy dose of skepticism.

Methodology. It can also sometimes be useful to question the scientific methods used in a study. There are a variety of ways of collecting, recording, and analyzing data, and a researcher's choices amongst these methods and techniques can affect the outcome. For example, sampling techniques should include the use of a group of test subjects that are representative of some larger body. A small sample size could invalidate the investigation by producing results that are atypical, or unrepresentative, of the larger body or population for which the study is being conducted. As a prime example, television commercials often tell their viewers that two out of three doctors (or dentists, or mothers, or kids, etc.) prefer a particular brand, yet without ever telling viewers how many doctors were surveyed in the first place. Alternatively, a random sampling might produce results that are far different from those derived from a sample of subjects that were carefully chosen according to particular criteria.

Location. For certain statistical data, the location in which the research was conducted really does make a difference. The political orientation, median age, or socioeconomic demographics of any particular region can significantly influence the findings of a study. For instance, a research project designed to investigate the predominant attitudes of Americans toward underage drinking might be expected to be considerably different in medium-sized college cities as opposed to either a rural setting or a dense urban environment. If a scientific study does not account for these variables, study results may not be as accurate as might be expected.

Interpretation. In addition to there being a number of challenges related to the process of data collection, so too the raw data accumulated can be interpreted in more than just one manner. It is therefore useful to determine, as far as possible, the relative values, beliefs, and other potential biases of those individuals involved in the interpretation of the data. Similar to those previous questions regarding the purpose of the study, the people who do the interpreting of the data might also be prejudiced by any number of influencing factors, including job security, discriminatory attitudes, and political or religious affiliations.[52]

Accuracy. It would be incorrect to assume that every fact that is observed and reported is completely free of error. Factually inaccurate data can result from distorted perceptions, clerical errors, miscommunication, preconceived expectations, and a range of other factors, and this is sometimes referred to generically as **misinformation**. As a result, what is reported as fact may not be factual at all. Although most journalists are generally well trained and report both impartially and accurately, it is well known that this is not always the case.[53] To slightly modify an old adage, do not believe everything you read, and even less of what you see on TV.

Manipulation. In addition to misinformation, there is also what might be called **disinformation**. Just as some facts are reported inaccurately due to the honest mistakes of otherwise well-meaning individuals, there are also instances of information being intentionally distorted.[54] This distortion may be carried out in an effort to generate fear for some political purpose, to arouse suspicion toward a minority group, or perhaps to generate undeserved interest in some commercial product. There are many who feel the Bush Administration

---

[52] It is not difficult to see, for example, how a person's religious affiliation might influence his or her interpretation of data regarding Americans' perspectives on gay marriage.

[53] Hanson, Gary and Stanley T. Wearden. "Measuring Newscast Accuracy: Applying a Newspaper Model to Television," *Journalism & Mass Communication Quarterly*, Vol. 81 Issue 3, 2004.

[54] In 2003, a Florida Court of Appeals supported the contention by Fox News Corporation that the First Amendment gives broadcasters the right to deliberately distort news reports on the public airwaves. NEW WORLD COMMUNICATIONS OF TAMPA, INC., d/b/a WTVT-TV v. JANE AKRE. Case No. 2D01-529. Although it was Fox News directly involved in the case, it should be noted that several other major media organizations supported Fox's position.

distorted a number of facts in order to compel the public to support the invasion of Iraq. This same kind of manipulation is suspected of having encouraged the American public to support greater involvement in the Vietnam War.[55]

TESTING AUTHORITATIVE OR INTERPRETATIVE EVIDENCE

It is a highly common practice in argumentation and debate to offer testimony as support for a claim. As stated earlier, this not only gives credit where credit is due, but it also offers a certain degree of credibility to the claim. However, it is unfortunately not nearly as common for people to be familiar with the various ways to effectively challenge arguments based on authoritative evidence. Below are a number of questions with which you might test authoritative evidence for its validity.

Credentials. Although it might seem somewhat obvious that the simple presence of significant credentials does not necessarily mean that a particular authoritative source of information is infallible, it is nevertheless not a bad place to start in making a reasonable judgment about a source's qualification. After all, there happen to be some fairly solid reasons why society tends to place considerably more trust in the diagnostic skills of someone who has actually earned his or her M.D. than the skills of a person who has gone through only one or two semesters of undergraduate level premed classes. It seems to be a rather safe assumption that the former has not only received substantially more thorough training, but has additionally been through a set of rigorous testing and examination procedures in order to ensure that his or her skills meet a strict standard of competency.

It is important to note, however, that credentials in one area or discipline should not automatically transfer over to another area or discipline. Whereas the person with an M.D. may well be an expert on the function of internal organs, he or she may not know a thing about international trade policy or the constitutional protections of free speech and assembly. Yet despite this reality,

---

[55] There is no shortage of sources either in print or on the Web suggesting that numerous efforts were undertaken by officials at the highest levels of government to intentionally distort information in order to manipulate public opinion in favor of American involvement in the Spanish-American War, World War II, the Vietnam War, the War in Iraq, and other military operations.

often when a recognized authority in one field makes a statement about something that is outside of his or her area of expertise the person is erroneously treated as a competent and qualified source, simply because of the credentials in his or her own field of expertise. It is quite possible for a person to be an expert in one area and a lay person in another.

Origin of Credentials. Knowing where a particular source's credentials were earned may affect how much credibility we choose to place on their opinions and statements. For better or worse, a degree from one of the Ivy League schools is likely to carry greater credibility than one from a small public university. Conversely, some of the most able and credible experts have little or no formal academic training whatsoever, having instead established their credentials through practical experience and hard work. Though this kind of qualification should ideally be held as no less valuable than that based on an academic degree, it is more difficult to evaluate and therefore might be seen as less credible. Further, one might question how recently a source's credentials were earned. In certain areas, progress is being made so rapidly that a degree earned a decade or more ago may not indicate as much expertise as the degree nominally indicates.[56]

Reputation. It is not all that unusual for someone to have a substantially different reputation among the general public from the reputation he or she carries within his or her own field. The criteria by which a peer group evaluates its own members' qualifications might be quite different from those of the public at large. For instance, it would be quite possible for an economist writing a weekly column for a regional newspaper about effective small business strategies to be well regarded by the local readership, but considered a fool by his or her peers. In most instances of such disparities, it is probably wise to give greater consideration to the judgment of those individuals in the source's area of

---

[56] The medical profession is a prime suspect here. A doctor who earned his or her degree more than twenty years ago might not be well trained in many of the significant advances in medical technology and practice over the ensuing decades. Likewise, a computer technician's degree becomes obsolete rather quickly if he or she does not vigilantly follow the rapid advancements in the field. For a dramatic illustration of the rapid changes in some of these areas, see the educational presentation titled *Shift Happens*. http://www.youtube.com/watch?v=ljbI-363A2Q. July 10, 2009.

supposed expertise than to that of the lay public. Although there are exceptions to every rule, the source's peer group is simply in a much better position to make an informed assessment of the quality of that person's work and the validity of his or her authoritative opinions.

Practical Experience. Even if an authoritative source of evidence has impressive academic credentials, the person's knowledge base may still be primarily, or even completely, theoretical in nature. There are legitimate reasons why the stereotypical ivory-tower scholar's interpretative judgments should sometimes be disregarded.[57] A white middle-class professor writing about the various challenges plaguing the numerous slums of sub-Saharan Africa's major cities, without having ever lived in or perhaps even visited the area, would hardly seem to be a qualified source on the subject. Theoretical or academic knowledge is unquestionably valuable, and it should not be rejected out of hand, but when it is purely theoretical in nature and scope, rather than being coupled with experiential knowledge, it lacks reasonable applicability and might therefore rightly be considered of limited use.

Objectivity. Although it must be recognized that total and complete impartiality at all times is virtually impossible for any human being possessing even minimal cognitive function, this does not mean we should not question a source's biases and subjectivity. If a person is known to have previously misrepresented facts and distorted information, then that person's credibility should be viewed as highly suspect. It is critically important, both when gathering evidence to support your own claims and when assessing the validity of evidence used by someone else, to maintain a constant outlook for the presence of bias in any source's perspective.

SUMMARY

Knowledge about the world around us can be obtained from a great number of sources, each of which differs in its level of accuracy, comprehensiveness, and consistency. In distinguishing between the reliable and unreliable in this endless

---

[57] The term "ivory-tower" refers to an attitude that is preoccupied with intellectual considerations rather than with the practicalities of everyday life, and use of the term often carries with it an implied criticism of academic elitism.

stream of information, we can and should test these factual statements in order to determine to what degree they meet the conditions set out earlier in this chapter. Alternatively, we can rely upon the authoritative opinions of others. However, we must ask ourselves to what extent we should trust those opinions. There are, of course, some people who are distrustful of virtually any authoritative opinion and feel that, rather than relying upon others, we should always try to figure things out completely for ourselves. On the other hand, some people are almost entirely uncritical about the degree to which they are willing to accept the words of alleged experts as the absolute truth. They may feel too pressed for time or perhaps too lacking in training to make judgments for themselves and thus become overly dependent upon others. It is our hope to find something of a middle ground, where we utilize authoritative evidence when it is called for, but do so with a healthy dose of critical assessment. In other words, we would call for neither the blind acceptance of authoritative opinion, nor the total rejection thereof. Rather, we would suggest that, whether dealing with raw data or the expert interpretation of that data, a thorough and comprehensive challenging of the evidence should be pursued in order to establish its validity. Upon carrying out such a challenge, we discern that which might offer proof to our audience, and that which should be discarded.

CHAPTER 8

CRITICAL ASSESSMENT: TESTING THE VALIDITY OF REASONING

Nowhere am I so desperately needed as among a shipload of illogical humans
Commander Spock

Logic is the beginning of wisdom, not the end.
Leonard Nimoy

For much of the past, the study of logic has focused heavily on those formal elements of reasoning, such as the evaluation of syllogisms, the use of models, proof theories, Venn diagrams, Boolean indicators, and a host of other fairly complicated methods. Although this kind of **formal logic** undoubtedly serves very important purposes, argumentation theory is primarily concerned with the study of **informal logic**. Whereas formal logic serves very specific and specialized purposes, informal logic is much more commonly used in everyday practice. Informal logic focuses on such things as basic reasoning, the discovery of fallacies, and critical thinking. It is a way to question and analyze arguments for their relative levels of validity. Most errors in argument occur well before the point at which formal logic is necessary to identify them. As such, it is informal logic with which we are interested here. To be sure, this text will not offer exhaustive coverage of even informal logic, but it will suffice to offer the reader a basis from which to utilize reasoning more effectively both in argument and in his or her personal life.

We might define **reasoning** as the capacity for logical, rational, and critical thought, to use sound judgment in drawing inferences or conclusions. Accordingly, "to reason" is to argue or deliberate logically or with good sense. Before we can test the validity of reasoning processes, which we will do later in the chapter, we must first understand some of the basic characteristics of reasoning. This has already been discussed to some extent in previous chapters, particularly Chapter 1 where some of the formal types of reasoning are addressed in relation to basic argument models, but here we will go into a little more detail.

BASIC COGNITIVE SKILLS

There are a number of basic cognitive skills (or "thinking" skills) that help us to become more effective critical thinkers. They include storage skills and retrieval skills, matching skills, elaboration, and constructive cognition (Figure 8-1). These tools and skills are the foundation of most cognitive functions.

STORAGE AND RETRIEVAL

Storage and retrieval skills enable a person to transfer information both to and from long-term memory. While focusing on the information being evaluated, the thinker associates it with information that is already in long-term memory. In this way, the thinker is treating the brain's memory capacity somewhat like a filing cabinet where similar information is placed together–existing information is retrieved from a relevant category while the new information gets filed away in the appropriate category.

As mentioned earlier, the brain tends to operate in patterns, as well as pictures, so storage and retrieval techniques that operate under this assumption will likely be effective ones. One commonly used practice is called **visual imagery**. The thinker may create a visual representation for the information that is to be remembered, or alternatively, may recall an existing visual image to be used in testing new information. For example, when a child is asked, "How long is a frog's tail?" they are likely to retrieve an existing image of a frog and see that a frog has no tail. The process of creating and then later retrieving visual images can occur either consciously or subconsciously. Beyond visual images, someone could also create an auditory, kinesthetic, or emotional impression (or some combination of these elements) for storage and retrieval, depending on his or her more preferred learning style.

The exercise of mnemonic devices is also a useful strategy for building good storage and retrieval skills. **Mnemonics** is a memory technique that uses a system of acronyms, rhymes, unusual phrases, and other means to help in the recall of specific data such as facts and figures or perhaps historical sequences. First invented by the Greeks 2500 years ago to assist in memory training, the word comes from the Greek words *mneme*, meaning "memory," and *mnemon*, meaning "mindful."[58] In Greek mythology, the goddess of memory, and mother of the Muses, was Mnemosyne. The Greeks assumed that "artificial" memory, developed through training with a variety of memory techniques, was capable of recalling far greater amounts of information than the "natural" memory, or that with which a person is born and uses on an everyday basis, was capable of on its own.

Still used quite commonly today, mnemonics utilize associations between easy-to-remember verbal constructs that can then be related back to the data that is to be recalled. The idea is that the human mind can more easily remember personal, surprising, or funny tidbits than data that follows some seemingly arbitrary sequence. For instance, the phrase "Richard of York Gave Battle In Vain" is regularly taught to British schoolchildren as a way for them to remember the order of the colors of the rainbow. Similarly, we use the phrase "spring forward, fall backward" as a means for remembering which way to

---

[58] Feinstein, Sheryl. *The Praeger Handbook of Learning and the Brain*, Westport, CT: Praeger Publishers, 2006.

adjust our clocks for Daylight Savings Time. Students often rely on mnemonics when studying for exams as a way to recall difficult sets of data.

MATCHING

The effective storage of information further relies upon **matching skills** which enable a person to determine how newly received information and concepts are either similar to or different than those concepts and data that are already stored in long-term memory. We will address three types of matching skills: categorization, analogical reasoning, and evaluation of logic.

Categorization is a process by which a person classifies ideas as belonging to a particular group due to the presence of certain attributes that are characteristic of that group. Categorization tends to speed up the thinking process by allowing generalizations of incoming information that go beyond the limited set of data that has been received. When someone is walking in the woods and sees an animal they have never seen before, they must go beyond the exclusive set of data provided by the sighting and refer to other information stored in long-term memory. When comparing the new animal's wings and feathers to animals the thinker has seen before, it becomes quite simple to categorize the animal as a type of bird. Any time we classify something as being part of a group or concept with which we are already familiar, we are categorizing.

Analogical reasoning, sometimes referred to more simply as "**extrapolation**," is a strategy that assists thinkers in matching similar patterns of data from one area to those in another. In this manner, someone need not unnecessarily start from scratch when encountering new information. Rather, they simply adapt existing knowledge for application to a new situation. For instance, if you have grown up playing tennis and are therefore fairly familiar with the rules and techniques, you could perhaps extrapolate and apply some of that knowledge when it comes time for your first racquetball match. Although the two are certainly different, the similarities may be sufficient to transfer much of your knowledge to the new game. Likewise, if you are familiar with the motivations behind the Boston Tea Party, you might extrapolate that information in an effort to help you better understand the many popular uprisings that took place across Central America throughout the 1980s. Analogical reasoning provides the basis for understanding a new idea or subject simply by applying an existing set of knowledge to a new context.

The **evaluation of logic** is a process of checking newly received information against an individual's existing internal system of logic, whether innate or learned. In other words, sometimes newly heard ideas will simply cut against our general impression of what makes good common sense, while other data might conflict with specific rules of logical thinking which we have learned. In either case, such a conflict should give us cause to question the validity of the new information we are receiving. Of course, once we have learned some basic styles of reasoning, we can use them to better watch for errors in the arguments that we read and hear.

ELABORATION

Above, we discussed how we match new information and ideas with those we already have. In some cases, however, the listener must actually supply some of the necessary information themselves. **Elaboration** is the process of inferring information that was not explicitly stated. We use some of the previously mentioned skills, such as categorization and analogical reasoning, to help us make these inferences. For example, many books and films contain what might be called the "moral of the story" which is intended to share some life lesson with the reader/viewer. Although not always the case, the author or filmmaker usually subtly cloaks this moral in the storyline rather than coming right out and throwing it in our faces. We typically have to surmise what the author or filmmaker was intending to share by elaborating upon what we have seen or read. Similarly, many of the great teachers of history, such as Jesus, Muhammad, Buddha, and Lao Tzu, used parables or short stories to share important concepts with their followers. Rather than explicitly detailing the purpose or moral, these stories often required the listener to infer meaning by adding some details to what they had heard.

There are at least two situations in which elaboration might be considered necessary: (1) if the message being heard or observed provides incomplete information, or (2) if the listener does not comprehend all of the information that

135

has been made available. If the listener/viewer has good elaboration skills, then neither of these situations should prevent them from filling in the blanks accurately enough to allow them to make a reasonable decision as to a message's validity. On the other hand, some people will invariably make inaccurate inferences that will lead to poor comprehension and misinterpretations. As a listener, we must be vigilant to use good judgment when elaborating, while as a speaker we should be as clear as possible in order to avoid the possibility of our listeners making poor inferences.

CONSTRUCTIVE COGNITION

The final set of basic thinking skills is called **constructive cognition**, which involves either the constructing of entirely new thought patterns and associations or perhaps considerably restructuring existing ones. We will look at two skills in this set: problem-solving and exposition.

Problem-solving is the process of discovering new information and/or developing a strategy to achieve a desired outcome, or to overcome a particular challenge. In education, typically the desired outcome or goal is to build greater knowledge and understanding in a particular field or discipline. For example, a student may be tasked with determining how conflict can best be managed in a stressful workplace environment or how to calculate the time it takes a train traveling at a certain speed to reach a particular destination. In each instance, the student must not only supply additional information through either elaboration or observation, but must also devise a strategy for resolving the question at hand. Argument plays a crucial role in problem-solving in that it is often the case that, when faced with a problem, many different solutions might be available and one must discern which among them is best.

Although this final skill might reasonably be considered a subset of problem-solving, it is unique enough that we will address it separately. **Exposition** involves the practice of creating new information in order to more effectively express an idea or position. As a problem-solving mechanism, its aim is to overcome either the obstacle of uncertainty or the absence of information by finding ways to communicate new ideas in an appropriate and persuasive manner. Although typically referred to in the context of written communication, the concept applies equally to the oral communication of thoughts and ideas. For example, a history student may need to utilize exposition skills for the purpose of assessing the causes behind the success of the civil rights movement or the failures of the Vietnam War, and the end product of their efforts could be either an essay or a speech. In either case, the student is essentially creating new ideas by integrating and synthesizing their various thoughts on the matter. In this same vein, **expositional rhetoric** is that discourse that explains or describes a concept more fully in order to enhance its persuasive effect.

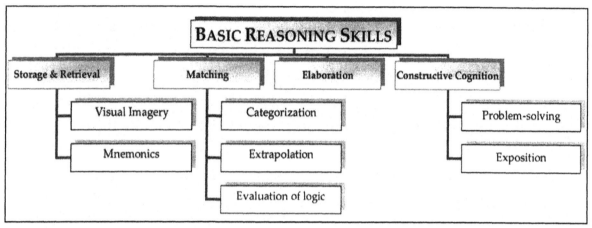

Figure 8-1 Basic Reasoning Skills

THE TESTING OF REASONING

Now that we have defined some common forms of reasoning and have basic skills in place, we can begin to challenge the validity of some of the reasoning we hear. In this section we will begin by identifying a lengthy series of generic logical fallacies before offering some specific questions for each of the previously mentioned types of reasoning.

IDENTIFYING LOGICAL FALLACIES

A **fallacy** is a flawed form of reasoning or logic, and an argument that uses flawed reasoning or logic is said to be *fallacious*. It is quite possible that the reasoning will initially seem to be valid, but upon further reflection is found not to be. It is important to understand that a fallacy is a flawed *method* of support—the claim itself may be true, but not for the reasons given.

It should be clarified that a fallacy refers specifically to an argument that uses faulty logic or reasoning as support for the claim. Although a claim that uses faulty data, such as the quoting of a scientifically flawed study or out-of-date statistics, would be considered invalid, it would not be said to be a fallacy—this term only applies to the use of flawed reasoning in support of an argumentative claim.

When the Greek and Roman philosophers came up with the various fallacies, there were dozens and dozens of them, and they were separated into a number of categories and families, much like biological taxonomy. Since that time, the fallacies have been categorized in numerous ways, any of which could be considered appropriate. For our purposes, we will try to simplify the process by offering three categories: irrelevancy, misrepresentation, and misdirection. By no means are the lists below exhaustive; rather, we are including only those fallacies that seem to be the most commonly occurring.

FALLACIES OF IRRELEVANCY

The fallacies in this category all make use of supporting logic that is irrelevant to a determination of the validity of the claim. For instance, if someone argues that a dog is better than a cat "because there is a blue milk van in the parking lot," the reasoning offered is irrelevant and therefore fallacious. The Latin term *non sequitur* means "the conclusion does not follow." In other words, the support offered is irrelevant and does not prove the claim. With regard to the example given, it may or may not be true that a dog is better than a cat; we simply do not know because the support that was offered neither proves nor disproves the claim. Fallacies of irrelevancy include[59]:

- **Appeal to popularity** (*argumentum ad populum*). Just because something is popular, it does not necessarily mean it is correct. For instance, if the answer to a multiple choice question on an exam is "c" but

---

[59] Some of the fallacies include their Latin names in parentheses, whereas for others, the Latin term has become commonly accepted into English usage, in which case the English translation may be included.

70% of a class circles "d," it does not mean that "d" is a valid answer. Likewise, just because the majority votes a particular way does not mean they are right about the question at hand. Indeed, it is quite possible for a majority of people to be wrong about something.

• **Appeal to authority** (*argumentum ad verecundiam*). Just because someone is an authority figure does not necessarily mean they are correct. It takes more than simply a position of power, a fancy title, or letters after one's name to make a valid assessment of a situation. While there is nothing particularly wrong with using an authority figure's opinion as part of the support for a claim, that in and of itself is not enough to sufficiently prove the validity of a claim. It is not uncommon for even an authority figures to be wrong from time to time.

• **Appeal to tradition** (*argumentum ad antiquitatem*). Just because something has always (or for a very long time) been done a certain way does not necessarily mean that is the correct or best way. Otherwise, we might well still be using slave labor. Likewise, simply because the concept of marriage has traditionally been between one man and one woman does not mean that it should continue to be exclusively so. Some traditions should rightly be abandoned.

• **Tu quoque** ("you are another"). This is the "two wrongs don't make a right" fallacy, and it is quite common. If your roommate gives you some flak for not having done the dishes last night when it was your turn, is the retort, "Well, you didn't vacuum the rug last week when it was your turn," a valid defense? Indeed, it is not. Someone else's inappropriate behavior does not justify your own—both are wrong.

• **Ad hominem** ("attacking the person"). Sometimes simply referred to as an "ad hom," this fallacy occurs when someone makes a personal attack against the individual rather than their argument. Calling someone a bad name or disparaging their fashion sense does nothing to dispute the validity of their argument.

FALLACIES OF MISREPRESENTATION

The fallacies in this category all attempt to establish a claim by relying upon false or misleading representations of the truth. They may falsely depict a relationship or portray a connection that is flawed. This might be done in an intentionally fraudulent manner or simply due to unconscious error, but either way prevents a clear understanding of the issue.

- **Inductive fallacy.** Also known as a "**hasty generalization**," this fallacy refers to an incorrect assumption that what is true of the individual parts is also true of the whole. When someone takes the characteristics of one small part of a group and applies it to the entire group, they have generalized too hastily. For example, if we suggest that penguins do not fly, penguins are birds, therefore birds do not fly, we have committed an inductive fallacy.

- **Deductive fallacy.** Also known as a **fallacy of division**, this is roughly the opposite of the inductive fallacy and refers to the incorrect assumption that what is true of the whole is also true of the individual parts. Reversing the above example, if we were to suggest that birds fly, a penguin is a bird, therefore penguins fly, would be to commit a deductive fallacy.

- **False dichotomy.** A dichotomy is a division or split, so a false dichotomy is to create a division or separation that is not an accurate one. It is a misrepresentation when someone is offered only a small number of choices (either/or) when in fact there are additional options available. Whenever you are presented with a limited number of options in life, always search for another.

- **Straw person.** Is it difficult to knock down a person made of straw? Not really. Like a person made of straw, presenting an opponent's argument in an undesirable or weak manner so that it is easy to knock down is a misrepresentation of the strength of the real arguments on the other side.

- **Complex cause.** When one thing is held to cause another, it may be so in part, but it might also be insignificant compared to other causes of the effect. While cause and effect reasoning can be a valid form of logic, it is only so if an actual causal relationship exists. It is quite common for two things to exist side-by-side and assume a cause-and-effect relationship, but this really only proves *correlation* (a simple connection, or co-incidence, rather than causation). It may be, for example, that both are the result of the same prior cause. Genuine causation is difficult to prove, and a speaker claiming to do so is often also hoping that their causal assertion is not heavily challenged.

- **Post hoc, ergo proctor hoc** ("after the fact, therefore because of the fact"). Just because one thing follows another does not mean the first in sequence is the cause of the second. The sequential relationship may be a mere coincidence. Just because your friend borrows your blender and the next day the blender stops working does not necessarily mean your friend broke your blender (they may have, but not as a general rule). There very well may have been some unseen or unknown cause.

- **Slippery slope.** Similar to a domino effect, a slippery slope is a generally superficial connection between a series of statements that often lead to an exaggerated conclusion. For example, if someone is opposed to a new government regulation against alcohol advertising near high schools, they might argue that it will cause a shift toward hard drugs, resulting in a rise in crime and the total disintegration of society, and therefore we should save our society by allowing alcohol ads to be displayed near high schools. The slippery slope is often resorted to in emotional situations where careful consideration is easily replaced with irrational appeals.

FALLACIES OF MISDIRECTION

When a speaker or advocate avoids proving their argument by somehow distracting the audience, they have committed a fallacy of misdirection. Some of these fallacies distract the listener from what is really going on, while others make use of vague and ambiguous language to cause confusion. Some appeal to emotions rather than logic and reason. Whatever the case, these fallacies attempt to take the listener's focus and attention away from the actual argument.

- **Appeal to Emotion or Desire.** Some arguments are constructed to elicit an emotional reaction from the listener in an effort to use that reaction to get them to agree to the conclusion. For example, while a prosecuting attorney may have convinced a jury that the defendant is a mean and terrible person, that does not necessarily mean they committed the crime in question. There are several subordinate fallacies that fall under this general heading: appeal to poverty/money, appeal to fear/coercion, appeal to pity, appeal to flattery, etc. These fallacies could also fall under the category of irrelevancy because an emotional reaction, although sometimes a powerful motivator, is irrelevant to determining the actual truth or falsity of an argument. A listener very well could be motivated to agree or act out of fear or pity or any other emotion, but they are not acting on the rational and logical merits of the argument.

- **Shifting the burden.** Sometimes, rather than proving their own claim, an advocate will challenge the audience or their opponent to *disprove* the claim. It is not, however, the audience's responsibility to disprove a claim that has been asserted before the advocate of that assertion has offered a defense. In other words, if a teacher enters a classroom and tells the students that "there is no God," then challenges the students to prove there is, the teacher has shifted his or her burden of proof onto the students. The general guideline in this context is, "he or she who asserts must prove."

- **Begging the question.** Also referred to as circular reasoning, this fallacy involves a restating of the original claim in different words as a reason for the claim. This may occur in a single, simple statement or through a more extensive set of statements and claims that go around and around in an elaborate circle in an effort to eventually prove the original statement true, and may be either intentional or purely accidental.

- **Red herring.** This is an attempt to change the direction of a conversation by diverting the listener's attention to something that is irrelevant to determining the validity of the claim (and, therefore, might also be considered a fallacy of irrelevancy). The source of the distraction can be something completely unrelated or somewhat related but not very relevant. Either way, the purpose is to change the focus.

TESTING REASONING BY ANALOGY

When testing reasoning by analogy, we must question the significance of both the similarities and the differences between the two things being compared. For instance, are the items being compared not only similar, but more specifically, are they similar in the most essential characteristics? There may be a number of similarities, but if they are of a nonessential nature then they do little to validate the comparison. The same could also be said of the differences. Are meaningful differences being minimized, overlooked, or perhaps even altogether ignored? Alternatively, are insignificant differences being exaggerated? And finally, are there a greater overall number of similarities or differences? All of these questions can be useful in determining the strength of the comparison being made.

TESTING CAUSAL REASONING

The obvious question here is whether the relationship between the variables is actual causation or merely correlation. This is one of the most common mistakes made in reasoning. The correlation versus causation mistake is so common, in fact, that there is a unique fallacy named especially for it—*non causa pro causa*. Simply because two items or events are associated with one another does not mean one caused the other. There are also some specific fallacies that might apply to attempts at causal reasoning (such as *post hoc, ergo proctor hoc* [after the fact, therefore because of the fact], which is discussed above). Finally, because causal reasoning runs a high risk of oversimplifying a situation by reducing a complex problem down to a single cause, the complex cause fallacy is also often applicable. It is probably apparent by now that causation is rather difficult to prove and subject to a large number of potential errors.

TESTING REASONING FROM SIGN

When testing reasoning from sign, we should look primarily for the possibility of misinterpretation, particularly if the sign is ambiguous or vague, and therefore a challenge to interpret. If the sign has been misinterpreted, then obviously the reasoning is invalid. Further, how relevant the sign is to the matter in question is significant in determining the strength of the claim. If the sign is largely irrelevant, any reasoning based upon it should not be taken very seriously. We might also ask whether there are a sufficient number of signs to draw a meaningful conclusion. And finally, if there are any contradictory signs present that point in a different direction, both the relevance and interpretation of the competing signs must be ascertained.

TESTING INDUCTIVE REASONING

As was mentioned above, inductive reasoning runs the risk of hasty generalizations. If we generalize too quickly, we may make incorrect assumptions and jump to faulty conclusions. As with causal reasoning, this type of generalization frequently results in oversimplification and distortion. We must also determine whether or not a large enough number of observations was made, or a large enough sample size was used, to validate the conclusions made. And finally, we should evaluate whether or not the samples used, or observations made, were typical of the larger category. If the sample is unrepresentative of the whole, the inferences made from them could quite easily be inaccurate.

TESTING DEDUCTIVE REASONING

There is primarily one way for a deductive claim to be shown as being faulty, which is that the presumed characteristics of the group are determined not to be applicable to all members of the group. In other words, when there is an exception to the rule. For example, the deductive claim about penguins flying because they are birds would display an obvious fallacy. This commonly occurs when assumptions are made about groups of people and certain attributes are assigned, sometimes quite arbitrarily or in a discriminatory manner, which do not apply to all members of the group. Such faulty characterizations or overgeneralizations, also known as stereotypes, are used all too often.

SUMMARY

As a skill set, reasoning and critical thinking help us to better analyze and evaluate the strength of arguments—both our own and those of others. The ability to challenge thoroughly our own reasoning is perhaps even more important than becoming more adept at refuting others' positions, in that by challenging our own reasoning we offer ourselves ever greater opportunities to learn and grow as individuals. When we begin to examine and question our own thoughts and perspectives in an intentional and deliberate manner, we have truly become critical thinkers. We figure things out better, make more sound decisions, and gain knowledge more proficiently when we use the proper tools. We begin to take part in the learning process more completely and fully. And, of course, we are then better prepared to interact in a purposeful and skillful way with the world around us.

CHAPTER 9

RESEARCH

"Research is formalized curiosity. It is poking and prying with a purpose."
Zora Neale Hurston

"If we knew what id was we were doing, it would not be called research, would it?"
Albert Einstein

"All I'm armed with is research."
Mike Wallace

One of the key themes of debate is that you have to have something to say before you can speak. Rather than being a simple disagreement of opinion, or simple negation of what another has said, debate requires that we prove our positions and to do so requires we use support that identifies its source and allows for evaluation independent of the way we may feel. Gathering that support is both an exploratory and a guided mission and it is important, just as in argumentation, to have a strategy and stay organized. One of the unique problems of the information age is the problem of information overload versus scarcity or lack of access. Not only are we interested in researching a topic for its own sake, but we also want to learn how to be critical consumers of information. Debate gives us an opportunity to do both, while we investigate often multiple sides of a question as we are preparing the side we are assigned (or choose).

GETTING STARTED

Right from the start, research can seem daunting because it is such a blank slate from which to begin. You may have some idea about what the debate will be about, but not necessarily know what type of literature you need to access to find evidence. It is fine to not know where to start; sometimes starting with the obvious and learning as you progress is the best way to get going. Do not get frustrated early on in your research as you try various search terms and databases. It may take one news story or article to clarify what is going on and then from there you can easily conceptualize and find what you need. Most of the ideas that get debated are very complex, and so even if you know what side you are supposed to be researching it may be very hard to figure out what the arguments are—much less whether they are good or useful.

WHAT TO RESEARCH

Starting with a somewhat general approach may be your best option. Trying to find some general knowledge on your topic, or even the history or development of the topic, can help you better conceptualize the controversy. With that goal, sometimes a basic Internet search in a search engine of your choice can be a good beginning. You will have to strike a balance between being overwhelmed by what comes up in terms of total hits and getting too tied up in the minutia that presents itself as part of that astronomical hit total. Web pages and sites that are designed to summarize information, or are more encyclopedic in nature, can be a great way to familiarize yourself with the ideas and terms associated with the issue you will be debating. As you understand the topic more, you will be able to not only come up with better search terms, but also have a better understanding of how to combine search terms and refine what you are looking for more efficiently.

Journal Databases

When you feel you have some basic knowledge and understand some of the language and terms as they are specifically used for your topic, try to find information in the most sophisticated database you can access. Rather than only using an Internet search engine, you should utilize the resources that are associated with academic libraries and the portals they provide. These databases are incredibly helpful in gaining access to high-quality information and essentially operate the same way that Internet search engines do, they just access higher-quality materials. The materials that they catalog are valuable to those doing research for a variety of reasons. They are materials that often have some form of review before publication, so they provide evidence that can be represented in a debate with few concerns about credibility. These materials also represent a variety of disciplines like economics, political science, the social sciences in general, and scientific and policy oriented journals. There is a very good chance that there will be a plethora of material specific to your issue no matter the nature of the controversy. These journals are not only from a diverse range of sources, but often the contents take on discussions of controversial issues and engage in a discussion of the exact topics you may be debating. These articles are also the product of the authors' research and therefore have an extensive bibliography that may end up being more useful than the original article in pointing you to specific information that is useful.

News Sources

Rather than doing a general search on an Internet search engine, you should try a search within the news section as an option. You may also go to specific news portals as ways to look for different perspectives. Along with mainstream news sources, be sure to seek out more regional or alternative sources as well. You will also want to become familiar with the perspectives they represent in terms of being commercially oriented or public oriented. Are they government sourced? Who are they quoting or interviewing as the authorities? What journalistic devices are being employed that may be distorting the information? You will need to be critical of news and treat it as potentially as opinionated any other source you may encounter. It certainly will contain a perspective even if it is not intentionally trying to be ideological. Even so, news can be a great way to stay informed of pending actions on your issue and to find updates on certain statistics or the status of some harm that is continuing or impending. News sources also allow you to use the most current sources available and to be sure that your materials are consistent with current understanding about the topic.

Books

An increasingly underutilized resource is books. Admittedly it can be daunting to think you have to read an entire book or even several books to be doing research, but it is worth taking a look at the relevant books because you may find some extremely helpful material. The right book might be a whole case built for the position you are researching. Often books have themes of what should be done about social or foreign policy issues. Finding one of these can really help you understand and organize your thoughts on the issue. Often books are edited volumes, and that may mean that, rather than having to read an entire book, there may be a chapter or two that is relevant that ends up being a very efficient way to cover the issue. Books also have the time and space to develop issues more completely and to be more exhaustive in their presentation of support. In the Internet age you may even be able to access e-copies of books if going to the library seems rather archaic. However, the library should still rightly be considered the "center of knowledge" on any college campus.

Government Documents

For those willing to go on full policy wonks, searching out the relevant government documents can be a rich source of data and a variety of perspectives on an issue. You will want to search the form of government documents that are most often issued by the agencies on the topics you may be trying to research. You will also want to look at the form of government documents that represent hearings by committees of Congress on issues you will be debating. Often these hearings are arranged to include a wide variety of both pro and con perspectives on issues being considered for legislative action. Many of these types of documents are now publicly available on the Internet.

Policy Papers from Think Tanks

There are a variety of organizations that are dedicated to studying and offering policy recommendations to government and public actors. These organizations also span the political and ideological spectrum. Even if you do not end up using materials from these types of organizations, it is important to be aware of them in case the other side ends up quoting them. Often they are high quality, using information that is publicly available rather than generated in house. Of course they may also be unfounded diatribes that only feign intellectuality. These types of documents can be found at these organizations' web sites, or they are often published as periodicals and indexed that way. A general search engine may return them as well, or you can use search terms that increase your odds of returning them in your search.

WHAT ARE YOU LOOKING FOR?

Of course, having materials to look at is only part of the story. Just what are you looking for in those sources? Evidence and support can take a variety of forms; there are also facts and historical elements that may help provide context, but may not necessarily add good reasons for your position in the debate. Of course, sometimes that context can help build the basis for analysis or explain data that can only be understood by knowing the timeline of the situation.

General Background

While it may not provide supporting evidence, looking up information on background may help you better understand the information you do use as evidence. The general background information may also evaluate the way things are now or explain the dominant or conventional wisdom on the topic you are debating.

History

This is one to be careful on as often presenting the history of the issue only seems like filler rather than being a reason to support your position. In some cases, an understanding of history is essential to knowing what has been tried, or past conflicts and the basis for them. It may be the type of evidence you collect and brief but may not bring up in the debate unless it proves necessary.

Statistical Data

The difficulty of statistical data is that it can often be overly abstract and difficult to put in context. Even if what is being measured is relatively straightforward, it may not in itself prove any particular claims. The value of statistical data is that it can be used to express numerical significance in terms of quantifying impacts and costs. Statistical data can also be useful in cases where what is being measured, and how it was done, is easily understood and the relationship between what is being measured and the point being drawn is clear.

Expert Testimony/Use of Authorities

Often, much of what you are looking for is concentrated in the testimony or advocacy of noted experts or authorities on the topic. These experts might be government officials who have addressed the issue, members of the academic community that have studied the issue, or persons with experience in the area speaking from their experiences. These sources may use statistics or historic examples in their own testimony to help support their argument, which makes it easy for you to use their comments on your behalf. Even if they are not offering supported arguments, their analysis and reasoning in itself can often be useful for explanations about how things work or why they are good or bad.

Narratives

Often the use of statistics alone may indicate a large number, but the real impact of that number may require a narrative explanation for how the harm identified really impacts people. Knowing a certain condition impacts hundreds of thousands of people is one thing, but to understand what it means to one individual severely impacted can help emotionally amplify a number in a vacuum. Narratives can also represent a viewpoint that is not present amongst the people involved in the debate. Some people may be so marginalized that they do not have access to the privileges of education or public participation. Including narratives can bring their perspective and voice into the discussion. Narratives also represent an element of pathos that can help round out a strictly logic- or reason-based argument.

Court Decisions

Often in court decisions, the rationale of the court can be useful for supporting why a position is appropriate or not. While establishing the law, often the basis for the decisions reveal the values or purposes of the law in terms of social good or order. In dealing with issues of crime and the law, this type of information can be invaluable.

SETTING UP A RESEARCH PLAN

Once you are comfortable with the basics, you may want to approach research in a more organized fashion. As you take on more complex subjects and requirements involving the debates you are in, there will be a higher level of research quality that you will want to bring to your efforts. You will want to be able to save time and avoid repetition, as well as pursue more challenging resources as you learn to access them.

BEGIN WITH THE OBVIOUS

The first step is similar to getting started. Begin with a basic approach by starting with basic search terms and getting background information on the issue to make you feel more comfortable going into greater depth. You should also make sure that you have identified all the main issues, even if you decide they are not ones you will pursue.

IT IS A BUILDING PROCESS

It is important to acknowledge that you do not know everything as you begin working on your topic. But you should have a quick learning curve as you immerse yourself in the topic. Reading a few articles of high quality early on can really help unlock other sources and ideas, so do not try to collect a bunch of materials without reading a few along the way to help make sure you are really collecting what you are needing.

KEEP RECORDS

As you try key words, and especially combinations of key words, you will want to keep a record of those lists in case you need to recreate them later, or to know what terms are useful or not. If you go through specific databases but only get partially through them try to note where you stopped by date or result number so you can start there later. You also want to keep track of where you have searched or what articles you have found so you do not duplicate efforts.

SKETCH OUT YOUR ARGUMENT EARLY

As you get a few materials you may come to figure out what the main points of your case will be. Take the time to brainstorm those ideas, and from that outline you can target which areas need more support or research. You may also want to think about the other side's arguments and start to look for materials that would support them, to see if that reveals ways you may want to answer them.

BEING A CRITICAL CONSUMER OF INFORMATION

As you learn more about argument and the quality of claims, you are learning to be a critical consumer of information. Use those skills as you assemble your own arguments to make sure you are constructing a sound and well-supported case.

UNDERSTANDING BIAS

It is not really possible to avoid bias or individual perspective when viewing controversial issues. The ideal of unbiased or neutral presentation of facts is a construct to strive for, but unlikely to exist. Rather than rejecting information as biased, it is important to understand that sometimes that bias is not necessarily a component that disqualifies it as valuable; instead it may require that the information be presented in the right context. However, bias can also undercut the value of evidence as it may reveal blatant self-interest or blatant discriminatory views represented as fact. You should be sure you understand and can justify the perspective of the evidence that you are using.

Propaganda can be a loaded and controversial term. Upon simply hearing the word, many people automatically assume someone is lying to them. However, a technical definition of the word simply implies the spreading of ideas and information for the deliberate purpose of supporting or opposing a particular position or cause. It is a form of communication intended to influence the thoughts and attitudes of either an individual or an entire group. As opposed to the impartial or objective presentation of data and information about a topic, propaganda comes from a particular prejudice or preconceived perspective; it is subjective. That does not, however, mean that the information and ideas presented are necessarily false—the validity of the claims still need to be either established or discredited. In other words, propaganda comes from all sides of a controversial issue. Each side is simply presenting that body of evidence that supports their position, and excluding that which does not. This is to be somewhat expected from people who are advocates of a particular idea or action.

Propaganda takes on some of the more nefarious overtones commonly associated with it when it is practiced by either government officials or in the news media. In these contexts, consumers have at least a reasonable expectation that they are receiving valid and objective information that is as free as possible from preconceived notions and ideological bias, as opposed to the "intentional use of suggestion, irrelevant emotional appeals, and pseudo-proof to circumvent human rational decision-making processes."[60]

The Propaganda Model[61]

The influential economist Edward Herman and well-known scholar and political critic Noam Chomsky have developed what they call the Propaganda Model for evaluating the information we receive in the form of "the news." They suggest that the news passes through five filters before it reaches the consuming public:

Box 9-1 The Herman and Chomsky Propaganda Model

Raw data—the actual event or issue

First Filter—Size/Ownership/Profit

The vast majority of news sources (print, TV, radio, Internet, etc.) are all owned by a small number (6-8) of massive corporations, and they share the same value structure: profit.

Second Filter—Advertising

Advertising dollars are by far the primary source of revenue for most media. Advertising revenue is far more significant than subscription base in terms of income.

Third Filter—Source of Information

The media is reliant on information from two main sources: Big Business and Big Government, and the "experts" funded by these primary sources.

Fourth Filter—Flak/Discipline

Flak is negative criticism the media receives from the agents of power for disagreeable reporting. It is used as a means of disciplining the media.

Fifth Filter—Anti-communism

The control mechanism of the dominant cultural bias of the day. Today, anti-communism might be replaced by anti-Islamic fundamentalism.

The "News" we read, hear, and see

The question raised by Herman and Chomsky is whether or not, and by how much, the news is different from the raw data. They would argue that public consent for economic, social, and political policies is somewhat manufactured or manipulated by powerful entities.

---

[60] Richard L. Johannesen. *Ethics in Human Communication,* 5th ed., Chicago: Waveland Press, 2002, p. 115.
[61] Herman, Edward S., and Noam Chomsky. *Manufacturing Consent*, New York: Pantheon Books, 1988, Ch. 1.

BE AWARE OF METHOD

You do not have to be a quantitative or statistical whiz to be able to process the method by which the data you are researching was obtained. Was it a study with subjects and how many, or was it a comparison of isolated events? Was it done by a survey? What types of statistical measures or tests were involved? What variables were utilized and are they appropriate to measure what they say they do? If the material is qualitatively derived, in what ways were the data conceptualized or analyzed? What is the overall intellectual perspective that is the organizing principle behind the method? Even a partial understanding of these constructs can be helpful in gaining insight into what is really being proven.

SUMMARY

Research skills are one of the most transferable of abilities that being involved in debate helps to develop and refine. Many find the search for ideas and support to be one of the great joys of being involved in debate. It certainly does provide a reward for the intellectually curious. The research involved in debate is also more than just a fact-finding mission. Being able to put information in an argumentative context can add to the understanding of the issue in unique ways.

CHAPTER 10

REFUTATION, STRATEGY, AND TACTICS

"As for the assertion that nuclear weapons prevent wars, how many more wars are needed to refute this argument?"
Joseph Rotblat

"In boxing you create a strategy to beat each new opponent, it's just like chess"
Lennox Lewis

While there are a variety of formats for debate you may participate in, they will all share the basic aspect of having a side start the debate in favor of the proposition, and a side assigned to refute that advocacy. This section will start to take some of the theoretical parts of argument discussed in theory and explain which of those elements are used to make up a basic way of presenting a debate argument that can be adapted to a variety of contexts.

STARTING THE DEBATE

If you are the side assigned to be in favor of the proposition, you will start the debate by presenting your advocacy for the proposition. You may be asked to propose a policy or action, or you may be asked to be critical of some action or behavior, or you may even be asked a question of values or fact to which you must respond. In any of those cases, you will be identifying things that are good about the ideas embraced in the proposition, or explaining how the absence of the constructs contained in the proposition cause some harm that needs to be remedied.

BUILDING A CASE

Your goal in advocating the proposition is to build up a good reason why supporting the ideas or actions of the proposition are beneficial in the abstract or concrete. There are some basic components you will use to help build that case and present good reasons for favoring the proposition.

Harms

The identification of some **harm** or problem is often the beginning to building a case for support of a new idea or policy action. In debate, that issue is most often identified as "harm" specifically. You are demonstrating that there is some state of affairs that exists that warrants our attention and response, as it is a significant issue in terms of its impact on individuals and society. Most propositions will identify some major issue in society that is controversial or unresolved. At the core of those issues is some form of violence of a physical or psychological nature. The issue of Gay Rights can examine the issue of bullying and violent hate crimes as well as the issues of discrimination and exclusion. Both harms are significant in terms of their weight of impact on any person who might encounter such violence, but also significant in terms of numbers of persons who have had harm done to them.

As a debater you will identify some harm that needs to be addressed and express how that harm is one of great impact and affects a great number of people. While quantitative aspects are one way to make a point, it is also important to remember the qualitative aspects. As much as a statistic may show the extent of a harm, which is indeed a valuable piece of evidence, it is also important to show the personalized element of the harm by taking the time to explain how such violence really is destructive to people's lives, or even to introduce a specific story of someone harmed to add depth to your presentation. In classical rhetorical theory, this is the element of *pathos*, or emotional appeal. It recognizes that logic alone is not enough to persuade or compel a response, but that the audience must also be able to feel that the idea is a good one or a true need exists.

Statement of Advocacy (Plan)

One of the many things that makes debate a useful tool for critical thinking is that identifying a problem is often not enough in debate to build a case. There must be some identification of a means to resolve the problem through the ideas or actions embodied in the proposition being debated. It is easy to identify problems, but to be able to propose a means of solving them means you possess an understanding of the costs and benefits of addressing the problem and that you can show how acting is better than not acting in response to that problem.

In debate the language for what you would advocate is often embodied in the wording of the proposition itself, as in "the Federal Government should pass the Dream Act" or it may require you to identify an action that fits under the ideas in the proposition such as "the Federal Government should reform immigration policies." You may say something as simple as a statement of advocacy about what you think should happen, or it may be a more detailed list of actions that you support that you formally identify as your "plan." In either instance you make clear what you stand for at some point in your speech that is a direct means of addressing the harms you have identified.

Solvency

A natural extension of having a statement of advocacy, or presenting a plan, is to show how that response actually can address or alleviate the harms that you have been identified. **Solvency** is one of those words that debate has come to use that really only has meaning in the world of debate. In this case, solvency is a shortcut for saying "the explanation for how when the things we say should happen do happen things will get better, or how we show how we solve the problem."

One of the things you are likely to come across as you are preparing for your debate is the explanation of how certain policy actions or regulatory responses will affect the behavior of abstract concepts like markets, or specific aspects of human behavior. It is important to identify those explanations and to present them to your audience so they can understand how your plan works and will want to support it.

For example, for those advocating drilling in ANWR, explaining how horizontal drilling technology will be the specific technique allowed can help alleviate fears of environmental damage; while accessing the oil can help address the economic harms of high-priced oil and foreign oil dependency. You cannot just assert that your plan is a good idea; you have to present evidence and analysis about why changing the way we do things now to the way you want them will actually bring about positive results.

ORGANIZATIONAL STRUCTURE

A simple approach to organizing that first speech may be to gather your evidence and supporting materials and start to identify which ones develop harm, what are the plan ideas, and which elements help you to explain or demonstrate your solvency.

You can group the assorted ideas that you use to develop your harm into a single organized main point with supporting structure. You can refer to that first main point as your first **contention**. The identifying title of that contention could be generically called "harms of the status quo" or you could give it a title that identifies the specific context of the proposition and the harms that make up your case in support. If you are debating the issue of opening ANWR to development, your first main point might be "Contention I: The Harms of Low Domestic Oil Production." The supporting structure of this point might include statistics on oil imports and the harms of dependency on foreign sources of oil along with points that present statistics and evidence on the high costs of oil due to low supplies. Both of these ideas are expressions of harms that exist in a world where there is not more oil available from ANWR.

The next main point that can be presented would be a contention that is the expression of or development of your statement of advocacy or plan. It makes sense that after identifying a problem, you immediately identify what should be done to address it. This particular contention may not need to be as long as the other ideas you develop. In some cases it may be one sentence or simple statement that says you embrace the actions identified in the proposition. In some cases you may have a bit more detail on the exact nature of your action, including the agent you think should act, and details about the exact amount or level of response you specifically endorse, or the change in policy you effect.

The third main point is your expression of solvency, and it becomes the third contention. The presentation of solvency involves not only an explanation of how things work functionally, but also an expression of the benefit of having that action in place. Solving the problem may alleviate the harms identified, but they may also lead to additional benefits beyond lessening harm. In some ways you can also conceptualize the issue of solvency as being the description of the advantages your advocacy creates. In the ANWR example we have been working with, not only might an increase of supply lower oil costs, but those costs being lowered may significantly increase economic growth because of lower transportation costs. Not only are people's pocketbooks helped (harm alleviated), but the entire economy becomes stronger (additional advantage accrued).

You may need to modify the above format depending upon the format of the debate, but the core ideas will remain relatively constant. Debate is very similar to the ideas presented by Monroe in the Motivated Sequence organizational pattern. In order to persuade, Monroe conceptualizes that people need to have attention drawn to a problem, a need demonstrated, an action proposed, the benefits of the action identified, and a final call to action based on what has been presented. In a rough sense, the attention-getting step is a strong introduction to your speech, your presentation of harm is the demonstration of need, your plan is the action proposed, the benefits are your explanation of solvency and advantages, and the call to action is your appeal to the audience to accept your advocacy in the debate.

While we treat debate as a technical and unique animal in the world of public speaking, at its core it is a persuasive speech. Remembering basic persuasive structures and modifying them for debate use is always a great place to start building your case.

BASICS OF REFUTATION

While any particular debate is unique, there are some general strategies or options every debate shares. While much of what you will refute will stem directly from what the other team has said, there may be ideas you can introduce that bring in issues they failed to think of or address. You may also find quickly that debate and refutation is not simply negation of everything the other team has said. It may not be necessary to counter every argument or to challenge every point. You need to think at both a micro and a macro level about what is going on. While for any specific argument you may have a strategy, it is also important to remember how all your approaches to refutation fit together overall to avoid self-contradiction, and to help remind you what issues matter the most.

STRAIGHT REFUTATION

The most basic approach is to address the other side's argument in a manner that touches on all of the points they have made. Earlier we discussed the notion of the **stock issues** in a debate, and how a side advocating for the proposition is required to have a *prima facie* case. A straight refutation challenges those stock issues and tries to make the point that the proposition side has failed to present a *prima facie* case. You may challenge the extent of their harm, or the representation of impact. You may challenge the evidence or supporting materials they are using to uphold that claim. Your general strategy is to show in what ways things are not as bad as they claim, or that there is very little chance even if there is a problem that their approach will make it better.

Many of the ideas you know about argument fallacies and poor argumentative structure would be appropriate to bring out in a straight refutation of case. There may be counter evidence that you wish to introduce to challenge the claims of the other side, or you may incorporate your own analysis pointing out flaws or incongruent arguments. This strategy relies heavily on the concept of **presumption**, or the idea that you don't fix it if it is not broken. Your goal is to show that the reasoning that calculates the harm is in error, or that the costs of trying to fix it would be greater than leaving it as it is. Straight refutation strategies are a way to guard against the **pathetic fallacy** (where the root of pathetic links directly back to the construct of *pathos*, the use of emotion in argument) of acting just to act.

It is important to remember that not every point has to be refuted. In some cases it may be insensitive or inappropriate to try to deny that there is a significant harm that needs addressed. It may also be that the facts introduced by the other team do not need to be disputed, but may actually be helpful to a point you want to make if interpreted appropriately or in a different context. Going back to the issue of drilling for oil in ANWR, it may not be important to dispute the amount of imported oil the United States uses, or the list of countries that are top exporters. That information might be useful in proving that oil dependency actually leads to greater stability since the incentive of the exporter to be hostile to the United States is minimized and a simple understanding of the economics of capitalism points out that nations with only one export cannot afford to shoot themselves in the foot for long by shutting off supplies.

The opposition side also gets to rely on the burden of proof most strongly being applied to the proposition side. If the proposition has introduced a main point then they must defend that point the whole debate in order to win. The opposition team may only have to win one point in the debate if they have picked the right one, or it is a big enough issue. You may successfully point out that they omitted a key element they needed to prove and, while they could be right about everything else, it still is an argument that can be rejected. They may fail to fulfill proof of a harm they initially claimed, and the judge may feel their case is undercut enough not to vote for, even if they like the idea behind the plan. So clear advantages of the opposition are that there is no need to be perfect and there is far greater latitude of choice about what arguments to make or to leave alone.

INTRODUCING ARGUMENTS NOT STARTED BY THE PROPOSITION

While straight refutation is a valuable tool for debate, often there are other arguments available to use that do not stem directly from the main points brought out by the proposition side. These arguments can be introduced as a way to show the true costs of doing the action advocated, to suggest a better alternative, or to challenge the very basis for considering the view of the world that is embraced by the proposition. It is very important to be clear in how these arguments are introduced, both in the organizational structure and presentation of the arguments, but also in the conceptual justification for bringing them into the debate.

Disadvantages

In decision-making, most people are familiar with some form of benefit to cost analysis. The proposition side usually has set their main points up to support a calculation that is stating that the actions they are advocating are worth the costs because they lead to the benefit of alleviating the harms or accruing additional advantages that are worthwhile. A **straight refutation** approach attempts to deny there is a significant harm or a way to solve it. The **disadvantage** approach points out that, even if they can address the harm they state they will, they will lead to some greater harm that is the true cost of taking their action or supporting their advocacy.

The basic elements of the disadvantage are to show that right now (in the status quo) things are basically OK. There may be some warning signs present we should be aware of, but absent any changes, things are on course. This is an attempt to show a snapshot of what is going on to be able to compare the way things are with the way things will be if the proposition's actions or ideas are embraced. It is a way of showing things that paint the scene that the proposition team leaves out that need to be considered. Debate shorthand for this concept is to say you are showing the **uniqueness** of the situation. It is also a way to show that there is a **threshold** of action that has not been crossed, but can be identified that should not be pursued.

The next piece of the disadvantage is to show what the proposition side does to change things so events change to start causing harm. It is an attempt to "link" the action of the proposition to the bad end results you will be identifying. In this part of the disadvantage you are being specific about what it is about the proposition's advocacy that is the action or idea that pushes us over the edge.

You may want to directly show in their plan text the action or policy they advocate as the cause, or how embracing the idea or philosophy embedded in the proposition is the driving impetus behind the changes to the way things are now that lead to the undesired consequences. Often world events and policies are quite complex, so your explanation of how the proposition causes bad things may be a chain of several events or actions that lead to the final result, starting with their action and then showing how that spins off into other actions and reactions.

The final piece of the disadvantage is the explanation of the harm caused, or **impact**. It is important to be able to show that the net result of the proposition's advocacy leads to greater harm than the harm they are aiming to solve. Just as they are claiming the benefits and costs add up for their side, you need to show that the costs they failed to recognize end up outweighing the benefit.

If you want to introduce a disadvantage into the debate, you should make sure and clearly identify it as a separate main point you want to make that is not directly related to a main point brought up by the proposition. One aspect that can be useful is to offer a thesis statement for the argument before presenting all of the component parts.

Again using ANWR as the basis for the proposition, it may be hard to deny that, given the laws of supply and demand, providing more oil will lower prices to consumers. All of the main points that the proposition team is offering up that make economic sense are somewhat seamless within the logic of economics (though still debatable). But, they have not mentioned the ramifications to the environment of doing their proposal. In this case you could offer a disadvantage that points out the environmental risks of oil drilling in a nature area. Your first main point would set the stage for how ANWR is like no other place on earth. It would also point out its current protection (the uniqueness and threshold ideas). Your next main point would talk about how their plan opens up ANWR in ways that have not been done before and how oil drilling leads to a variety of adverse effects, both unavoidable and unintentional (the links). Finally, your last main point would develop the impacts of an oil damaged wildlife refuge. The highlighting of rare and endangered species may be a part of this explanation along with general defenses of a habitat that cannot be recreated if permanently scarred. Your goal is to show that, yes, there may be the result of saving a few pennies per tank of gas, but the cost would be vast environmental destruction. In this case the costs would clearly outweigh the benefits.

Counter Proposal

After evaluating the harms presented by the proposition, you may decide that it would not be a good idea to try to minimize or try to diminish the issues they have addressed. You may even agree that responding to the problem identified is worth some risks. However, you may want to point out that there is a better way of addressing the issue than in the manner endorsed by the proposition. If that is the case, then you would want to offer an organized means of forwarding your **counter proposal**, or counter plan, that highlights why it should be done over the original proposal.

A counter proposal involves offering a clear description of what you are doing, similar to the plan text or advocacy statement of the proposition. It should be clear what the differences are between the original proposal or actions and what you would prefer instead.

A way to highlight that difference after giving your counter plan text is to offer a main point that explains how the two actions compete with each other. In explaining the disadvantage we made note of the idea of cost-benefit analysis. In dealing with the counter proposal, we will borrow from the idea of opportunity cost. By offering a counter proposal you acknowledge something should be done, and the original proposal could be put in place, but by doing so you are forgoing another opportunity that would be more optimal. Your ability to explain how the two differing proposals compete with each other is a way of highlighting the differences that lead to differing costs of action. Often your explanation of competition between the two proposals includes examining a world wherein both might be happening at the same time, and a rationale why your proposal alone would be superior to even that world.

The final element of your counter proposal is to move beyond the explanation of how the two ideas create a form of forced choice by competing with each other to highlighting the benefit or advantage of your proposal compared to the original of the proposition. This main point develops the clear "opportunity" that is not available by doing the proposition proposal and ends up being the cost to them.

To help illustrate, consider the issue of alternative energy. As an opposition debater you may find it hard to dispute that petroleum is a poor choice as it is finite, and does much environmental harm when utilized. So the proposition team may sound like they have a good idea when they support a proposition that calls on the Federal Government to create subsidies for alternative fuels and they have a plan that picks corn to be subsidized. So rather than having to try to deny the problems with petroleum, you might offer a counter proposal that acknowledges a need to move away from petroleum but not by using corn, you may offer a counter proposal that has a plan to subsidize sawgrass (or pick your favorite biomass source) instead. You would state your counter proposal to subsidize, but note that you support sawgrass instead. You would then state that you compete with the plan that subsidizes corn because they are completely different infrastructures and doing both means doing neither well. You might also point out that there is limited funding so you cannot pay for both at the same time. Finally you would make your last main point of the counter proposal in explaining how much better sawgrass is for the environment and how it avoids the problems related to corn like making food prices go higher and cutting our ability to offer significant food aid. Your goal is to show that corn is a less desirable alternative, or has greater opportunity costs, than your proposal of sawgrass instead.

Philosophical Critique

Sometimes, the way in which the proposition has set up their advocacy, or an idea at the core of the proposition they advocate, is based on a premise or worldview that needs to be challenged before even getting to the action itself. These objections are often based on philosophical or ideological perspectives that are used to shed light on unchallenged assumptions or beliefs that perpetuate bad actions and behavior. By engaging in criticism of the proposition's case you are showing what flawed assumptions are being made and how they lead to negative consequences that cannot be understood from their worldview.

The criticism approach begins with a main point that explains the thesis of the criticism and the assumptions that it is intended to challenge. By presenting this point you are bringing a new awareness to those listening than was presented by the proposition. It shows an alternative means of viewing what or who is harmed, and what the response should be. It is the ability to reveal a new perspective that can help explain what is wrong and what needs to done instead of old ideas that keep repeating the problem even as they try to solve it.

The next main point would be to identify what assumptions the proposition team is making in error. In what ways do they show that they are embracing a view that is really missing the point or fails to account for important aspects they end up ignoring? You are showing the blind spot they exhibit by the way they frame the problem, or by how they think it should be addressed.

Your final point would be to explain the implications of your analysis. You should be pointing out how the flaws embraced by the proposition perpetuate harms and continue problems of which they are not even aware. You should also show that the perspective you are presenting with your critical view is a way to resolve problems in a better way. There is a need to change mindsets before we start offering policies or actions.

One of the propositions competitive debaters most want to avoid being on the opposition of is a proposition to allow same-sex marriage rights. It is difficult to point out ills to society at large from making such a policy (even though some may claim personal harm to their own values or beliefs). In this case, the opposition cannot really offer a straight refutation strategy because they do not want to say people are not really discriminated against, and there may be no disadvantage to the public at large, and alternatives like civil unions may be a worse idea. One alternative that was developed was to offer a critique of marriage as a state-based contract. The thesis was that the state should not be in the business of brokering economic relationships among individuals (remember you get a "license" to be married from the state, the church ceremony is unofficial!). And essentially a marriage license is a form of business contract that now dictates economic ownership rights and obligations between two persons. As such, marriage is a flawed institution for heterosexual couples as well as for same-sex couples. Therefore, one should reject same-sex marriage because one should reject the concept of marriage for all. While certainly a unique take on the issue, it allowed opposition teams to engage in a theoretical debate that did not have to rely on supporting discrimination or offering up piecemeal solutions that were inadequate.

SUMMARY

Breaking down debate into its component parts may seem somewhat complex and overly technical, but in reality it reflects the way that people argue with each other every day. When someone is complaining about a problem we may challenge them by asking how bad it really is. When someone has a suggestion how about how moving the furniture around the apartment will make it seem bigger we may point out that they failed to account for electrical outlet or heating vent placement so it will not really solve the problem. We may point out the harms that will occur if someone wants to drive when they are impaired. And we may offer up numerous alternatives for getting home that do not involve them driving. So while in debate we may call it straight refutation, or a disadvantage, they are all forms of reasoning we are very familiar with, they just end of being used in more formal and organized ways with evidence and support.

While we have discussed straight refutation and arguments not started by the proposition in separate ways, it is important to note that most often they are used in conjunction with each other. You may find that it is a valuable strategy to try to minimize the harms and solvency the proposition may be trying to claim while also pointing out disadvantages or other alternatives at the same time. By using both approaches, you may find that comparing the costs and benefits may be easier to do in your favor.

Our example of the disadvantage of the environment being harmed by oil drilling is far more compelling if you can in fact establish that people will save only a few pennies on each fill up. But if the difference is a dollar for each gallon of gas sold, then the plight of the caribou may not matter!

There is also just the strategic value in engaging the other side with a variety of points to keep them from being able to have clear control of any point. Much like a lawyer works to create reasonable doubt, on the opposition you are

169

trying to create doubt about the value of the whole proposition case, and any flaw or minimization may be the key to having your audience doubt the worth of their claims.

GENERAL STRATEGY

Having examined the proposition and opposition individually, let us now consider how the two might interact. Obviously both sides are trying to win their facts and evidentiary battles, but in some cases both sides will have issues that are undisputed, or relatively uncontested. But just because an argument stands in the debate does not necessarily make that a winning argument. There is always a process of contextualization and comparison that needs to be actively done by the participants to try to maximize their chances of winning the debate. One of the key distinctions made about arguments is whether they provide offense to your side (a reason that you win), or do they provide defense (a reason that you do not lose). Neither team should get stuck in a pattern of exclusively trying to show they are not losing or that the other team is losing. It is important to say, "here is why we are not losing, but also here is why we are winning these arguments" or if on the proposition, "here is why the other team is losing and why we should win the debate." It seems like a slight nuance, but at the end of the debate people are not looking for who survived the debate, but which side made the best case or won the arguments.

Comparison of arguments, or often the impacts or advantages claimed, is the core of any strategic choice in a debate. You tried to have the best issues in advance, but now that both sides have been heard, you need to show how they stack up against what the other team actually said.

IMPACT COMPARISON

Magnitude, probability, timeframe, and **irreversibility** are four lenses with which to compare impacts. Each of these ideas can be used by a speaker to manipulate the impact of his or her advantage or disadvantage, showing that it is more important than the impacts that the opponents present. Impact comparison could be viewed as a form of argumentative "Rock, Paper, Scissors," but in a debate any one of the four concepts can beat the other three, depending on the skill of the advocate.

The size and scale of any given problem can be a persuasive reason to act to fix it (the advantage) or to avoid it (the disadvantage). **Magnitude**, which is sometimes referred to as "body count," suggests that the problem is so large that it should be avoided at all costs. Many of the more unlikely results of a given impact story suggest grave consequences. It is probably unlikely that society will collapse into anarchy without the social glue of the death penalty, but the horror of that impact can be used to show that the advocacy statement should be rejected. Speakers can also suggest that the magnitude of an impact is a more significant concern than when an impact will happen: "even if it is several years before crime becomes pervasive, the level of violence will pale in comparison to the harm from the very controlled use of the death penalty." Like the other impact comparison tools, the speaker can get creative in developing why the magnitude of an impact is the most important thing to consider.

Speakers can show that the **probability** of a given impact is the most significant thing to be weighed with the criteria. The more direct control the advocacy has over a given problem, the more that problem should be taken into consideration relative to the other impacts that are less likely to occur. People would generally agree that it is better to certainly save one person's life, than to try to save ten people with only a million-in-one chance of success. Relative proximity to a given outcome is more important than how long the outcome takes to occur, as the eventual outcome can be predicted. Speakers can also argue that "many problems are complex; it is rare to be able to solve one problem comprehensively; preventing one innocent person from being put to death is far more important that the infinitesimal risk of social implosion."

There are three different aspects of **timeframe** to consider. The first reason that timeframe is an important concept in debate concerns impact comparison. The timing of when an impact story is likely to come into effect can be a way of prioritizing its importance when the debate is evaluated. Speakers can argue that impacts that occur more quickly should be considered as more important in that they are more directly caused by adopting the "For" advocacy. Longer-term impacts are less likely to be directly related to the advocacy statement, as with increased time there is a larger chance that another change will intervene. An impact that occurs twenty years in the future is likely to be affected by a later development in the status quo that is not controlled by either the "For" or "Against" side. New policy is constantly being suggested and implemented by the government; this will continue to occur after the "For" advocacy is implemented, so future action could interrupt the long-term impact, preventing it from occurring. Thus speakers can argue that their impact scenario, which will occur quickly after the advocacy statement is adopted, is more significant than their opponent's impacts, which will occur many years down the road.

The second aspect of timeframe that speakers should consider is how all of the arguments of the debate fit together. Participants should consider how long a given impact from an advantage or disadvantage will take to occur, and whether different impact stories will interact. Often a disadvantage or advantage will make it less likely that the impact from an advantage or disadvantage that the opposing side presented will occur. If the "Against" team presented a "deterrence" disadvantage against an abolish-the-death-penalty advocacy, a disintegration of the social fabric would make it less likely that an advantage of "Ending Racist Laws" would ever happen, as people would attack each other as the government collapsed. Conversely, in the next speech, the "For" speaker could then explain that the advantage of "Fair Justice" would help make all people feel a part of society as they are treated more fairly, reducing or eliminating the risk of the disadvantage by strengthening the social fabric. Participants should feel free to use either or both conceptions of timeframe presented here when delving into impact comparison.

The third aspect of timeframe to consider is fairly simple. Once a change takes place, it will stay in effect until another change is made. So if a given advocacy saves some people every year, over the decades, all those people's lives will add up. Conversely, if an advocacy statement once implemented causes a disadvantage, the problems last for some time and aggregate over the years. Not all impacts are best thought of in this last form of timeframe. Some things are intangible, others are one-time occurrences; but when the advocate can, he or she should emphasize the longevity of a given impact.

Finally, if it is appropriate, speakers should emphasize that one or more of their impacts are **irreversible**. Death, some forms of pollution, suffering, bereavement, and many other potential debate impacts cannot be alleviated once they have happened. Many problems can be fixed with future government actions; with others, once the harm is done, no amends can be made. Impacts that are irreversible, because of their finality, are often highlighted as the most significant, even if they do not have the largest magnitude. Speakers should consider irreversibility and the other tools of impact comparison as they prepare for their debate and structure their cases, deciding which advantages and disadvantages to bring into the debate.

MACRO VERSUS MICRO VIEW

While there may be many points developed in a debate, it is important not to lose sight of the forest because of the trees. As was discussed in the section on opposition strategies, not all arguments are equally important or need to be disputed. There may even be some value in conceding some minor points that hurt you a little to be able to spend more time on things that have a better chance of helping you win the overall argument. It is important to remember that debate is not a quiz bowl, battling over statistics and the details of facts may not help build an overall case for either side. Sometimes people spend too much time on an issue because it is the one they have the most comfort talking about, rather than it being the most important issue in the debate.

Debate involves not only strategic management of arguments, but also time management. Like most public speaking opportunities, debate has time limits imposed on those participating that require choices to be made about what order things are talked about and for how long. Your audience will always think the thing you talked about the most is what you think is most important, whether that was your intention or not. Also, ideas that come earlier in the speech are always seen as more important or fundamental. Be careful about leaving important ideas for last; the audience may not see them as clinchers, but after thoughts, particularly if you have very little time to talk about them once you get there. You may take a more balanced approach to the issues and ideas in the debate earlier on in the first few speeches, but as the debate wraps up, it is imperative to prioritize your most important arguments and be sure to identify them clearly in your speech and to allocate enough time to be able to explain them, especially in context of what the other team has said or done.

SUMMARY

At some point in the debate you will need to engage in some form of meta communication about what has happened in the debate in a manner that acknowledges the arguments made by the other side, and how the judge or audience should deal with those arguments in light of the ones you have made. It is important to not get caught up in the trap of explaining the debate as if only your arguments are the ones that were made. You also should be able to speak about the arguments in comparative ways that show why your arguments provide offense for you. You need to use language that emphasizes how you win the debate versus how you avoid loss or the why the other team should lose.

SOME OTHER CONSIDERATIONS ABOUT "HOW TO"

While this chapter so far has focused on basic strategies and ways to present those strategies, there are a few other aspects of being involved in a debate for which you will want to be prepared. Depending on the format you are participating in there will be some variations in what is expected and how things are done, but the ideas that follow are easily adaptable to a broad range of contexts.

STRATEGIC USE OF QUESTIONS

Effective use of questions in argument is a difficult skill to master, and debates provide an excellent opportunity to practice asking and responding to pointed questions. There may be differing question formats: sometimes there is an allocated time to ask questions, sometimes you can ask questions during the speech if the speaker allows, sometimes you may take questions from the audience during a designated Q & A period. Regardless of the format, the aspect of questioning is the most interactive aspect of a debate, and can really show a difference between not only the thinking and ideas of the two sides, but also their credibility and likeability. Asking your opponent a stunner of a question can turn the tide in a debate, and a devastating response to your opponent's question can throw a team off rhythm for the rest of the debate. In theory, each speaker is individually responsible for responding to questions after his or her speech, but in practice it is occasionally beneficial for one's partner to chime in if the partner has some additional and more specific information to add. There are four general ideas about questions that participants should consider before the debate and even practice if they get an opportunity.

The most basic function of a question is to provide clarity. In debates, speakers are often less clear in presenting their arguments then they think they are, and often there are a few ideas that were not expressed clearly. It is necessary to understand an argument before you attempt to refute it, so it is vital to ask questions to clarify what the previous speaker intended to mean with his or her argument. There is an added benefit to doing this: doing so highlights that the previous speaker was not clear in her or his speech, and it is likely that the audience will be happy that more clarification is included. Having to explain himself or herself a second or even third time makes a speaker look weak, so participants should look to make a speaker clarify their thoughts via questions.

Related to creating clarification, opponents can ask questions to lock a speaker into defending a position. Once participants know what the major arguments are on both sides of the topic, speakers may be intentionally vague in order to avoid a potential argument of their opponent's. Asking a leading question can make speakers commit to an idea that they may not want to support. Sometimes speakers will be vague without purpose; in that situation it is still a good idea to ask a question to lock a speaker into defending an idea so that your side is able to create clear links to your arguments. The clearer the debate, the more everyone benefits, and the easier it will be to connect your arguments to the material presented by your opponent.

Be assertive when asking questions; be firm in your phrasing and try to look as if you are the expert and are simply trying to understand the garbled mess that your opponent just stumbled through. Unlike the panel debates, the opponent, not the speaker who just finished a speech, controls question time. Speakers who are being questioned should try to extend their speech into the question time and continue to pile on arguments into the debate. People asking questions should not feel bad about politely interrupting a speaker who is rambling on once they have had their question answered. Often in a debate, someone asking questions will say "thank you; and now this question . . ." as soon as they have the answer that they were looking for.

Finally, participants should avoid revealing their hand too much when asking questions. People naturally want to bring up their best arguments against what the speaker just said and try to throw the speaker off balance. In reality, though, the person asking the questions does not want to tip off the other team to what the major arguments coming up will be. Asking questions that reveal your side's best arguments only gives your opponents more time to think about how to answer the argument in their next speech. Even worse, a really crafty speaker will take a question that reveals what an opponent will argue in the next speech, and attack and beat the argument quickly. This is bad, because now a speaker who wishes to use that beaten argument needs to rehabilitate it even before it is formally presented into the debate.

TAKING NOTES

One of the key differences between debate and other forms of public speaking is that so much of what is said in a debate depends on what the other team is going to say, so there cannot really be a full outline or manuscript ready to read from for your speech. You must make up some of your arguments as you are going as well as track the arguments of your opponents. In debate we call the notes that you take your **flowsheet**. That terminology references the dynamic nature of the debate as it progresses, and that at any point in the debate things may change or take a different direction.

The Basics

Rather than a format you may use for taking notes in a class, in debate you will have a specialized way you record what happens. Rather than keeping track of the debate in sequential paragraphs, you will have your paper divided up into columns that represent each of the speeches in the debate. You are essentially going to put things in a column, so that in the next column if those things are talked about you have a space directly next to those items to write down what is said (or for you to write down what you will say about them).

Your flowsheet serves not only as a record of what has been said in the debate so that you can follow it and remember it, but it also serves as your script for the things that you will say in your speech. It is a way to jot down the ideas you want to be sure to bring out when you hear what the other side is saying.

176

The way you take notes can vary significantly based on your own preferences, but it is a good idea to start with the basic model of using columns. Flowing the debate is a physical skill that people do not often think of when they imagine debating, but many a debater can lament the argument they lost because they did not remember to make it because they did not write it down.

Consider the following example of a flowsheet that covers a proposition constructive, followed by the opposition, and in a third column, the response to the opposition (Figure 10-1). It includes a basic case by the proposition along with some arguments that the opposition want to introduce that are not directly related to main points in the first speech along with some straight refutation of the case ideas. (Note that there are a bunch of shortcuts taken with abbreviation and brevity of sentences. Often your notes will be more of a prompt to remind you what you want to say rather than the exact language you will be speaking.)

Shortcuts

Once you become familiar with a topic you may find that there are abbreviations or symbols you can use to save time as you are taking notes. You also should get used to the outline form of arguments and how they are presented so that you will flow more intuitively. Some people like to use two different colors of pen as well to create a more clear contrast between the two sides visually so it is easier to use while speaking. It is important to write large enough to be able to read your notes as you are speaking, and to give each argument plenty of room in case it develops into a major point.

If you are working with other people in your debate, it can be useful to coordinate your symbols and abbreviations so you can more easily share your notes in the debate. A benefit of using good handwriting is that it makes it easier for your partner to read your notes if they missed something (or vice versa).

First Proposition Speaker	First Opposition Speaker	Proposition Response to Opposition
Prop: The US Fed Gov should Ban GMOs D/C: Team which best upholds stability of the food supply	>Grant D/C: GMO's best uphold stability	>OK, but will Prop will show GMO's not stable

I. Harms: GMO's are dangerous
 	
A. Unknown Consequences to Enviro
  1. enviro break out
  2. impact on non-GMO
  3. long term growth patterns
  4. long term genetic drift
  5. trans species funkiness
	>wrong. Enviros can't have both ways—say humans have irrevocably changed planet, and then must rely on natural processes
	>GMO's help with drought
	>GMO's help with heat
	>T/H already crossed: GMOs out of the bottle
		>GMOs never justified, even with compromised nature
		
		>GMOs not better than nature
		>GMOs unpredictable
		>GMO results only short term
		>T/H justifies ban, not continuation

B. Human Health
  1. not natural
  2. unforeseen consequences
  3. untestable
	>no impact
	>hybrids are natural in nature
	>TA: solve for food allergies
		>genetic sickness is serious impact
		> hybrids not transgenetic in nature
		>Re-Turn: GMOs create new allergies never seen before

PLAN: US not allow GMOs for commercial products or applications		
Solvency: A. Traditional Means sufficient B. More Costly most safe C. Look to Long term survival not short term profit	>No international Solvency >Traditional methods will fail >Cost is important factor: need to save farms 1st, then worry about quality of product >Long term survival requires genetic flexibility	>US does impact GMO use worldwide as producer and importer /exporter >save farms by abandoning GMOs >long term survival requires natural evolution
	ICounterplan: USFG will require labeling of GMOs II. Avoids the Disadvantages III. Gives consumers and market choice	1. Case is DA to CP—GMO's are bad 2. Consumers won't look to long term 3. corporations will eliminate choice
	DA: Farm Destruction A. GMOs central to farm production B. NO GMO's devastates family farm C. Farm Crisis equals final corporate takeover	1. TA GMOs destroy farms: terminator seeds 2. TA: Monocropping encouraged which is devastating strategy 3. GMOs cost only possible with corp farms scale and finances 4. small farms best for organic 5. will return profit to small farms with no GMOs

	DA: 3W disaster
	A. GMOs available to 3w now
	B. Removal Crushes 3W
	C. Impacts
	  1. Nutrition and starvation
	  2. economies and self sufficiency
		1. TA GMOs colonialize 3W
		2. Nutrition only sympton GMOs not solve
		3. GMOs expand world crisis

Figure 10-1 Sample Flowsheet

Summary

Keeping a good flow is never easy, but most participants will have had some practice through the course of the class and the use of this text, and will be getting more comfortable with their notes. Practicing is always useful preparation; speakers should take advantage of when they are the audience for the in-class debates by flowing them. When participants flow debates in which they are not competing, they gain a better understanding of how the parts of the debate fit together and are able to see "the big picture" more easily. When advocates do not have to worry about giving the next speech, they are more relaxed and can concentrate on recording arguments without worrying about what they will have to say in response. The more participants can use their flow in debates, the greater their understanding of all the concepts that make for good debate.

BEING ORGANIZED/USING BRIEFS

Not only will you be using your flowsheet during the debate as your notes for speaking and as a way you remind yourself to make arguments, you can also do yourself a big favor by having the materials you gathered to collect evidence and arguments organized so you can access and use those materials during the debate as well. The idea is to organize **briefs** on topics that you know you will want to talk about in the debate as well as those you think may come up from the other side. These briefs are helpful in organizing information and supporting evidence, but also to catalog the ideas and analysis you have of issues that are contextual to the specific debate you will be having.

As you practice debate you will notice that you will need to be multi-tasking at a pretty high level. You may be listening, taking notes, thinking about what your answer will be, and writing that answer down pretty much simultaneously. The more you have prepared before the debate, the easier it will be to respond. For example, you can just note on your flowsheet, "apply brief on harms here" and then pull that specific document out and refer to it in your speech and thus be capable of presenting numerous well thought-out arguments without having to write them down or try to mentally recall them while you could be listening more carefully to what is being said.

Evidence Briefs

One type of brief you may prepare is a compilation of evidence and supporting materials on a specific issue or on sub sets of arguments on the issue. You may literally cut and paste key passages of articles or news stories you have read into a document and identify the source along with a summary sentence to identify what that particular quote or passage does for your argument. You might also paraphrase key concepts, and give them appropriate attribution of source even if you do not include a direct quote or transcript. Sometimes these briefs are useful for compiling sets of facts or statistics that may be useful to have even if they are not required for any of the arguments you may be making.

Imagine a stack of note cards you have prepared for a speech, with key quotes, statistics, and empirical examples that all support your argument. You could "shuffle" the order of that information to meet the needs of your debate, or draw from that pile later in the debate when you need an additional support you may not have used earlier, or you know specifically refutes a point made on the other side. You could have a stack of note cards like that, but often if you have more than one supporting idea or piece of evidence that go together, it is more convenient to have them all on one page, or set of pages. This may not be the case for some of your in-class practice debates. They will be less formal and more limited in nature, and thus will not need extensive and duplicative sources of support.

Argument Briefs

Your approach to the debate may also involve one in which you may be reacting more than initiating. Or, as you anticipate what the other side may say, you are thinking through answers you might make that are based on your understanding and analysis of the situation versus directly being tied to a piece of evidence. An **argument brief** is a way of cataloging and keeping track of those ideas to keep them accessible and to remind you of them as you are debating.

It can quite simply be a document that you create that has a list of the ways to respond to an issue. By preparing it in advance you can take advantage of putting the arguments in an order that prioritizes the most important ones at the top, so that if you are in a hurry you know the best or most important point is the first one on the page. You can also add ideas as you come up with them even up until the start of the debate! Even though your brief may be prioritized, ultimately what ends up being a priority in the debate may change, so your familiarity in preparing and organizing it may allow for you to remember the third or fourth argument on the page that becomes the best answer in the context of the debate.

Using your own analysis and evaluation of the arguments in the debate is a perfectly legitimate way of responding to arguments made by the other side. Rather than relying on coming up with them all in the debate as it happens, as you will certainly want to think of arguments in the debate itself, having thought about the arguments and hypothesizing what might get said or how the other side may respond will give you an edge in participating in the debate and eventually summarizing the issues overall as your side presents its rebuttals.

Summary

Each debate or persuasive situation will vary, but being prepared and anticipating what will be said to your arguments is essential for doing well. For the beginning debates you are participating in you may find that a "hybrid" form of brief that mixes evidence, and your own analysis, and potential responses is the best way to go. You can organize those by issue or specific argument, and have all of your ideas and evidence together.

However, you are more than likely to experience a situation where you do need to organize a variety of materials that help to support a textured or complex issue. Not only in school, but also in your job you are likely to have to build a case for a project or business model that will require complex analysis and support. Thinking of how you build a case and support it and what materials you need to do that are skills you will be directly enhancing by participating in debate.

SUMMARY

While each debate and argument that you get into will be unique, there are some basic starting points that will be the basis for what you do. At core you are being an advocate for the actions or ideas embodied in the proposition or conversely challenging the advocacy of the other side while presenting your own counter advocacy. So while the argument is in general a persuasive speech, it is one that is based on a specific question being developed from the ideas in the proposition. The construction of your argument emphasizes the awareness of some harm, some way to address it, and demonstration of how that action solves the problem or creates some advantage. Whether you are supporting or opposing the proposition, even though you may at times try to discount the arguments of the other side, at root you need some good reason to vote for your position on the proposition.

Not only must you intellectually approach the debate, but there are also organizational and presentational elements you should prepare for as well. Being able to take good notes on your flowsheet and being able to access your arguments as the debate is in progress are elements that make it easier to demonstrate the superiority of your position. Other chapters will give more details about the expectations for specific formats of debate that will help you flesh out the exact organizational patterns and types of arguments you will want to emphasize. Being able to adapt a general way of constructing arguments and engaging in a discussion of public action and advocacy will allow you to not only practice better argumentative and persuasive skills but also to hone your critical engagement of public controversies and policy choices that affect you.

Being able to argue well involves an understanding of argument theory and an understanding of the issue you will be debating. While the topics debated in your class are for educational and training purposes, imagine the confidence and advocacy you will be able to bring to situations where you must engage in persuasive manner over an issue of public policy or the creation of rules or decision-making in groups you are a part of. Even though the emphasis on preparation may seem quite intense, putting that effort in early makes the actual performance in the debate much easier and less stressful. An engaging and informative conversation that is structured as a debate can in fact be quite enjoyable and invigorating to the participants. It is something that you should look forward to as a fun and unique learning opportunity.

CHAPTER 11

PRESENTATION AND DELIVERY

The genetic hardware a bird uses to learn to sing probably isn't far from what a mouse uses to learn to run a maze, and what you use to learn to speak.
Constance Scharff

Deafness has left me acutely aware of both the duplicity that language is capable of and the many expressions the body cannot hide.
Terry Galloway

One of the key values of being in a debate is the ability to have face-to-face immediacy with the others who are present, not just the person or persons who may be debating, but also those who are listening. While the strategic considerations and substantive ideas that are the core of debate are foremost in having a good quality debate, the element of presentation is also one to consider. The way that debate is practiced, even when informal, involves the use of oral communication. In more formalized situations, such as tournament debating or the public presentation of a topic, the idea is to have not only a conversation with the person you are debating, but also with those who are observers. Those observers may be part of an interested audience or have a stake in the outcome of the issue being discussed. They may be people who just want to learn more about the topic, and hearing a variety of perspectives is useful to them to understand things more quickly. In some circumstances an observer of the debate may also be serving as an evaluator or judge for the event. All audiences include the speaker's ability along with their content in their overall evaluation of the influence of the speech. In this section we will look at some of the basics of delivery and identify some ways you can be comfortable with this element of debate as a specialized form of public presentation.

BACKGROUND: THE EVOLUTION OF SPEECH

There are important lessons about how the body works that are necessary for understanding why body language is so important in argument. It is important to note that the authors are practitioners of argument and not physiologists, evolutionary biologists, anthropologists, sociologists, or specialists in communication disorders; we have, however, incorporated knowledge from these fields with our argumentation background to create the following chapter. Body language is a subject that is ripe for multidisciplinary examination, as it involves both complex biological and metaphysical processes. Before we address the various kinds of nonverbal communication, we must first examine the way that the human body has evolved into the speaking machine it is now and how that machine works.

The biological origins of human cognition and speech are hotly contested topics in several different academic disciplines, with the exact physiological mechanisms still being described and debated. However, there is general acceptance that the two capabilities—which provide much of the differentiation between humans and other species—evolved over time, with each having an effect on the other. Neither the ability to communicate nor the ability to engage in rational thought is unique to humans; many different animals communicate simply and rationalize to some extent, but the level of complexity of human thought and the ability to communicate it does appear to be unique among the animal kingdom.[62]

COGNITION AND LANGUAGE[63]

Cognition comprises self-awareness and the ability to rationalize the information provided by the senses to interact logically and predictably with the physical and nonphysical worlds. Humans appear to be the species that best processes the wealth of information our body gathers about the world around us, contemplates it, and then formulates actions based upon calculated desires. We are conscious of this process and ourselves. It appears that all of these traits evolved before the emergence of humans from within the mammalian line; however, with larger brain capacities, early humans were able to distinguish the species as a thinking machine. Early humans are clearly distinguished from great apes in posture; the evolution of an upright body position rearranged the physiological organization of the throat and airway. Changes to the hominid (early human species) airway were biomechanically necessary for the articulation of more complex sounds: noises that slowly became words. The flexibility of the human tongue and the space between the tongue and voice box are necessary for the complex vocalizations that make up spoken language. Anthropological work suggests that advances in the development of human consciousness appear to be influenced by the emergence of complicated vocal communication. There is disagreement as to when exactly early vocal communication became language, and when humans began to think in a modern way. There is, however, some consensus that language evolved as a mechanism to coordinate ever more complex human social interactions between 120,000 and 70,000 years ago. Changes to the human airway, a result of the evolutionary pressure to walk upright, created the capacity for complex vocal articulation. Increasing brain capacity, and the growing ability to express concepts, created the modern

---

[62] Think about a dog barking and dragging its leash. It is communicating in a way and also showing that it can "think" by connecting disturbing you and presenting its leash with its desire to go for a walk.

[63] Three sources were consulted in the creation of this section. They provide for interesting further study if readers are curious to learn more.
Goodenough, Ward H. "Evolution of the Human Capacity for Beliefs," *American Anthropologist*, New Series, Vol. 92, No. 3, September 1990.
Ochs, Elinor, and Lisa Capps. "Narrating the Self," *Annual Review of Anthropology*, Vol. 25, 1996.
"The Day We Learned To Think"; Horizon Series, BBC Two, aired Feb 20, 2003.

thinking human. It is important to understand that modern human thought and language are co-productions of each other, both gradually gaining complexity as humanity evolved. For students today, recognizing the origins of language and thought should help emphasis how vocal communication works and why it is so important to humans.

MIRROR NEURONS[64]

The human brain is very complex, and scientists are just beginning to understand how it works. A fairly recent discovery may help to explain some particularities of human behavior. Mirror neurons were recently isolated in the brains of primates, and as a result of MRI study on human brains, many scholars believe that they, or a mirror neural system that is very similar, exist in humans. When an animal with mirror neurons acts, the mirror neurons fire in conjunction with the other neurons that fire to control the animal's action. What makes mirror neurons special is that they also fire when an animal observes other animals acting. In a way, when humans watch someone speak, they "feel" through their mirror neural system what the speaker is doing. The scholarship on mirror neurons and their role in the human system is still in its infancy, but many believe that mirror neurons are part of the explanation for complex human thought and behavior. Human mirror neurons, or a mirror system, most likely have motor, visual, and auditory components. Many experts believe that imitation is a key process for human language acquisition, and mirror neurons may form the base of this mental process. Mirror neurons may also form the base for human empathy; an emotional response often considered representative of complex cognitive functioning.

The existence of mirror neurons is important for students of argument in that they help to explain several aspects of human communication. Mirror neurons are likely tied to gestures. Some anthropologists and linguists believe

---

[64] Literature consulted for this chapter that would also be good resources for further learning: Gallese, Vittorio. "The Manifold Nature of Interpersonal Relations: The Quest for a Common Mechanism," *Philosophical Transactions: Biological Sciences*, Vol. 358, No. 1431. Mar 29, 2003. Le Bel, Ronald M., Pineda, Jaime A. and Anu Sharma. "Motor—Auditory—Visual Integration: The Role of the Human Mirror Neuron System in Communication and Communication Disorders," *Journal of Communication Disorders*, Vol. 42. 2009. Kendon, Adam. "Gesture," *Annual Review of Anthropology*, Vol. 26. 1997.

that language evolved in tandem with gesture, and that ever more complicated abstract verbal expressions gradually replaced more literal gestures in a primitive sign language. The communicative power of gestures would be heightened if the scholarship on mirror neurons is correct, and humans are communicating in two ways: in a conscious manner, where the mind is self-aware while processing the communication; and in a subconscious manner, where mirror neurons are triggered, and the brain is feeling the communication without filtering the information through the conscious self. Mirror neurons also help to explain the way that humans process information; the neurons help the brain tie external information to an individual, creating a "like-me" reaction. The "like-me" reaction helps to explain how abstract ideas are interpreted by the receiver in communication. Although the research on mirror neurons is still developing, it is fair to conclude that mirror neurons may be a key explanation in how humans think and communicate.

DIAPHRAGM

Humans make noise by controlling the passage of air through the voice box (larynx). The diaphragm is the muscle that separates the lungs from the digestive tract, and it is critical for respiration. When the diaphragm contracts, it puts pressure on the lungs, forcing air out and through the throat. While exhaling, humans can manipulate the noise they make by contracting their vocal cords and adjusting the final section of the airway with their tongue and palate. This is important for good communication because proper posture allows the diaphragm to operate most efficiently. Singers are often told to "sing from their diaphragms" in order to gain power in their voices; presenters of argument should "speak from their diaphragms" as well. The diaphragm underwent complex changes as hominids began to walk upright, and this evolutionary change, coupled with the changes already discussed, help to inform the physical way that modern humans speak.

PREPARATION

Before the Debate: Have Something to Say!

The easiest way to be comfortable and relaxed when speaking is to know you have put together your information in the best way possible. If you are confident in what you are going to say and have it well prepared, the speaking part can be easy, and even sometimes fun.

In terms of debate, the preparation has the substance phase, where you gather your evidence and strategize and anticipate arguments that may arise. Those elements are what the rest of this book discusses and are what conceptually you should have in place. In many ways, some of the choices you make about content end up organizing your presentation. The order in which you think that the ideas should be addressed in essence becomes the outline for your presentation or speech.

Extemporaneous Delivery

Often, the working through of how you want to present your ideas for presentation can help you crystallize your ideas and remember your main focus or thesis. This can happen as you prepare the specific notes you will use for presentation. In many other forms of public address, speakers often choose to work from very detailed notes or even a manuscript. This style of presentation can often be stale, and certainly cannot deal with the inherent interactive nature of a debate. As you prepare for your presentations, you should emphasize the use of an **extemporaneous delivery**. That means that, while you do not have your speech memorized, another technique not endorsed for debate, you also will not have it be completely made up as you go. You will have some notes available, but you also may be referring to evidence, or other materials that you may or not use verbatim, but still have prepared in advance.

One the best ways to prepare for debate is to review your evidence and materials so that they are at the forefront of your thoughts, so as you hear what the other side is saying, you can remember your information and how it applies to what they are saying. It can also mean that you remember to introduce issues they did not, but should have, that you are prepared to talk about.

Extemporaneous delivery basically means that you will rely both on notes and material you have prepared in advance, but also introduce and refute ideas that arise in the debate that you have not specifically prepared. Rather than being completely impromptu, or making it up as you go, you do have some ideas that are ready to be presented; you just may change the order or emphasis on them as you get involved in the debate.

YOUR MATERIALS

How you prepare your materials for use in the debate can vary greatly based on the type of debate you are in, and how you feel comfortable organizing yourself. As we present some ideas for presentation, remember that often trial and error is the best way to find out what works for you. It is also possible that you may see someone doing something different than you that seems to work well. Do not be afraid to adopt that technique! There is no single right way to prepare your materials, but it is always true that the better prepared your materials are, the better your debate.

Evidence Briefs

As you have researched the topic you have come up with evidence that has helped you to construct your argument. Often in complex debates, this evidence is compiled into materials that are easy to reference in the context of the debate. This may be statistics that you want to quote absolutely accurately, quotations that need to be used verbatim, or other types of data that need to be included but you do not need to memorize since you can access them during the debate.

For some, having the articles with the key parts highlighted is a simple and effective way to have evidence available. If the debate is not too complex, or the issues will be over a well-defined set of ideas, then having the materials you collected in preparation available with the most important parts made clear is one possibility. You can also make some notes, or have some keywords written in the margins or made note of on the text in some way to both help remind you what you have, and to make it easy to access as you need it in the debate.

In more complex debates, you may not want to have a bunch of articles or copies from books all over the place. In that case, the main ideas that you have found are, quite literally, cut and pasted from the original source and compiled onto a separate page with the bibliographic information on the original and some notes that identify it or the "tag" for the argument that it supports. By compiling the material into a new document, you can customize that document to address specific elements of the debate. If you are discussing economic issues, you may have an evidence brief prepared that has a variety of statistics referring to employment rates, the interest rates of mortgages, the size of the GNP and GDP, and other relevant pieces of evidence or facts that you want access to in the debate. These pieces of evidence also are likely to come from a variety of sources, but by digesting them on one page you have organized your evidence into a brief of related ideas that make them accessible and easy to use in your debate.

Argument Briefs

Along with the actual pieces of evidence and supporting materials you have collected, you may also have prepared in advance a special form of brief that anticipates a specific argument that you think may arise. For this type of brief, rather than having evidence be the basis for the document, you will catalog your ideas about how you want to handle arguments, or reminders on how you want to carry out your strategy in the debate.

For example, you may be debating the economy and employment rates and what they mean specifically. Your opponents may present arguments that say that employment rates have improved over that past few months. The case may be that factually they are correct, but the assumptions that are behind those facts may be what you want to challenge. So even though their data may indicate that for two months employment has gone up, you could have some arguments ready that will help counter their conclusions based on the data. You may point out that their figures are likely to be only seasonal employment due to a holiday shopping season; their data could reflect jobs that are clearly temporary, like persons responding to natural disasters; or maybe they have not included the number of jobless claims, which may have gone up at the same time. Your argument briefs may be a combination of logical ideas or analysis along with supporting counter evidence that may not directly refute their facts, but give them a different meaning or context.

The organizational pattern for this type of brief is usually to have a separate document for each main idea that you think is or will be an argument. For both the evidence and the argument briefs, remember that being able to use them easily in a debate is their primary function. You should ensure they are clearly organized and are easy to read during your presentation.

Your Notes (Flowsheet)

Along with materials you have prepared in advance for your debate, it is also highly useful to take notes during the debate. These notes should not only be used to record the main ideas or points of the other side, but also function as notes to yourself about what you want to say in your speech.

One of the things that can be most difficult for many beginning tournament debaters is to get used to listening, taking notes, and making notes practically all at the same time. But having good notes of the debate is essential to keep track of all the ideas being addressed, and also to serve as a strong template or script for your own presentation.

It is likely you will use a combination of your notes taken in the debate along with prepared briefs while you are speaking. Just as in your prepared briefs, it is important to make sure the notes you are taking are in a form that you can actually read and use easily in your speech. You may also want to make notes to yourself to remind you to use any evidence or argument briefs that you have ready to go to respond to what the other side is saying. Some debaters even go so far as to have notes made in advance on removable sticky note paper to place on their notes as they are taking them that have key arguments or pieces of evidence already identified as being what needs to be said in their speech.

Summary of Prepared/Written Materials

Your prepared materials that you can use to present your arguments and respond to those of the other side are the basis for what you will do in your debate. Putting these materials together in a way that is mindful that these are working documents for you to use, rather than a paper you are writing for others to read, will help you keep them clearly organized and easy to use in your extemporaneous presentation. The preparation and organization of these materials will also reveal to you the areas that you are the deepest on and the areas in which you may have less information or strategic use. You can always bolster your prepared materials as you go along, up until the time of your debate. Your organization of these materials will also help to remind you of the ideas that you want to talk about and give you a better chance of being able to emphasize your strengths and make the debate about the issues you choose rather than letting the other side dictate what happens.

DELIVERY

We started this chapter by emphasizing the mental and physical organization of the materials. Having those elements well in hand makes everything else about the debate much easier. In some ways the debate becomes simply the sharing of those ideas rather than emphasizing the speaking style of the presenter. Of course, there still is the presentation element that occurs and that should still be addressed.

Speaking in Public

One of the greatest fears reported by the population at large when polled about such things is public speaking. Often, more people would rather jump out of perfectly good airplanes (go skydiving) than have to speak in front of people. This is only natural, and to be expected. Even very experienced performers often feel a little nervous before going in front of a crowd of people. However, this nervousness need not be all bad. In fact, if a speaker is able to learn to control this fear they might be able to use it to improve their performance. In a fear situation, the body tends to react automatically; adrenaline pumps into the muscles, the heart beats faster sending more blood and oxygen to the brain and central nervous system, and the liver and pancreas work together to convert more stored sugar into quick energy. Under such circumstances, you are both stronger and in a way smarter than usual. Of course, uncontrolled nervousness can make a presentation more difficult, so it is important to do everything possible to manage it.

Rather than seeing debate as a way to exacerbate those fears, we see debate as a way to become more comfortable with those anxieties. Debate helps to build confidence in one's abilities and allows for a feeling of success that builds greater positive feelings and expectations for future experiences. Even debates that do not go well for the participants still give them valuable experience and, while rather rote and mechanical, do build up a desensitizing effect toward fear of speaking.

One key to help with any anxiety you may have is to remember that it is the content and substance of what you are saying that is the focus of the debate. Your delivery does not have to perfect in order for you to get your ideas across. A smart argument presented humbly is always stronger than a weak argument presented flamboyantly. It is helpful to understand that an audience may not have as high expectations for a performance as you have for yourself. While you may want your own presentation to be perfect, your audience is not likely to be as demanding. Audiences often fail to see the small errors that seem huge to ourselves, and even if they do notice they are often far more forgiving than we might expect.

You also will be using an extemporaneous delivery style, which means that you can make choices as you speak that can help you tailor what you are saying and how you are saying it to the debate context. Rather than practicing a speech in advance where you might try to build in dramatic pauses, and consciously manipulate your pacing, your extemporaneous delivery frees you to respond as needed at the time, and rewards authenticity of presentation over polish.

Finally, have a sense of humor and try to avoid taking any situation too seriously. It is inevitable that at some point we will all stumble over our words or say something that makes little sense. In such a situation, being able to laugh at yourself can turn a potentially awkward and uncomfortable situation into a chance to build your credibility with an audience. Being able to laugh at our own mistakes not only helps us manage our nervousness, but might also improve our standing with an audience because they perceive us as being genuine and honest.

Of course, all things being equal, there are some things you can do regardless of your style or manner of presentation that can help make your delivery stronger. While speaking can be a physically technical operation that involves a multitude of components (as per the evolutionary discussion above), there are several basic elements related to speaking that you can have some control over and practice to make better

Auditory Elements

Many people consider the way that words are spoken to be part of verbal rather than nonverbal communication—and the line between is fuzzy—but your authors would like to quickly explore the impact of the way that words are spoken, regardless of their linguistic meaning. Two important topics should be considered, the tonal qualities of the words expressed, and the way that they are delivered. We are not focusing on the meaning of words here, but rather on the way that they are spoken.

Tonal Qualities

Tonal qualities such as pitch, volume, and strength shape the way ideas are expressed and received by speakers and their observers. **Pitch** is where the sounds made during communication fall on the register, commonly expressed as how high or low (deep) the sounds being made are. High-pitched speaking often indicates nervousness by the speaker; squeakiness is generally off-putting to receivers of communication and can lead people to pay less attention and listen less carefully. Volume and strength are related concepts, but slightly different. **Volume** is simply how loud the speaker is. Speakers must be conscious of their volume, making sure to speak loudly enough for their observers to hear them, but being careful not to shout or yell. Speakers who have trouble controlling their volume will likely not communicate as effectively as speakers who do control it. In some circumstances, a speaker might wish to speak more softly or loudly to emphasize particular points. Changing the volume of speech will signal the receivers of the communication that the speaker holds the particular point in high regard and that the audience should as well. **Strength** is volume in addition to projection; speakers should look to project their voices throughout the space in which they are speaking. Richness and depth are often concepts used to define the auditory strength of speech. Speakers use their diaphragms to create strength in their voices, forcing a higher quantity of air through their larynxes, and giving their voices resonance.

Speakers should attempt to vary the way they speak in regard to the two concepts discussed. Monotone speaking is likely to bore an audience, decreasing the overall absorption of the material presented. Speakers should vary their tonal qualities to connect better with their audiences. Changing the pitch, volume, and strength of speaking patterns helps speakers control the attention of their audiences and maximizes their effectiveness as presenters of information.

Delivery

The majority of the comments on delivery in this text are covered in the sections concerning debate; however, a few brief ideas can best be explored here. The rate and pacing of delivery, organization, and pronunciation of words all affect the way that communication is absorbed, above and beyond the meaning of the individual words used. Speakers who are in control of these aspects of speaking will better connect to their audiences, and the points they deliver are more likely to be persuasive.

When people are nervous, they tend to speak more quickly. The largest potential issue is that speakers may move from idea to idea too quickly for their audience to absorb them, rendering their communication less effective. However, even if the audience is able to absorb ideas expressed more quickly than is optimal, speakers will be judged to be less persuasive when their thoughts are rushed. The audience will pick up on the speaker's nervousness and assume that it correlates to the speaker not being confident about the points being presented. Rushed delivery undermines a speaker's credibility.

Audiences will also have difficulty absorbing information that is presented in a disorganized manner. Beyond absorption of information, lack of order will undermine a speaker's credibility, as it is difficult reconcile the disorganization of the information presented with the idea that the speaker is an expert on the material he or she is presenting. The audience will subconsciously judge the presenter of the information, and will assume disorder to indicate a lack of confidence and expertise, decreasing the persuasive power of the speaker.

Proper pronunciation of words is also an important aspect of what is communicated beyond the meaning of the words used. When speakers mispronounce or emphasize the wrong parts of words, it indicates that the presenters are not familiar with the ideas that they are expressing. Judging a speaker to be unfamiliar with words leads the audience to question the credibility of the speaker, and that perceived lack of credibility in turn undermines the power of the speaker's persuasion. Pronunciation problems are also associated with nervousness and with a lack of self-confidence, further suggesting to the audience that the material presented by the speaker is not necessarily as believable as it might otherwise appear.

Speakers should make an effort to deliver their ideas in a manner that exudes confidence. Human nature pushes most people into attempting to fit into the norm. Observers of argument will subconsciously want to believe the side that they determine is right. This process does not occur solely in the rational mind, but rather affects the way that the rational mind constructs and evaluates arguments. Appearing confident and assured in the validity of the material they present allows a speaker to tap into this subconscious process, resulting in an increased likeliness that the audience will agree with the arguments presented.

BODY LANGUAGE

The complexities of body language is the subject for another class, or perhaps for a lifetime of research; however, some basic observations will help readers understand how the body is involved in communicating and processing arguments. This section will begin with an examination of personal space and a look at combined processes; finally it will address some of the specific parts of the body. A speaker should be conscious of what he or she is communicating with his or her body, shifting from uncontrolled expression to effective manipulation complementary to the verbal ideas being expressed.

PERSONAL SPACE

In debates, people are often physically close to one another, and it is important that people respect each other's space. Humans also pick up on encroachments of personal space as a sign of aggression. Speakers should be considerate of where they physically are in relation to their audience, and, if they are in a debate, in relation to their opponents. A great example of the importance of respecting personal space was demonstrated in a 2000 debate featuring Rick Lazio and Hillary Clinton, the two major candidates for the open New York Senate seat. In the debate, Lazio left his podium, waved a piece of paper in front of Clinton's face, and demanded that she sign a pledge not to use soft money. After the debate, commentators were surprised that many voters found Lazio off-putting and viewed Clinton more favorably. Political pundits have debated the importance of this example, many viewing it in narrow gender terms, but the lesson to be taken should be to respect other people's space.

Related to personal space, aggressive movements while a person is speaking or listening can be misperceived. Humans have an instinctual fight-or-flight response that is triggered subconsciously; body movements that are very quick or aggressive can trigger this response in someone, shutting down that person's cognitive processes. When we are trying to convince someone, an accidental triggering of this response will certainly decrease the chance of successful persuasion.

COMBINED PROCESSES

Many of the most important lessons to be taken from an understanding of body language involve many individual body parts and are best explained organized around a concept. The facial responses speakers and receivers of communication make, their body positioning, and twitching are three key areas to be examined. Humans receive and process multiple streams of information simultaneously; although concentrating on multiple, different occurrences at once can be difficult, humans subconsciously process many different aspects of communication, with each process shaping the overall reception of a given set of ideas.

Faces are among the earliest things that infants recognize while their minds develop, and facial expressions are a key part of body language.

Emotions are easily expressed on the face, and the human mind can read and assess the emotions of another person quite quickly. Speakers should be mindful that negative expressions will adversely affect their connection to their audience. Looking angry or upset will break down the connection that a speaker is hoping to establish with an audience. Audiences should also be mindful that speakers will absorb their facial reactions while communication is being delivered. All participants should be mindful of how their emotions are being perceived, and they should adjust their communication accordingly. Facial engagement is a key component to effective body language communication. Consistent eye contact indicates interest either in a speaker or in a member of the audience. Rolling your eyes indicates disbelief and signals a lack of interest or respect in what is being communicated. Head nodding sends the message that a person agrees with what is being communicated, whereas a stiff neck with a tilting backward of the head indicates non-acceptance. Smiling and frowning are simple ways for humans to signal their engagement with a given piece of communication.

Body positioning is the second major grouping of body communication to be considered. The overarching "openness" of body positioning communicates a tremendous deal. Crossed arms and legs generally signal that a person is not receptive, and, if listening, is unlikely to be open-minded about what he or she is receiving. "Closed body position" can also involve posture; slouching indicates inattention and disinterest in the receiver. Related to "open/closed" body positions are the shoulders. Good posture with flat or raised shoulders indicates attentiveness and interest; slouched shoulders indicate the opposite. The way that the head is positioned can also show relative interest in a receiver of communication, with a slight tilt forward indicating a positive and interested reaction, and tilting the head back indicating inattention. Of course nodding the head up and down generally indicates agreement, whereas shaking the head left and right is indicative of disagreement.

When people fidget or twitch, there are three possible things happening, each one communicating something nonverbally. People often twitch when they are nervous, and when a speaker is shaky it can often be perceived that he or she is unsure of himself or herself. Shaking at the knees is the most common expression of nervous twitching. For nervous twitching, deep, calming breaths can aid in relaxing a person, helping the twitch to subside. Breathing deeply increases the oxygen content in the bloodstream, and oxygen has a calming effect on the brain. Audiences will often note that a presenter is nervous, and again this lack of confidence can signal weakness and will hurt the persuasiveness of a speaker. People are also more likely to fidget and twitch when they are bored or not paying attention. This fidgeting will take the form of tapping fingers, scratching arms, and playing with hair or jewelry. Speakers should recognize this in their audiences and consider changing the vocal qualities of their speaking to snap their audiences back into attention. The third form of twitching is completely uncontrolled and is often mistaken for one of the two previous forms discussed. Some people twitch, often shaking their legs or tapping their feet subconsciously. This is rarely a sign of nervousness, and scientists are as yet unsure why some people have a natural fidget; however, there is some agreement that it is likely genetic. Speakers and receivers of communication should be careful and not necessarily base their assessment on the relative level of confidence of the speaker, or the attentiveness of the audience, based solely on a simple tapping of the foot.

SPECIFIC BODY PARTS

Eye contact is often difficult for people to engage in and maintain. The discomfort associated with eye contact can be overcome with practice, and it is preferable to make good eye contact when speaking or receiving communication. Maintaining eye contact shows attentiveness and confidence and can significantly improve the persuasiveness of communication. While a person is building his or her confidence up so he or she can engage in good eye contact, there is a useful shortcut that will help people simulate true eye contact. Instead of looking someone directly in the eyes, shift your gaze to a person's nose or to the spot between his or her eyes. From most distances it is impossible to detect that a person is looking at your nose and not at your eyes. Within about four feet, this trick does not work, but in most debate situations you are more than four feet from an audience.

Arm and hand gesticulations can also have a significant impact on communication. As mentioned earlier, current anthropologic research suggests that the complexity of human language evolved in relation to human gesticulation. Research now confirms that people perceive information more completely that is presented with gestures. Too many gestures, or gestures that are jerky, can be distracting for an audience, so a speaker needs to be in control of his or her arms and hands while presenting. Effective gestures help a speaker indicate transitions between points, and highlight the most significant ideas that he or she is presenting. Small circles or chops are frequently used by effective speakers to visually depict the ordering of their thoughts. When speaking from a podium, it is important that speakers consider how they will use their arms; people tend naturally to grip the podium, making it more difficult to use their arms effectively.

GENERAL PRACTICE STRATEGIES

While each debate is unique, there are some things you can do to help your presentation abilities in general. For any particular debate you will always want to remember your audience and their needs, but these basics will serve you well no matter the situation.

Speaking Out Loud

As obvious as it may seem, debate is a physical as well as mental activity. And while many of us have no problem talking for hours upon end with friends in social situations, most of us never have to speak uninterrupted for minutes at a time. Just as if you were planning a bike race you would practice riding a bike to get used to the physical demands, you will want to practice speaking out loud for extended periods of time to get your body used to those unique demands.

A simple exercise is simply to read a newspaper out loud while standing for several minutes. Newspaper text is usually very dense and information packed, which is a good way to get used to you being verbally efficient. There is the pleasant side effect of being more aware of current events as well! You may surprise yourself at how difficult it is to speak out loud for a sustained period of time. You will begin to tax your breathing, your posture, and other physical aspects that you never notice when you speak only in short alternating messages with friends. You will also become aware of your volume, rate, and pitch. As you become more fatigued you will be quieter and slower, not something you want to have happen in a debate where you will still need to make important points at the end of your speech as well as the beginning. Try five minutes at first and work your way up.

Increasing Fluency

Of course you do not want to just be able to speak for an extended period of time for simple duration; you want to have good clarity and verbal dexterity with words as well. So in addition to reading out loud, there are some drills you can do to give your vocal skills a real workout. These are also good ways to warm up for your debate, things that you can do in abbreviated fashion a few minutes before your actual debate.

Read out loud faster

While rapid delivery in your debates would not be appropriate, there are times when your adrenaline kicks in or you simply are in a rhythm that has you going faster than average. You want to make sure you are physically capable of doing so comfortably. Even if you never speak fast in your debate, your practice at doing so is still going to strengthen your voice and vocal capabilities so that a more leisurely presentation is still easy to do. One surprising thing this drill can show you is how disconnected your eyes are from your mouth and your brain! Trying to keep your vision, brain processing, and vocal abilities in sync takes more skill than you may think.

Put a pencil between your teeth

The idea here is to make your speaking muscles exert extra effort. When you take a pencil and put it across your back teeth and then grip it lightly with your jaw as you try to talk, you can immediately tell all the muscles that have to work to speak and how difficult it is to enunciate. Try reading a passage from a paper with the pencil in your mouth for one minute, and then take it out. You will be amazed how easy it seems to speak once the pencil is gone!

Read with emphasis

A long-time debate coach referred to this exercise as the "ham" drill as you try to read the text you have with extra drama and emphasis. While you would not want to fake emphasis in a real presentation, it is important in practice to realize the range you can create, and also to help guard against being monotone.

Give Practice Speeches

In many cases, you can practice your debate before it even happens. If you are the first side to begin, then your case is a great thing to practice giving. If you are the side that is going second in the debate, you can anticipate what the other team is going to say, and practice what your responses might be.

By practicing your speeches you not only become more familiar with the specific material you will use in the debate, but you also become more aware of how much time it may take to make those points. Debates can often come down to who can manage their speech time better, and your practice will help you understand how much you can still say, or what you may need to prioritize if you find you have less time left than you had hoped.

Debate practice also helps you to get familiar with merging your spontaneously generated ideas with the evidence and argument briefs you have prepared. It will take practice to work from the notes you take in the debate and to get comfortable with an extemporaneous form of delivery. You should also make sure that any briefs you have prepared are in fact easily read and usable, not confusing and difficult to interpret.

Practice with an Audience

As uncomfortable as it may seem, speaking in front of a real person for practice is an invaluable way to be motivated to do your best, and also just get more used to people listening to you. You will find that speaking for a real person will cause you to be more dynamic and less monotone. You may also be more involved in and enthusiastic about what you are saying. Such practice also helps make speaking in front of your real audience less daunting.

You should also solicit feedback from your audience. It is important to know if they thought you were speaking too fast, or not clearly. They may also be critical in reminding you that maybe some things you were trying to say were verbally good, but just did not make sense. Maybe you used too many acronyms or verbal abbreviations that are not familiar to them, or to your real audience. As we will discuss later, debate is unique in the amount of feedback you can get formally; do not be afraid of informal feedback early in the process.

Record Yourself

While nothing beats a live audience to give you feedback and get you used to speaking, often recording yourself so you can hear and see for yourself what is going on is a good idea. Given the myriad of recording options available, probably even in your pocket now on your phone, there is no reason why you cannot get a recording of your practice to view. You may notice things you were unaware of, and it gives you a chance to analyze the content as well. Did you spend too much time on a certain point? Did you have good eye contact? Were your words clear? If your roommates do not owe you a favor and you cannot find someone to listen to you practice, you can still use this method to give yourself feedback and do some self-evaluation.

USING FEEDBACK

Debate easily takes us out of our comfort zones. One of the things that can be most difficult to handle is the feedback that debates generate for the participants. In some cases of competitive debate, that feedback takes the form of winning or losing. In public debates that feedback may occur with the audience being asked to applaud for the side they felt did the better job, or to physically move to the side of the room on which the side they favored is positioned. That feedback may be informal as well, such as the nonverbal responses of the audience as you are speaking. No matter the form, debate is set up to elicit a response that is unique to most forms of public speaking. Dealing with criticism can be difficult, but most would agree that any comments can be useful in trying to improve, even negative ones.

The key is to keep the feedback in context. Just as the other side of the debate is challenging your arguments, they are not attacking you personally. The judge who does not vote for your argument is not saying you are a bad person. The audience member who is not persuaded is not personally rejecting you, but the intellectual idea that you were presenting. It is quite likely in academic and competitive debates you may have not even have had a choice on which side you were assigned, so there is no need to see a negative outcome or response as a referendum on your personal worth.

As you get feedback, try to determine to what the comments relate. Was the comment related to what you said or how you said it? Also, the comments may be empathetic to your position, but questioning of how you chose to present it. Someone might even preface their comments with acknowledgment that they in principle agree with your position, but may not have understood clearly the argument you were presenting. Even if they state a disagreement with your position, knowing the specific element that they had issues with can be a means to research that point further, or reconsider how you might approach that element in the future. It may also reveal an idea that you never even considered before.

Just as you get comments on papers you have written with the goal of making you a better writer, comments you get on your debate performance are a means of helping you grow as a debater and speaker. Many competitive debaters find that getting feedback that is not positive is far superior to getting no feedback whatsoever, even if they won the debate. Remember, in the context of this class, the goal of your debates is improvement in critical thinking and presentation skills, not victory! Winning or losing is far less important than being able to receive feedback and be self-reflexive about what others have to say.

SUMMARY

A poor physical presence can damage your credibility with an audience; a positive physical presence can likewise suggest many constructive things about you to your listeners. Effective physical action and composure can send signals of knowledge, confidence, conviction, and enthusiasm. A physically confident speaker makes his or her audience feel more at ease, encouraging them to listen attentively to the message being delivered, rather than concentrating on the speaker's jerky movements or nervous fidgeting. Strong, fluid movements not only help you to hold an audience's attention, but they also use up some of the nervous energy that often accompanies either public speaking or argumentative situations. Each movement should have a purpose. Whether it is to write something on the board, moving away from the speaker's stand to offer a visible demonstration for your audience, or otherwise, be sure the purpose is clear to your audience. When you make a move, decide where you want to go, get there, and stop. Try not to let your movements become indefinite and distracting. When you make a gesture, make sure you complete it. If you drop a gesture in the middle, it is left hanging in the air, where it weakens your presentation by interfering with the flow of your ideas.

The process of communicating is more complex than most people realize. Your actual words and tone of voice, though obviously critical to your message, do not by themselves account for the total impact you make on an audience. A substantial portion of your message is communicated physically, through facial expression, posture, gestures, and so on. Although these signals may go unnoticed by the person sending them, they are often quite perceptible to an audience or argumentative opponent. You are most effective in your communication when you are communicating the same thing with your physical presence as you are saying vocally. If the two are markedly different, your listeners may well pay as much attention to what you are doing as to the words that are coming out of your mouth. What you are doing physically may be more revealing to your audience than anything else, making the old adage "seeing is believing" rather meaningful in relation to persuasive appeals.

PART IV

ARGUMENTATION: WHERE WE DO IT

CHAPTER 12

DEBATE FORMATS: SPAR DEBATE

SPAR stands for <u>SP</u>ontaneous <u>A</u>rgumentation and <u>R</u>efutation, and the name accurately describes the format.[65] The debate is an extremely limited preparation event, often with only one or two minutes of preparation time; essentially it is a spontaneous debate. There are typically two participants, with each delivering two short speeches; just enough time for a few quick arguments and some brief responses. SPAR debates are a simple and easy way to get people used to the basic argument structures and feel of a competitive debate. As the overall debate

---

[65] The format is used in some high school debate tournaments, and it is often used as a training exercise in many debate leagues.

is short, the format is great for allowing lots of practice. SPAR debates will be used extensively in the class as an exercise that builds the foundation for developing more sophisticated argument techniques and building familiarity with the debate process itself.

Students enrolled in any basic argumentation course will need to get comfortable with arguing in front of others. While some may feel that the idea of engaging in a formal debate before an audience is a terrifying prospect, SPAR debates offer a unique method that allows virtually anyone to participate in a way that is really not very scary. SPAR debate topics are typically common knowledge issues that are familiar and fun, and once announced generally bring up a couple of quick ideas in everyone's heads (i.e., "Dogs are better than cats"). Fortunately, the debate itself is so short that a couple of ideas are all that anyone

> **Box 12-1 SPAR Debate Format**
> 1 Person vs. 1 Person
> 1 Minute Preparation Time
>
> 1 Minute "For" Constructive
> 1 Minute "Against" Constructive
> 30 Seconds "For" Rebuttal
> 30 Seconds "Against" Rebuttal

really needs to fill up his or her limited speech time. In the formal debate, participants will use the outline explained in this chapter (see Box 12-1). When the SPAR debate is used as a practice tool in class, the times of the speeches or even the number of the participants may be modified so that a specific argumentative technique can be practiced. Of course, SPAR debates can also be rather chaotic, as there is limited time to think of ideas and then present them, as well as a nearly limitless variety of topics. The SPAR debate format is basically just a simple way to help people get used to the process and become more comfortable debating in front of other people. Even if one debate does not go well, you will have plenty more, so enjoy the experience and try to make the most of it.

FORMAL OUTLINE

Two people participate in a SPAR debate, with each speaker assigned to be either "For" or "Against." The participants are then given the topic, or perhaps several to choose from, and one minute to prepare for the debate. Following the minute of preparation, each person delivers a one-minute constructive speech and then a thirty-second rebuttal speech, with the "For" speaker presenting their position first, then alternating back and forth, with the "Against" speaker concluding the debate in their rebuttal speech. The whole debate takes place within five minutes.

Topics for SPAR can be quite diverse: funny or serious quotations, pop culture trivia, favorite rivalries; in reality, just about anything. The best topics usually put two ideas in direct contrast, or suggest that one particular thing is superior to all similar things.[66] Because the purpose of the SPAR debates is simply to introduce the back-and-forth nature of a debate, the topics tend to be simple, with a few basic potential ideas to be explored that are at the surface of the topic.

The names of the speeches in a SPAR debate are intentional, and these names will be used throughout all of the debate formats introduced in this text. **Constructive** speeches are used for building arguments and exploring the topic. These speeches should contain all the major points that each side intends to introduce through the course of the debate. **Rebuttal** speeches are to summarize a debate; these speeches focus on comparing the most important arguments in the debate, and rarely offer new elements for consideration. The total breadth of ideas and arguments in the debate expands throughout the constructive speeches, and then becomes narrowed down through the rebuttal speeches. There is logic in presenting the ideas of the debate in two phases. Participants first need to offer up and explain their ideas and then compare them to the best features of the offerings of their opponents; construct, then rebut.

PREPARATION

Though the time allowed for preparation is brief, it is invaluable for a good debate. It is important that participants be ready to begin once the topic is announced; so being situated and comfortable, with all necessary debate supplies ready, is vital. Any questions participants have about where to sit or speak from

---

[66] Example topics: "Those Who Will Sacrifice Liberty for Security Deserve Neither," - Benjamin Franklin; Brittney Spears is Better than Madonna; Twilight is Better than Harry Potter; Batman is More Super than Superman; Crushed Ice is Better than Cubed Ice; Red is Better than Blue; Summer is the Best Season; Macs are Better than PCs; School Uniforms are Good; etc.

or when and for how long they are to speak should be addressed before preparation begins. Once the participants are ready, the topic will be determined. The speakers should plan to spend just a few seconds making sure that he or she has understood the topic. Speakers should then quickly try to brainstorm as many different ideas as they can. Obviously the speaker does not have time to write out entire parts of their speech, but should rather take a few brief notes to remind him or herself of the complete thought; often a word of two will suffice. You can write down a few organizational headings in order to offer a little bit of structure to your arguments. Be sure to save a few seconds to take a nice deep breath to calm yourself and sweep your eyes across the audience to show your confidence. Remember, it is just a simple exercise.

CONSTRUCTIVE SPEECHES

"FOR" SPEAKER

The "For" speaker in the constructive speech should try to fulfill some very basic requirements. The most fundamental obligations is for the speaker to support the topic. The speaker should begin the speech by introducing and **framing** both the topic and the debate. This is done by providing any definitions that may be necessary in order to clarify what is to be debated, and by providing basic **criteria**—the standards an observer should use in prioritizing arguments in the debate. Ideally, the debate should be framed in a manner that creates a fair division of ground for each side. In other words, each side should have some reasonable arguments available to use in supporting their position on the topic.[67] In most SPAR debates, the definitions are fairly self-evident, in which case the speaker may simply say, "Definitions will be provided contextually." In later formats of debate, the definitions will become more significant.

The second part of framing the debate is providing the **criteria**, a concept that is sometimes a little difficult for people to get their minds around. The criteria can be viewed as a decision-making tool, or as a measuring stick, a guide, or a rubric; or as a combination of all of the above. The criteria filters, sifts, or strains all of the arguments in the debate, focusing them and making sure that

---

[67] For example, if the topic is Brittney Spears is Better than Madonna, the first speaker should clarify that the debate is between two singers, and not one pop star against the Holy Mother.

they are all responsive to one another and fit together. The criteria helps to prioritize the various arguments offered and may limit which ideas should be more heavily considered in making a final decision about the topic. Not all arguments that are presented are necessarily useful ones; the criteria help to exclude tangential arguments. Many SPAR topics will use comparative terminology: "Red is *better than* blue." The criteria serve to explain what the comparative term "better than" means for the debate.[68] Each side wants to use the criteria to constrain the arguments that can be used in the debate and to create an advantage for themselves. If the "For" speaker knows a lot about food, then a criteria of "Best Tasting Food" could be appropriate for a topic such as "The Southwest is Better than the Northwest." The more clearly the criteria is deployed in the debate, the more likely the arguments presented in the debate are to interact with each other, creating good clash and a fun and rewarding debate.

Framing the debate should not take a significant amount of time, say ten or fifteen seconds; the speaker will want to spend the majority of the time explaining why she or he is on the right side of the topic, not what the topic means. However, framing is still very important, as it helps to keep the debate organized. In clarifying what the debate is about the "For" speaker can help to avoid a common phenomenon in debate known as **Two Ships Passing in the Night**.[69] This occurs when the "For" side presents some points in support of its side, and the "Against" side does the same, but the actual arguments used do not interact with one another. For example: "Red is best because it is the color of fire engines and it symbolizes passion," versus "Blue is best because it is the color of the sky and ocean, and blueberries are the tastiest berries." All four ideas can coexist at the same time, but they do not directly engage one another. The more clearly the debate is framed, the less likely it is to be like two warships passing

---

[68] For example, a criteria for the topic on color could be "fashion: whichever color provides the best clothing" or "food: whichever color has the best tasting foods." In the Brittney vs. Madonna example, the criteria could be "tabloid seller" with the winning pop star providing the juiciest gossip.

[69] This is a commonly used expression in debate circles. The phenomenon is probably most clearly observed in political debates where the candidates talk past one another with dueling lists of bullet points. It is not always easy to have clash in a debate, and while it is the "Against" speaker's obligation to engage the "For" speaker, it is also important for the "For" speaker to provide good points with which to clash.

each other in the depth of night, neither firing a shot because they could not see one another.

The majority of the "For" constructive should be devoted to developing substantive points in support of the speaker's freshly framed topic. The speaker now must make a few well-supported arguments to show why his or her side is right. The remaining forty or so seconds of the constructive speech is actually a fair amount of time to fill, and it is important that the topic be presented in an organized fashion. Natural instinct for most participants is to rattle off many points, one after another. However, this may not be easy for your judges, opponents, or audience to follow. The speaker should organize her or his ideas, examples, reasoning, and evidence into larger argumentative headings called **contentions**.

Exactly how to organize the ideas inside a contention is not too important at this time; however, it is important that all the fragments of thought in a contention are related to one another.[70] So, a contention is really a grouping of smaller arguments around a common theme, and when they are presented together, the strength and persuasiveness of the arguments should be heightened. It is good for contentions to have short names, one or two words that sum up the main idea or connection between the ideas. A contention should tell a brief story and have a logical beginning point, supporting information, and finally a summary sentence. The "For" speaker is attempting to show that, with a combination of the ideas presented in the contentions, the topic is correct and should be supported. The framing points, in addition to the developed contentions, are called altogether the "For" side's **case**.

"AGAINST" SPEAKER

Just as the "For" speaker has obligations, certain elements are also necessary in a proper "Against" constructive speech. The "Against" speaker has the **burden of rejoinder**—an obligation to engage and respond to the arguments that the "For" side presented, also referred to as **refutation**, or colloquially as "**clash**." It is vital

---

[70] In successive debate formats the idea of a contention will be further refined, and how to arrange all the different parts will be discussed. For now we are just getting familiar with some of the terms.

for the debate that the "Against" speaker directly attack the points made by their opponent; failing to do so will almost guarantee a "Two Ships" problem. The "Against" speaker should also advance **counter-contentions** in support of their side of the topic. The "Against" speaker thus has two fairly basic and simple avenues for attacking the "For" speaker's case. And while the "For" speaker gets the benefit of speaking first and an assumed deference in framing the debate, these benefits are balanced with the "Against" speaker getting what is functionally twice the preparation time.[71]

The "Against" speaker also has a bit more freedom in discharging their obligations for the debate—it does not matter as much in what order the "Against" speaker presents his or her arguments. The "Against" speaker may begin with the burden of clash and quickly respond to a selection of the points by the "For" speaker. It may be easier to start this way, as the speaker has something to work against; and of the two duties of the "Against" speaker, clash is the more important one. However, after your first few SPAR debates, you may begin to see why, in some situations, presenting a counter-contention first would be the more logical organization of your speech.

To begin clash, the "Against" speaker should address the way the "For" speaker framed the debate. Often the "Against" speaker will agree with the way that the "For" speaker framed the topic for the debate and may simply say, "I agree with the definitions and criteria." Although the "For" speaker has the right to frame the topic, they also have the duty to do so fairly. If the "Against" speaker feels that the definitions or criteria should be modified in some way, they are encouraged to say so. The more complex the topic, the more complex the issue of definitions can become, sometimes even dominating and distracting the debate away from a discussion of the issues. The way of resolving definitional arguments is highly complex in competitive debate, so for debates in class it is sufficient for the "Against" speaker to note their objection and move forward.[72] The speaker should try to do the best he or she can to react to the

---

[7] Everyone gets one minute of preparation, but the "Against" speaker also gets to use the time while the "For" speaker is speaking. It is necessary to listen to what their opponent has to say, but the "Against" speaker can also use this time to think of what they will say in response.

[72] In competitive formats, definitional debates often decide who wins and loses. Entire debates can revolve around the meaning of a single word. While some people find this fun and/or

"For" speaker's framing, and perhaps advance a point or two that may relate only to their own interpretation of the topic. After considering the way the debate is framed, the "Against" speaker gets into the more substantive rejoinder.

The "Against" speaker should pick out a few of the weakest and a few of the strongest points that the "For" speaker made, and directly challenge them. This action should take up the majority of the speaker's time while clashing. It is important for the speaker to attack more than just one point raised by her or his opponent, as doing so shows the judge and audience that the speaker has a broad understanding of the scope of the debate. It is also important to cover some of the stronger arguments the "For" speaker advances, so that that speaker has a harder time using those arguments persuasively in his or her rebuttal speech.

It is important for the "Against" speaker to not only refute their opponent's case, but also to advance arguments their own arguments independent of what the "For" speaker brought up. This provides the "Against" speaker with something specific to refocus the debate away from his or her opponent's points. Similar to the structures used by the "For" speaker, by using a counter-contention, the "Against" speaker can provide a grouping of ideas into one thematic argument. This is particularly important when the topic is asking for an evaluation of two things, as the "Against" speakers will not just show why the "For" side of the topic is not good but should also demonstrate why the "Against" side of the topic is *better than* the "For" side.

If the "Against" speaker finds that they do not have many arguments to directly respond to the "For" side's case, but they do have some significant counter-contentions, he or she should feel free to focus more on developing his or her own points.[73] Conversely, the "Against" speaker may find that they have many devastating arguments that directly clash with their opponent's claims,

educational, many do not, so we will seek to avoid overly detailed definitional debates with the formats used in this text.

[73] This can happen if the "For" side takes a very narrow interpretation of the topic. For example if the topic is "TV is bad for you" and the "For" side only discusses a single violent show that they happen to know a lot about, the "Against" speaker may try to refocus the debate in a broader context and bring up counter-contentions about education or cheap family entertainment to show that TV as a whole is not bad.

and again should feel free to focus attention where they believe their position is strongest.[74] In this circumstance a speaker need not offer counter-contentions and can focus only on direct refutation.

To **refute** is to respond to an argument and dismiss its validity as a persuasive tool. Successful refutation should make the influence of an argument less significant in the debate, rendering it less useful as a tool for persuasion. There are many ways of refuting an opponent's argument, and refutation is a concept that is developed more fully in other parts of this text. At this beginning stage of learning, participants should simply try to respond to their opponent's arguments and worry about more complicated refutation techniques later.

REBUTTAL SPEECHES

"FOR" SPEAKER

Thirty seconds is not much time, and the "For" speaker needs to be careful to use their time efficiently. The "For" rebuttal needs to accomplish two things: it must answer some of the new arguments from the "Against" constructive speech, and it needs to summarize and re-establish the "For" side's main reasons for supporting the topic. The speaker needs to rehabilitate his or her best arguments to show that their logic is superior overall. Rebuttal speeches can be more free-flowing in structure, as there is no way to respond to all of the arguments in the debate in such a limited amount of time. Thus the speaker has more discretion in how best to accomplish the two tasks of response and summation. Every debate is a little different, so it is important to find ways of tying together some of the different ideas in the debate in a manner that makes thematic sense in the context of the given arguments. Trying to prioritize one or two main threads throughout the debate can be difficult, but with practice, recognizing the connections between arguments will become easier.

The speaker should start by identifying the best reasons to support the topic and then respond to the "Against" arguments. By immediately

---

[74] In some debates the arguments will be fairly predictable and the ideas that the "Against" speaker could use as counter-contentions may be better used in direct refutation of the "For" case.

217

highlighting their best arguments, the speaker will draw in the audience and provide a nice change after all the negativity of the "Against" constructive speech. It is also important that the speaker respond to any counter-contentions that were presented in order to show that the "For" speaker is engaged in the totality of the debate and knowledgeable about the topic. If an opponent's larger arguments are conceded, it will provide him or her with good material to base the rebuttal speech on, which is an important advantage when the "Against" side gets the last word in the debate. Participants need to be careful, however, as many "For" speakers will get so caught up in responding to their opponent's claims that they run out of time.[75]

In the rebuttal speech, the "For" speaker will want to summarize the debate in their favor by advancing one or two overwhelmingly compelling reasons as to why his or her side of the topic is right. Utilizing the strongest contention, and developing an overall theme to summarize the best arguments are often the most successful strategies for this role in the speech. As the debate is over so quickly, and because humans have such short attention spans, it is great if you can pick up a powerful refrain from your earlier speech. If your strongest point is repeated in a slightly different manner several times throughout the very short debate, it is more likely to sink into your audience's heads. A really strong finish can make it difficult for the "Against" speaker to get started, which is significant because they only have thirty seconds to work with. Speakers who feel that they can master this quick speech can try one final thing—preemptively addressing the main arguments the "Against" speaker will use in his or her rebuttal. A speaker who can address and dismiss her or his opponent's points even before the opponent brings them up will appear to be in command of the debate. This is sometimes referred to as **preemptive** or **anticipatory refutation**.

"AGAINST" SPEAKER

Although the job of the "For" speaker in the rebuttal speech is probably more difficult than in the constructive speech, the opposite is true for the "Against"

---

[75] Thus it is often a good idea to have a quick summary statement about why your side of the topic wins, before jumping into your responses. This quick statement can also be tied into the last part of your speech, giving it strong organization.

speaker. In the constructive speech, the speaker's attention had to be in several places at once; the speaker had to generate new ideas very quickly in response to what the opponent presented. Now the "Against" speaker gets to benefit from that work. Given the time constraints, it is unlikely that the "For" speaker covered all of the points made in the "Against" constructive speech, so the "Against" speaker can really choose a mix of different strategies, depending on what best suits the situation and the debate. It is also important to recognize that the "Against" rebuttal speech is the end of the debate, the last say on how to view the arguments that were exchanged. With those dynamics in mind, it is often best for the "Against" speaker to summarize the debate in his or her favor by looking at what the "For" speaker was unable to adequately address.

It is not that the "Against" speaker should rely on the opponent's mistakes, but rather should look to highlight the points in their own favor that have not been fully refuted. In a debate format this short, it is important to show your strength in the limited time you have; highlighting ideas that have been largely conceded is very efficient. Often the "For" speaker shies away from arguments he or she does not have a clear response to, providing a good place to demonstrate that your side of the topic has the superior arguments. Combining and more fully developing a few uncontested ideas is the most important part of the rebuttal speech for the "Against" speaker. However, it is also important that the speaker appears fully engaged in the debate, so a denial of some of your opponent's more important arguments is also necessary.

As with the previous rebuttal, starting off strong is important and will help the speaker move through the rest of the speech more smoothly. People will occasionally stammer for a few seconds, or spend a few moments collecting their thoughts before speaking. If a person is speaking for several minutes, a few lost seconds, though not the most impressive start, is not really a big deal. In a SPAR debate, however, a few seconds can easily turn into 20 percent of the speech. First the speaker should be sure to have a good sentence to lead off with that sums up the most compelling reason why her or his side of the topic is right. After delivering the quick and powerful number one argument, the speaker should try to refute a few of their opponent's main claims, followed by some general reasons why his or her side of the topic is right. These reasons could be one single-themed argument, or a synthesis of a couple arguments. Two or three general reasons or themes will be all the speaker has time to address. Finally, the "Against" speaker has the privilege and benefit of closing the debate, and a witty pun or compelling zinger can leave a lasting impression on your audience and judge. If your mind does not work in a funny and fast way, no need to worry—a simple yet strong finishing line will work just as well.

JUDGING A SPAR DEBATE

As the debate can cover a wide variety of issues and happens very quickly, there is no real consensus on how to award a winner in competitive SPAR debates. Logical analysis and persuasive presentation are two concepts most judges look for when they evaluate a debate. For debates held in class, who wins and loses is unimportant—there will be no cheap plastic trophies handed out. However, it can still be beneficial to think about how the debate might be judged. Just as professionals of all sports and competitive games like to play pick-up matches, practicing and thinking about how to win can help improve your skills. However, for class debates, it is more important that everyone feel comfortable than to worry about winners and losers. People can choose to debate competitively, but in class we focus on learning, not on winning.

SUMMARY

The SPAR format provides a short but sweet debate that makes for good practice. Each speaker has some simple roles to fulfill in his or her constructive speeches; both sides have more freedom in their rebuttals. Keeping calm and connected to the debate as it whizzes by is important so that participants can fully engage with each other and provide a good clash of ideas. In short, the format provides a great place to begin learning competitive debate; formats presented later will use the strength of these concepts to expand the complexity of the arguments and ideas being debated, thus providing an increasingly fun and educational experience.

By jumping into a simple classroom debate quickly, we can break the ice, overcoming common fears about public speaking. The SPAR debates show that really anything could be considered a debate, and that many of the things that we do in daily life are directly connected to argument. The idea of doing debate can be daunting for many people, but a minute-long speech and a thirty-second follow-up are much less intimidating. The argument structures and speaker duties discussed in this chapter are for the ideal debate. Do not worry if you cannot get all the parts right the first time or even the tenth time—they are really just what people have learned to do in the activity over a period of trial and error, and are not necessarily the only way to approach the format.

CHAPTER 13

DEBATE FORMATS: PANEL DEBATE

Panel debates are most frequently demonstration, exhibition, or public debates; however, some competitive leagues do use a format with speaking roles and speech times similar to the format presented here. The name of the format is suggestive of the way the debate plays out, and you may already be familiar with the format, having viewed a public debate in the past. The idea is that each participant is familiar with the topic from his or her own point of view. Speakers are prepared to present an organized speech on the topic, and interact with the major arguments presented by their fellow participants. The debate may be intentionally divided into opposing sides, or each speaker may simply be responsible for presenting his or her own views as a stand-alone position. If the opposing sides are used, the ideal is that each side will share some basic points of agreement, but may also come at the issue from different perspectives.

The audience is a central feature of a panel debate, with topic education focused more on those who watch the debate than on those who participate. That is not to say that those who speak do not also gain something; rather it is expected that panel members already know a great deal about the topic, and that they benefit from organizing and presenting their views. For class, however, you will receive the benefit of doing research to prepare for your debate, and the added bonus of being the audience for your peers.

> ## Box 13-1 Panel Debate Format
> 6 Participants (3 on each side)
> Week+ Research and Preparation
>
> 5 Min. 1st "For" Constructive
> 2 Min. Questions
> 5 Min. 1st "Against" Constructive
> 2 Min. Questions
> 5 Min. 2nd "For" Constructive
> 2 Min. Questions
> 5 Min. 2nd "Against" Constructive
> 2 Min. Questions
> 5 Min. 1st "For" Rebuttal
> 2 Min. Questions
> 5 Min. 1st "Against" Rebuttal
> 2 Min. Questions

Panel debates share some similarities with SPAR debates. In both formats the "For" side frames the debate by using large groupings of arguments. Clash is required of the "Against" speakers in both formats as well. However, in panel debates, the contentions will become a bit fancier. Both formats have "For" and "Against" sides, and constructive and rebuttal speeches, but in panel debates some of the speakers' duties are different. Most of the lessons learned from participating in the formal SPAR debate, and the material covered in this text, as well as in class, can be applied to your panel debate. The largest difference between the two formats is the length and complexity of the speeches. The way participants prepare for the debate is another significant difference. One format is nearly instantaneous; in the other, the topic is known in advance for days or weeks. Panel debates often use topics that cover wide-ranging issues that affect public policy or cover problems of social significance.[76] The topic, and thus the debate, should focus on the breadth of the issue without getting bogged down in one specific point. With the wide variety of perspectives and the goal of audience education, there should be a fairly comprehensive coverage of the topic at hand. Embrace the large topic; you may not be able to cover all of it, but you will learn a lot. A respect for, and understanding of, the other side's position is essential to effectively promote a personal cause; panel debates can provide a wonderful practicum for understanding all sides of an issue, and why some social problems are so difficult to solve.

FORMAL OUTLINE

Five or six people participate in a panel debate, depending on the number of students in the class.[77] The "For" side goes first, and if there is an odd number of speakers, the "For" side should have the extra speaker. As the "For" team speaks first, they must do some more clarification of the topic and explain more background; thus with an uneven number of people, the "For" side can use the extra help.[78] Each participant gives a five-minute speech, which is followed by two minutes of questions from their opponents and their audience. The first speech for each team is a constructive, and when there are three speakers on a team, the second speech is called the "second constructive." The final speech for both the "For" team and the "Against" team is a rebuttal speech. The whole debate should take about forty-five minutes.

Questions are a key feature of panel debates, and they are one of the features that make the format fun. Questions allow for a more detailed exploration of a point that may not have been explained clearly. Speakers should look forward to the questions as an oportunity to provide more information and show off what they have learned. Speakers who have spoken

---

[76] Example topics: The US Government Spies on its Citizens Too Much; The War on Terror Has Improved the Security of the United States; The US Needs Immigration Reform; TV Plays Too Large a Role in Today's Society; Hurricane Katrina Exposed the Myth of Racial Equity in the US.

[77] It is hard to control exactly how many students will end up in any given class, so the format can allow for some mix in numbers. In public debates, occasionally an expert will cancel at the last minute and the debate still goes on. The format could even be expanded to allow for 7 or 8 debaters, or shrunk to 3 or 4 debaters, with only minor reworking.

[78] Many people also feel it is easier to attack something that has already been established, so the "For" side always has a harder job.

can use questions to bring up missed points, or to rehabilitate their attacked points. Many debate formats can be a little dry to watch, but with panel debates, the audience can get directly involved. Collective education is one way of thinking about the goals of a panel debate; questions allow the group to probe and explore in an organic manner.

PREPARATION

RESEARCH

Getting ready for a panel debate is an extensive task, as most likely the participant will not already be an expert on the issue that he or she is debating. But not being an expert may help the speaker focus on the bigger issues. A danger for experts in public debates is that they can become enamored with a detailed point and lose their audience. Ranting about or over-focusing on one aspect of a large debate misses one of the reasons for engaging in the debate in the first place. Coming at the topic from a fresh perspective allows the speaker to cover the breadth of an issue as they get themselves prepared. What is important is to have a broad understanding of the topic and know a few details to support major ideas within the issue. Speakers do need to understand the major points of contention and feel comfortable talking about several of them for a minute or more. To prepare, speakers need to read a variety of high-quality sources of information.[79]

READ YOUR AUDIENCE, NOT YOUR SPEECH

Debate is a spontaneous activity, and panel debates should be lively exchanges; in this debate format, overly prepared speeches can actually weaken a speaker's presentation more than they help. Though speakers will have an idea of what their opponents may bring up, they will not know all of what their opposition may say. All people in the debate have some responsibility to create and continue a clash of ideas and respond to what the last speaker or speakers have said. This is very difficult if a speaker simply sticks to a pre-written script.

---

[79] "High-quality sources" can mean a lot of different things, but a simple Google search will not be sufficient. For panel debates, longer public interest articles from magazines or newspapers, articles from academic journals, position papers from reputable interest groups or think tanks, government documents and reports, and books all work well for getting prepared.

Focusing on writing a speech is different from focusing on preparing for a debate; a debate is a more fluid activity and participants need to be dynamic. When reading, it is also harder to make as much eye contact with an audience, or to examine their body language. Talented speakers adjust the way they deliver their ideas to cater to their audience as they look for signs of understanding and support. When presenting complex ideas, it is difficult for a speaker to make sure that he or she has clearly explained a given concept; reading the audience and not the speech is a great way for the speaker to make sure that she or he has completely expressed the arguments. Finally, when people read a speech they often have trouble controlling their rate of delivery. A speech that is practiced slowly and perfectly fills five minutes can easily turn into a rushed four minutes when it is presented in the stressful conditions of a debate.

FINAL PREPARATION

A panel debate does require a fair amount of preparation, but this gives participants the experience of becoming something of an "expert" on a subject in a short period of time, a skill that should come in handy later in life. In the real world, a future boss will often be unreasonable and ask for things that are nearly impossible in a short period of time. Having done a panel debate will at least give participants the experience of having stood up and put on a good show while trying persuade people that they have extensive knowledge about a topic. Remember, each speaker will have to give a speech, and then answer questions, so preparing for and practicing these skills will be valuable. Even if you are not as fully prepared for the topic as you would have liked, this is valuable practice for the time when your paycheck is on the line.

In preparing for the debate, it is vital that the participant review the duties and obligations of their partner's speeches as well. The instructions provided here are for individual speakers, but they are written with reference to all speeches, and attempt to describe the connections in a debate. Knowing what is expected of his or her partners will allow the speaker to craft their speech in a manner that strengthens their team's overall presentation. The best participants in the panel debate set up their partners and create strong connections between people's speeches. The ideas and vocabulary of debate are confusing, but the more participants read the words in context, the more easily they will understand the concepts.

FIRST "FOR" SPEAKER

FRAMING

The job of the first "For" constructive speaker is a little different from the rest of the speakers' roles. Though there are differences, the overall burdens are not unlike those of the "For" constructive speech in the SPAR debate format. In the first speech of the debate, it is necessary to frame the topic. The speaker needs to define any words in the topic that may not be clear, and should also look for ways of defining the topic to focus the debate. Definitions should also be supportive of the "For" team's advocacy or plan of action. While the speaker is framing the debate, it is also important to provide a criteria and explain or justify why it was selected. Often the criteria in panel debates will be utilitarianism, or what is the greatest good for the greatest number. Some panel debates, however, will call for a criteria of "justice," or "economic stability," or "freedom," or another philosophical concept. After these similarities with the SPAR debate format, the duties of the first "For" speaker in panel debates become more complex.

The topics in panel debates are general statements that highlight social problems and suggest either that something should be changed about public policy, or present an idea about reality that needs to be better understood.[80] In order to justify that a policy or social perception needs to be changed, the first "For" speaker should explain the problems of the status quo—the current state of affairs.[81] While framing the debate, the "For" speaker needs to provide all the background information necessary for the audience to understand the status quo,

---

[80] For example under the topic, "The United States Should Reform its Immigration Policy," it is suggested that a new set of laws is needed. With a more philosophical topic such as "Hurricane Katrina exposed the Myth of Racial Equality in the US," the implied idea is that a tragic event showed that America is under the false perception that racism is a thing of the past.

[81] Or "reality," or the present situation. For example, your status quo is that you are reading a book; you are in college, learning about argument. The status quo in the United States when this book was written is that Barack Obama is president, there is no universal health care, and the United States is still fighting in Afghanistan.

and for the audience to see clearly the problems with the way things are now — sometimes referred to as the harms of the status quo.

Presenting the harms of the status quo justifies the final framing point the "For" speaker makes—the advocacy statement. Just showing that there are problems with the way things currently are (the status quo) is not enough. The topic calls for a remedy, so the speaker must have a way of explaining and defending the best action for the situation. The "For" advocacy statement is the action or belief the "For" team will defend, and in order for a debate to be fair it must remain stable throughout the debate.[82] An advocacy statement is a basic idea or concept that clearly explains how the "For" team thinks the problems of the status quo should be solved. The more specific and well thought out the plan of action, the easier it will be for the "For" team to show why the topic is right, and how current problems can be remedied. This is one part of the debate about which participants on the "For" side need to talk to each other before the debate occurs. In the debate, the advocacy statement should be very clear to all participants, including the audience, as it is the backbone of the debate.[83]

As each argument structure (definitions, criteria, background, advocacy statement) is more complex and detailed than in the SPAR debates, it is understandable that it takes longer for the speaker to frame the panel debate. Each one of these ideas should be clearly expressed by the speaker, either implicitly or explicitly. Some people are so clear in the way that they phrase their ideas that everyone clearly understands which argument structure they are expressing while they frame the debate. However, most people benefit from literally saying "my definitions . . . the criteria for the debate . . . etc." The more clearly the speaker expresses the structure of her or his arguments, the better the organization of the speech as well as of the debate.

---

[82] Meaning that no one on the "For" team can change it mid-debate, even if the other team has a good reason showing that the advocacy statement is a bad idea.

[83] For example, on an immigration topic: "Our Advocacy Statement is that the government should pass a law making temporary work visas easy to legally obtain." Or, "The government should build a border fence."

CONTENTIONS

The second major task for the "For" speaker is to present some contentions. Since the SPAR debate, readers of this text have learned to formulate their arguments in a more substantive manner using the CWI structure.[84] Thus the contentions are a bit more organized and expanded. The contentions serve the basic function of grouping ideas and explaining a large argument for the speaker's side. Having too many contentions will leave the explanation of the ideas spread a little too thinly, whereas having too few contentions gives the first "Against" speaker too easy of a job clashing in his or her speech and does little to persuade your audience.

A contention is one big idea or argument, so at first it must be introduced with an explanation of what is bad about the current situation surrounding the argument. The contention should have a quick summary tag line of a few words to be used to reference the argument in the debate. The speaker should then explain how the advocacy statement, if adopted, would make things better within the context of the argument. Finally, the speaker explains why potential changes resulting from the advocacy statement will be more beneficial than any potential negative consequences. It is also a good idea to have a quick summary and transition sentence at the end of a contention. After the last contention in his or her speech, a brief conclusion of the speaker's major points is a good idea. The speaker needs to spend only ten or fifteen seconds recapping the reasons why her or his side of the topic is the right one.[85]

FINAL DUTIES

The final burden for the first "For" speaker is to be preemptive throughout the speech. Although the speaker does not engage in direct refutation, he or she can still foresee some of the major arguments an opponent may present, and provide a defense. While expanding on her or his background points, and also in the contentions, the first "For" speaker can identify and dismiss potential "Against"

---

[84] In case you forgot, or have not gotten to this idea in class, CWI = Claim, Warrant, Impact. What you are trying to prove; the proof; and why if the argument is true, it matters.

[85] The most effective speakers do not repeat themselves; rather, they refresh the audience's mind concerning their best points, by emphasizing them in a manner that is slightly different from the way that they presented the points at first, tying all the points together.

arguments. For example, the speaker could say, "My opponents will suggest that reforming immigration will be too costly, but one of the major points of this contention is that our advocacy statement, if adopted, will benefit the economy and government tax revenues by making it easier for the best labor to find the best jobs, increasing productivity." It is hard to be preemptive, but when done effectively it can make the following "Against" speaker's job much more difficult.[86] Being preemptive also makes the speaker look that much more knowledgeable about the topic and boosts his or her credibility, or ethos.

As already mentioned, preparing for a speech is different from preparing for a debate; one way that this plays out is during questions. Speakers need to engage the debate topic in an holistic sense, and be prepared to answer questions from a wide variety of interpretations of the topic. Participants who just write a word-for-word speech are more likely to miss a key part of a topic, as their focus is too narrow. Speaker should have a developed structure and an outline of the main ideas they wish to convey, yet should also be flexible and knowledgeable enough to adapt to the situation as it develops.

To finish the speech, the speaker should provide some final statements summing up the benefits of their advocacy statement, thus showing why the topic should be supported. Providing a strong conclusion is also important in building up your confidence in preparation for answering questions.

FIRST "AGAINST" SPEAKER

The job of the first "Against" constructive speaker is to respond to the "For" case and present the majority of the main arguments the "Against" side will use in the debate. Just as in a SPAR debate, the "Against" speaker has the burden of clash as a principal duty in the panel debate. However, the duty of the speaker to provide counter-contentions is more pressing in a panel debate than in the SPAR format. Throughout the speech, one overriding thought should be kept in mind—the "For" speaker has presented a change to the status quo as a way of supporting the topic. The opposite of a "change" is to "stay the same," so the "Against" team needs to demonstrate that changing the status quo in the way of

---

[86] Now if the "Against" speaker wants to use that point, they must first counter the argument presented by the "For" speaker and then explain their point, basically working twice as hard.

the advocacy statement would be bad, thus showing that the converse of the topic is true.[87] The "Against" side will try to show that the topic is not true while using some combination of two general themes—that things are not really that bad in the status quo, and that the "For" side's advocacy would actually make things worse. To organize these two themes, the "Against" constructive speaker will continue to use clash and counter-contentions as the organizational principles for her or his speech.

CLASH

The "Against" speaker should begin looking for clash points by making sure that all the "For" speaker's framing points create a fair debate. Just as in the SPAR debate, if the topic is not framed fairly or clearly, the speaker should note this, and then continue on with the debate as best as he or she can.[88] Next, the background information provided by the "For" speaker is often a place where a good back and forth debate can occur. The "Against" speaker should look to challenge the "For" side's presentation of the problems of the status quo, showing that the problems that the topic highlights are not as severe as the "For" side presents. After looking at the way the debate is framed, the first "Against" constructive speaker should turn his or her attention to the contentions that the "For" side is offering. This first section of the first "Against" constructive speech is primarily focused on fulfilling the first goal of the "Against" team, showing that the status quo is better than the "For" side claimed.

COUNTER-CONTENTIONS

The "For" side's contentions are more significant for the panel debate in comparison to the SPAR debate, and the same pattern holds true for the "Against" side. Counter-contentions for the "Against" side highlight significant arguments that are somewhat independent of the materials covered in the "For" case. If the point a speaker would like to make with a counter-contention is directly relevant to a point made in the "For" case, the speaker may choose to

---

[87] If you are familiar with formal logic, this may strike you as invalid, or at least as needing clarification. We are oversimplifying some fairly complex debate theory here. Although the theory is very interesting to some competitive debaters, it can put most people to sleep.

[88] Look specifically at the definitions and criteria when challenging the fairness of the way the debate is framed. Often, the problem is a lack of clarity in the way the debate is framed, and providing some analysis here will help to get everyone on the same page.

simply clash directly with their opponent's contention rather than developing the argument as an independent counter-contention. It is not always easy to discern where the best place for an argument is in a debate. What is important is trying to keep the debate as organized as possible.

In addition to offering a defense of the status quo, the "Against" speaker should look for unintended consequences as a result of the "For" side's advocacy.[89] Also called a disadvantage, an **unintended consequence** shows that significant problems not currently happening will occur if the advocacy statement is adopted. For example, if No Child Left Behind were eliminated, then some states would start to change their curriculum and in a few years all students would be taught different things, making it very difficult for universities to provide a standard education, leading to more required general education classes in college. Disadvantages show that it would be better to stick with the status quo.

ORGANIZATION

The exact order and time allocation of the "Against" constructive speech is less rigid than the first "For" constructive speech, with the speaker adapting the content of his or her speech to fit the specific arguments in the debate.[90] The "Against" speaker should use their best judgment on how to organize their ideas, while fulfilling the duties of the speaking role. The speaker hopes to provide many points of attack against the "For" case for his or her partners to continue in later speeches. In most cases the first "Against" speaker will directly clash with the "For" side's contentions in the beginning of the speech, with the development of counter-contentions done in the second part of the speech. That said, there is no hard and fast rule for organization, and different debates will lend themselves to different organization; whatever works best for the speaker and for the given debate is what should be followed.

---

[89] For example, many people thought that Ronald Reagan's program of Amnesty in 1986 would alleviate the immigration crisis, but an unforeseen consequence of the Amnesty program was the "brain drain" of talented Mexicans out of their own country, damaging the economy and furthering the immigration crisis.

[90] This flexibility will continue in the following speeches. The content and the structure of the first "For" constructive speech really sets up a general blueprint for the debate and the following speeches; speakers need to react to the debate before them, altering their speech to fit the debate in the manner that they feel is best.

Like the first "For" speaker, the first "Against" speaker should have a clear introduction and conclusion. Having a lively introduction will gain the audience's attention, and counteract some of the power of the "For" speech that was just finished. Strong conclusions help to keep all the "Against" speakers on the same page, connecting their arguments. Finishing strong will also help the speaker make an impact on the audience, and makes the opponent's next speech more difficult. Sign posting is important in this speech, especially as the speaker has more flexibility in the way that he or she organizes his or her thoughts. The introduction should be a brief statement of the overarching problems of the topic, transitioning either into arguing against the "For" case or presenting counter-contentions as the situation may dictate. The speaker should make sure to be clear about which action he or she is beginning to discuss. While moving from argument to argument throughout the speech, the speaker should sign post as often as is logical.[91] When concluding the speech, the speaker should try to summarize, showing that overall more bad than good comes from the advocacy statement, and thus the topic should be rejected.

SECOND "FOR" SPEAKER

The second "For" constructive speech generally has three goals. First, the speaker needs to refute the new material presented by the "Against" speaker. Equally important, the speaker needs to reaffirm and extend the points made by his or her partner in the first "For" constructive. The final action that the second "For" speaker should be looking to achieve is the addition of a contention or two. However, while new material is important, the speaker should prioritize arguments already entered into the debate as he or she allocates speech time. As the speech is in the middle of the debate, it is very important that the speaker is organized and clear in expressing ideas; so again, paying close attention to the overall outline or structure of arguments will help the speaker give an efficient and effective speech. The organization of the speech is more dependent on the dynamic of the particular debate and the judgment of the speaker than on any preconceived structure. The speaker should take care to make sure that she or he is clear about which arguments he or she is refuting and/or reaffirming.

---

[91] The speaker will literally say, "The next argument against the contention is . . ."; "In response to the point . . ."; "My first counter contention is . . ."; etc.

After a brief introduction, the second "For" speaker should continue with either refutation of counter-contentions or the extension of his or her partner's arguments. These are the main duties of the speech, so making sure that the speaker spends the majority of speech time on these two actions is important. A speaker should look for points his or her partner made that the opponent did not address well, and try to explain why those points independently show why the "For" side is right. It is also important that the strongest points that your partner made are furthered in your speech, regardless of how well your opponent answered them. Identifying and dismissing the refutation of the "Against" constructive speech is vital in showing that the speaker is engaged in the debate, and critical in demonstrating that the "For" side of the topic is the right side. Remember that the overall theme of the "For" side is that there is a problem with the status quo, and that the advocacy statement, if adopted, will make things better.

Refuting the counter-contentions is just as important as extending the "For" case. Counter-contentions are big ideas that disprove the topic as a whole, so if they are left unaddressed, the job of the second "Against" speaker will be too easy, as he or she will need only to highlight the conceded points.[92] While preparing for the debate, it is important for all speakers, but for this speaker in particular, to anticipate what the other side will argue. Preparing two or three responses in anticipation of the likely opposing arguments in advance will be beneficial both to the speaker's organization and persuasive appeal.

New arguments can be presented in constructive speeches, and the second "For" speaker should try to have one or occasionally two new, major arguments or contentions. The speaker could prepare three or four of these arguments and be ready to deploy the one that fits the debate best. Adding a new argument into the debate not only strengthens the "For" side's overall position but also puts additional pressure on the second "Against" speaker. It also shows that the speaker is well versed in the topic of the debate. After offering the new material,

---

[92] For example the second "Against" speaker could start her or his speech with, "Though there is disagreement about whether the advocacy statement will accrue benefits, the "For" side has conceded the counter-contention showing that there will be serious unforeseen consequences. If the benefits are uncertain, but the drawbacks are clear, we should not adopt the advocacy statement or support the topic."

the speaker should have a brief conclusion tying together their side's best arguments, showing that the advocacy statement should be adopted and the topic approved.

SECOND "AGAINST" SPEAKER

The second "Against" constructive speaker has goals similar to those of the second "For" speaker: refute the new material of the previous speaker, extend the previous "Against" arguments, and potentially present some new material into the debate. Many of the other roles and duties of the "Against" speaker are similar: the "Against" speaker should pay particular attention to the flow and organization of the debate; throughout the speech he or she should make sure to emphasize why the advocacy statement is a bad idea; and finally, the speaker should provide a brief summary at the end of the speech. The speaker also has relative freedom in organizing the speech, deciding in which order to answer arguments, and when to move from addressing the "For" case into advancing the "Against" arguments. The speaker should also clearly sign post which argument they will be addressing next. This is critical at this point in the debate, as things are likely to be getting a little bit complicated by now.

Generally a speaker follows the order of the speaker who spoke before them, but this is not necessarily a hard and fast rule. For instance, if the previous speaker was disorganized and difficult to follow, the speaker should order the speech in the manner that makes the most sense to him or her. This keeps the debate more organized, and it allows the speaker to have some rhythm to his or her speech. The second speaker may also choose to shake things up a bit by changing the order in order to highlight a particular issue they feel is of great significance. Moreover, the "Against" side does not necessarily want the whole debate patterned around what the "For" side has to say, so it is important for the "Against" speaker to order their speech in a way that really best shows the strength of their side's arguments. In doing so, the speaker does not have to advance all of the arguments used by his or her partners, but rather should be selective about advancing the best ones. The speaker should look to develop the counter-contentions of their partner with additional facts or examples, and perhaps supplement these ideas with a new counter-contention.

New material is not as important for this speaker, but if there is time to add further argumentation, it may well benefit the debate. A new counter-contention should be added after the speaker has finished the first two goals of his or her speech, and it should not come at the cost of a good final conclusion. Presenting a new counter-contention into the debate will put added pressure on the third "For" rebuttal, and also show the audience that the speaker was well prepared to enter the debate. After any new counter-contention, the speaker must finish the speech. Again, the speaker should look to show that the "For" advocacy will do more harm than good, and that the topic should be rejected.

"FOR" REBUTTAL

The job of the rebuttalist is distinct from the roles of the first four speakers. It is important that this speaker focus on the arguments that have already been introduced into the debate, rather than adding a significant amount of new material to the debate. If the "For" rebuttal has two new arguments, the "Against" rebuttal will simply answer them, potentially with new arguments of their own which the "For" side will be unable to answer, as the debate will be over. Thus it can be strategically unwise to use new arguments in this speech. A rebuttal speaker must take a different view of the debate, to try to see the big picture and highlight the important arguments and how they interconnect. The speaker traces how arguments were developed during the previous speeches, highlighting how the "For" side is generally right. As any given debate will have developed uniquely by this point, the organization of the speech is more free. The "For" rebuttalist needs to be clear with sign posts, so that everyone can follow the arguments and share a similar version of the rebuttalist's vision of how the debate fits together. It is also important for the speaker to pay close attention to the flow of the debate round so that she or he can identify the important arguments on which to focus the speech.

The speaker's job is to show that there are problems with the way things presently are, and that the advocacy statement, if adopted, will make things better. The criteria comprises the weighing mechanism of the debate, so the speaker should use it to show that there will be more benefits than harm from adopting the advocacy statement. Generally a speaker should start and finish with their strongest point; it is hoped a point that has already been highlighted by his or her partners. It is important that the speaker cover all major arguments in the debate, as this the final opportunity for their side to make its case. Being preemptive in this speech is uniquely important. If the speaker can offer persuasive reasons for why the major arguments their opponent is about to use are wrong, the "Against" speaker has to work much harder.

All speeches in debates are persuasive, but this speech in particular is conducive to great speakers. Having passion and energy in the speech is important, and establishing a connection with the audience is even more precious. It is hard to wrap up all the ideas in the debate, but having some idea of what you plan to talk about before the debate starts is important. After doing your research, you will have a good understanding of the potential arguments that you will need to summarize, so consider the two or three most important points for each argument before the debate starts. Prepare a few different summaries, but also remember to be reactive to the debate that actually occurs, not the one you envisioned.

"AGAINST" REBUTTAL

Although the goal of the "Against" rebuttal is similar to that of the "For" rebuttal, the outlook is the opposite. As previously mentioned, in most panel debates the criteria is utilitarianism, so the rebuttalist is charged with showing that more harm than good will come from the "For" case. The speaker will generally do this with two major themes: that the status quo at present is not as bad as the "For" side maintained, and that the negative consequences of the advocacy statement, if adopted, are more significant than the benefits. The speech should not contain new arguments, as they are considered unfair because the "For" side has no opportunity to respond to them.[93] The organization of the speech is generally free for the speaker to choose, and again, it is particularly important for this speaker to sign post clearly.

This speech should generally begin with a brief introduction on the overall position of the "Against" side that transitions into some more detailed analysis concerning perhaps the one or two major reasons why they are correct. After explaining these largest points, the speaker is faced with some

---

[93] In competitive debates, the judge would exclude new arguments from their consideration.

organizational choices in covering the remaining important points in the debate. The speaker can follow the general pattern of the "For" rebuttal, or they can create their own order. The best strategy will depend on the debate at hand, as each organizational pattern has its own strengths and weaknesses. Following the previous speech generally helps the speaker organize his or her points and cover all the "For" arguments that could validate their case. On the other hand, breaking the rhythm of the debate and refocusing everything around the best "Against" arguments can make a bigger impression on the audience. However, creating a new organization for the debate can be tricky; the speaker may under-cover points that are key for the debate, cause confusion, or both. The speaker needs to think about what approach will work best for them and the context of the debate. After covering the major arguments of the debate, the speaker should provide a clear conclusion showing that the advocacy statement will do more harm than good, and that the topic should be rejected.

Though it is difficult to predict exactly how a debate will unfold over five speeches, the speaker can anticipate and prepare for this speech just as the "For" rebuttalist would do. Considering the major arguments, strong examples, and significant statistics can all be done ahead of the debate. The speaker needs to be organized so that the most appropriate arguments that he or she has prepared can be used where applicable in their speech. It is also very important that this speaker offer a clear organizational structure that will make it more likely that the audience can follow along. This speaker is the last speaker in the debate, and having the final word is often the difference in a close debate.

JUDGING A PANEL DEBATE

Most panel debates that are presented as public or demonstration debates are for educational purposes, so there is no formal judging. Occasionally a "division of the house" is called for, with those who watched the debate raising their hands or clapping for the team they feel won the debate. When a modified version of the panel debate format is used in competitive debate leagues, the judge is usually someone familiar with the topic. Although there is no consensus for how to approach judging, most judges are looking to see whether the "For" side's advocacy statement will bring more benefits than drawbacks. Judges also take into consideration the presentation of information and whether speakers were able to demonstrate a complete understanding of the issue raised by the topic. Like all competitive speaking events, persuasive speaking is also a factor.

SUMMARY

The debate centers on the basic question, "If there is a problem with the way things currently are, will the "For" advocacy statement provide more good than harm?" This concept should be kept in the participants' minds at all times as they think about the arguments for their side.

With so many things to do, and so many ways of doing them, participants will not necessarily organize all the arguments well in any given speech. Some good arguments will get ignored, and some poor arguments will receive more time than they deserve. This is an inevitable part of debate. No debate will ever be perfect, and it takes time to master many of the techniques and guidelines offered here. What is presented here is idealistic, so just do your best to accomplish as much of it as you can. It is also important to understand that the principles explained here are not the only ways to approach a debate. We have offered the speaker outlines here as a guideline, but not everything works for everyone, and if you believe you have a better way to do something, by all means give it a shot. And don't worry about "ruining" a debate. That can only happen if people give up.

CHAPTER 14

DEBATE FORMATS: POLICY DEBATE

The last format of competitive debate that will be explored in this text, though perhaps the most complicated, is potentially the most fun and educational. People often wish that they could change the way the government does things. **Policy debate** is the academic activity where this daydreaming is taken to the next level, where ideas for new laws and government programs are tested and refined. Like the other formats, the name of this format is descriptive of the agenda of the debate: public policy analysis. Topics utilized in this format are almost exclusively phrased as questions with regard to how different government actors should change the status quo. Although the construction of topics tends to be a bit more narrow in this format, the debates are actually often "bigger" in that participants will more thoroughly cover both the breadth and depth of the issue.

In competitive leagues, the same topic is used for an entire year, with participants switching sides from one debate to the next. Such a long-term focus on a particular issue allows participants to really get to know the topic, and encourages a very thorough assessment of the subject material. Participants in this format of debate role-play are, in a way, pretending to have the power to control the government in order to gain a better understanding of how law and public policy interact with existing social frameworks when changes are introduced. In the United States, policy debate is perhaps the most widely practiced format, particularly at the high school level, with the longest continuous use by competitive debate leagues.[94]

Policy debate maintains several of the features of the SPAR and panel debates, just with added complexity, developing certain aspects of the debate in a much more concrete and specialized way. Each side in the debate has the same basic burdens, with the "For" side defining and defending the topic, as well as provide compelling support that shows that the topic should be adopted. Likewise, the "Against" side still has the burden of rejoinder ("clash"), and the responsibility to present its own major counter-arguments. There are both constructive and rebuttal speeches in policy debates as well, and questions are also a big part of policy debate. Unlike the panel debate format, however, in policy debates the question and answer periods, sometimes called the **cross examination**, are exclusive to the debaters themselves, with each participant responsible for fielding a number of questions from his or her opponents following his or her own constructive speech.

Similar to a panel debate, the "For" team will show that the topic should be adopted by using an advocacy statement and criteria. In policy debate, the

---

[94] Parliamentary-style debate has recently gained in popularity in the United States, and it is hard to tell currently whether it is utilized more than the policy style. Parliamentary style has old roots, but only in the last two decades has it been commonly practiced outside of the British Commonwealth. At the collegiate level in the US, parliamentary and policy style debate are becoming more and more similar to one another.

advocacy statement is the central focus of the debate, with the "For" side presenting well-developed contentions and the "Against" side offering equally developed counter-contentions. Participants in panel debates use essentially all of the same basic argument structures, but the level of specificity in policy debates is greater, with more complex internal organization for each of the major arguments. The experience gained from panel debates will provide you with a better understanding of overall speaking duties and the roles for any given speech. Having a better understanding of what should be accomplished in any given argumentative speech is widely applicable to any number of future public speaking situations. Policy debate will provide an opportunity to delve deeper into advanced argumentation, to understand how ideas are both constructed and exchanged, and to gain vital knowledge about successful persuasion in the real world.

FORMAL OUTLINE

Box 14-1 Policy Debate Format:

2 people vs. 2 people
Week+ Research and Preparation Time
2 Minutes preparation time for each team

5 Minutes 1st "For" Constructive
2 Minutes Questions (Cross Examination)
5 Minutes 1st "Against" Constructive
2 Minutes Questions (Cross Examination)
5 Minutes "For" Constructive
2 Minutes Questions (Cross Examination)
5 Minutes 2nd "Against" Constructive
2 Minutes Questions (Cross Examination)
3 Minutes 1st "For" Rebuttal
3 Minutes 1st "Against" Rebuttal
3 Minutes 2nd "For" Rebuttal
3 Minutes 2nd "Against" Rebuttal

A policy debate typically has four participants, with each side having two members.[95] Each participant speaker speaks twice, giving one five-minute constructive speech and one three-minute rebuttal speech. After each constructive speech, the speaker must then take two minutes of questions from their opponents, in the cross-examination period.[96] There are no questions after the rebuttal speeches. Each team will also be allowed a certain

---

[95] The format can be adjusted to accommodate six participants as well.
[96] Traditionally the speaker must answer the question, but in practice sometimes the partner helps.

amount of preparation time during the debate to be used as it sees fit in between speeches in order to prepare for their own speaking time. The "For" team speaks first, after which each team alternates speeches until the final "Against" rebuttal has been given.

In the other formats of debate previously developed in this text, there have been diverse kinds of topics utilized: funny, short, and very flexible for the SPAR debates; social and philosophical for the panel debates. Policy debate topics are almost exclusively phrased with a government actor needing to change a current law to address the shortcomings of the status quo.[97] Though the topic is always centered on changing a policy, philosophical concerns can be and are raised in the debate. Ethical issues are often reasons for supporting or rejecting a given topic or a course of action suggested by the topic. Both the "For" team and the "Against" team can look for ways of including value issues into their side's arguments. With the topic being used for an entire year, and with participants switching which side of the topic they represent in any given debate, the topics are phrased so that a specific and complicated issue is addressed.[98] The issues debated can be approached from many angles, with the "For" side having many choices of what action to suggest, and the "Against" side having several different avenues for pursuing arguments to disprove the topic.

POLICY DEBATE ARGUMENT STRUCTURES

SPAR debates are far too short and limited in scope to be overly concerned with a fairly uniform overall strategic objective for each speaker. Panel debates, with longer times and more detailed topics, introduce more complex argument structures and speaker duties. Though the argument structures were introduced in some detail in this text, the pedagogical focus of the panel debates concerned the overall way each speaker should think about his or her duties in a debate,

---

[97] One actor which policy debates utilizes on occasion is the Supreme Court. When the Supreme Court is the actor, the debate is centered on changing a legal ruling or precedent, not on creating a new law. However, the same basic principle applies; the court should act to make a change.

[98] Example topics: "The United States Federal Government (USFG) Should Implement a Policy to Significantly Increase the Use of Renewable Energy"; "The USFG Should Significantly Increase Academic Achievement in Secondary Schools"; "The USFG Should Substantially Change its Foreign Policy with China"; "The United States Supreme Court Should Strengthen Fourth Amendment Protection of Civil Liberties"; "The USFG Should Abolish the Death Penalty."

and develop an understanding of the given "job" of each speech. Policy debate participants should continue to develop their understanding of the duties of any given speaker, but the educational focus will now shift to further understanding and developing argument structures. With this shift, the explanation of the argument structures in the debate will be presented before an overview of each speech.

CRITERIA

The role of the criteria, the decision-making tool for the debate, did not change from the SPAR format to the panel debate format, and it will stay basically the same for the policy debates as well. There is a great deal of flexibility in what is used as the criteria in the SPAR debates, with the "For" speaker choosing. In panel debates, what is used as the criteria is more narrow; often utilitarianism is used, but any number of ideas could serve as the filter or lens for the debate. In policy debate, the criteria are not exclusively utilitarian but predominantly so, with some variation in the way that utilitarianism is explained. In competitive policy debate, participants often use criteria that are referred to as **net-benefits**—whichever team shows that its side has more overall benefits should win the debate.[99] Net-benefits is subtly different from utilitarianism in that some kinds of benefits can be highlighted as relatively more important than others; however, functionally the two ideas are very similar. Net-benefits is also different from utilitarianism in that it focuses more on pragmatism; what is going to work the most efficiently and effectively given the political and moral constraints of the status quo.[100] In the rebuttal speeches of the debate, the debaters start to weigh the debate round using the criteria as a guide. Each side attempts to show that more net-benefits will be accrued from its side of the topic. The advocacy statement is a test of the topic: if the results of the advocacy are net-beneficial, then the topic is proven true.

---

[99] Net-benefits can also be called "comparative advantage," or "cost-benefit analysis." Each term is slightly different, but they are all getting at the same point, to add up all the "goods" and "bads" and weight them against each other.

[100] For example, taxing the richest 30% of income earners in the United States very heavily and not taxing the other 70% of workers would probably be utilitarian, but may not be pragmatic.

ADVOCACY STATEMENT

The change to the advocacy statement for the policy debate format is similar to the change in the criteria; overall the concept is the same, with some refinements made. In the policy debates, all topics will call for a change to the status quo, and thus all advocacy statements will include a specific plan of action. The topics used will usually allow for several ways for the advocacy statement to be put into action.[101] The stability and completeness of the advocacy is even more important in policy debates, as a result of the topic being more focused. Any change to reality is complex, and no advocacy statement could be as exact as an actual bill from Congress, but participants in the debate should view the "For" advocacy as an abstract for an actual proposed bill. Any proposed change of law is generally challenged in two ways: will it happen, the political question; and should it happen, the pragmatic question. In the real world, the answer to the political question is usually recognized as equally important. However, in the world of debate, where we know the proposed change will not actually take place in the real world, participants focus instead on the question of pragmatism.

If the topic for a debate in the real world were abolishing the death penalty, the first way of challenging the topic might be to say that such an action is not likely to be taken. The debate would then center on the likely voting patterns of the 535 members of Congress and what the President is likely to do. Although more realistic in some ways, this would be a very boring and potentially hyper-specific debate, and very well may completely ignore the actual costs or benefits of abolition itself. The second way of challenging the topic, the pragmatic question of whether or not the death penalty *should* be abolished, is the better one for an academic debate.[102] In order to answer this question, the "For" side will affirm the topic by showing how the reform would work and why it would be better; the "Against" side will negate the topic by

---

[101] For example, with a renewable energy topic, a plan could focus on one or more of the kinds of renewable energy, on how to promote use of renewable energy through tax policy, carbon markets, etc.; or have the government use only renewable energy in all government offices and vehicles. The advocacy statement needs to be only one way of supporting the topic, not all ways.

[102] By better, we mean more educational, fun, exciting, rewarding. By looking at the pragmatic side of the question, participants get to role-play how the government works, and try to look at a given issue as a policy-maker would. The hope is that by role-playing, participants learn about the issue, how the government works, and how to argue.

showing that the "For" side's advocacy is undesirable. For this role-playing to be meaningful, the participants agree to suspend their assumptions concerning whether a bill would actually pass through Congress, and focus the debate upon the question of whether the advocacy should be implemented. This assumption has a specific name: **fiat power;** and like some of the other terms in debate, this one is based in Latin. Literally meaning, "let it be done," fiat is the idea that a given outcome will happen. The "For" side gets to use fiat power in order to assume, or pretend, that the change is implemented, allowing the debate to focus on whether the plan is a good idea, not on whether it will happen in the near political future.[103] The participants in the debate assume that the advocacy has been fiated into existence, and then they speculate about whether it is a good thing or a bad thing to have had the advocacy enacted in the new hypothetical world.[104] Though it may seem like a minor point, it is important that this assumption be well understood so that the debate can take place in the speculative realm, where sound logic and factual analysis are more important than memorizing the voting patterns and preferences of hundreds of different members of Congress.

ADVANTAGES

So far in this text, contentions have been explained as big groupings of small arguments on a given theme combined together to advance a complete reason to either support or reject a given topic. Policy debate utilizes more complicated contentions in a manner that is similar to the refinements made to the criteria and advocacy statement. Here we offer a more specific understanding of how those particular parts function to prove the topic correct. Contentions for policy debate are renamed advantages and disadvantages. The overall function of the arguments, developing substantial points in support of or against the topic, is the same for both sides in the debate, but the perspectives are directly opposite each other. As in the panel debates, the advantage tells a story of what good things

---

[103] It is important to note here that the political ramifications of an advocacy statement are most definitely open for debate. The "Against" side can say whatever it wants about what happens after the advocacy is implemented, but should not argue that the "For" advocacy will not happen simply due to political opposition in policy-making bodies.

[104] Said another way, the "For" side will talk about all the benefits that would happen if the advocacy were adopted, and the "Against" side will talk about all the problems resulting from the passage of the advocacy.

will come from the advocacy statement. In policy debates, the order in which the story is told is broken into three parts that help to explain the idea in a more compelling fashion. The three parts in an advantage are **uniqueness**, **link**, and **impact**, each concept helping to show specifically why the proposed change to the status quo is beneficial.[105] To begin the advantage, the speaker should give it a quick heading or tag line that functions as a name by which everyone may reference the advantage later in the debate. After the brief tag line, the speaker should explicitly present each of the major parts in order, literally saying "The uniqueness for the advantage is. . .; The link...; The impacts..." This level of clarity helps everyone stay organized and focused on the same elements.

Uniqueness is a description of the existing problem the advantage will be addressing, that is, what is uniquely bad about the status quo right now. An advantage to abolishing the death penalty might be "ending a racist law," so the "For" speaker will argue, "uniqueness point one: the death penalty is disproportionately applied to minority populations, even when all other factors are controlled for."[106] An advantage can have multiple arguments in the uniqueness point, each showing part of the problem of the status quo that the advantage is hoping to fix. Without uniqueness, the "Against" side could argue that "if there is nothing wrong, we should not fix it," or "if it is such a problem, we will solve it later, but now is not the right time."

The **link** is an explanation of how the "For" side's advocacy statement will solve the problems identified in the uniqueness section; it is the connection between the current problem and the way the "For" side's advocacy will solve the problem. Continuing the death penalty example, "The link for the advantage is that when the death penalty is abolished, it will be impossible for the state to execute anyone, so racial bias will not continue to take life." Usually the link is not one argument, but rather a chain of arguments (internal links), building progressively; sometimes debaters will refer to them collectively as their "link story," or "link scenario." Some advantages will have two or three different links, "abolishing the death penalty will send a signal that all are equal under the

---

[105] Disadvantages also contain the same three major components.
[106] The example provided here is very simplistic; more detailed analysis would be expected in an actual debate.

law; that will affect the society overall, helping to show that everyone should be treated equally; and in the long run decreasing racism." The "For" side hopes that it is clear why the link is important to the advantage, but there is one additional thing to note: the link provides a place where the speaker can further explain how his or her team's advocacy will work. Most changes to current policy are complicated, so it is important to continually clarify and explain the advocacy statement.

The **impact** is the big benefit that comes from solving the problems of the status quo. For example, "government is by the people and for the people—*all* the people, and decreasing racism will decrease violence and hate in our society, improving everyone's quality of life." Like the link, the impact is also a chain of connecting arguments. Overall the advantage is really just a more complicated and specific kind of story, and with the impact point the speaker can really use narrative skills to persuade. Telling an impact story and graphically describing the benefits achieved from the advantage can be very compelling. Speakers should try to start with the most realistic impacts, but should feel free to push their story further into less likely but significant benefits.[107] The line between qualified risk analysis and gross exaggeration is a fine one; using advantages in debates allows participants to hone this very important tool of persuasion.

DISADVANTAGES

Just as counter-contentions are the "Against" tool similar to the "For" contention in SPAR and panel debates, the disadvantage in policy debate is very similar to the advantage, only with an opposite outcome. The advantage is the major tool for the "For" team, and the disadvantage is the same for the "Against" team; it presents a major drawback of a proposed change to the status quo. A disadvantage is similar to a counter-contention, with one important exception; it cannot simply attack the topic in a generic fashion. In SPAR debates, the counter-contention just needed to show a reason to reject the topic. In panel

---

[107] For example, "increasing harmony within U.S. society is very important because the United States is looked up to all over the world. When the United States is more equal, maybe other conflicts in other parts of the world where people are divided along ethnic lines will calm down, leading to peace and justice for all across the globe." In a later section we will examine how to weigh these more extreme points.

debates, the counter-contention should be responsive to the "For" advocacy, but because the criteria and advocacy statements are constructed more loosely, the counter-contention can still relate more broadly to the topic. With the topic in a policy debate there are always several options for different advocacy statements that the "For" side could choose. The "Against" team cannot simply present an argument that is against the topic as a whole, as it might not apply to the specific advocacy statement presented by the "For" team. Aside from the application, the specific parts of the disadvantage are the same as the advantage; presenting a problem that the advocacy creates.

In the uniqueness section, the "Against" speaker shows that currently nothing is wrong with the part of the status quo to which the disadvantage applies. When debating the death penalty topic, a speaker presenting a disadvantage on "deterrence" would say, "Uniqueness: currently in the status quo, heinous crimes are punished with death, making people less likely to commit them." The argument shows that the problem the disadvantage highlights is uniquely caused by the "For" advocacy and not an alternative explanation. Not all disadvantages are completely unique; sometimes the "For" advocacy simply makes a current problem worse. In that case, the uniqueness section is used to describe the status quo presently, and why the "For" side's advocacy could make it much worse.[108] Uniqueness can be a single argument or a series of arguments; the "Against" team should just make sure that it shows why all of the problems it highlights later in the impact are not currently happening.

After showing that there currently is not a problem with the status quo, the speaker needs to show that the plan links to, or causes, the disadvantage. For example, an "Against" debater could say, "the 'For' advocacy links to the disadvantage because the absence of the death penalty as a punishment would make more people willing to commit crimes." Like in an advantage, the links in a disadvantage can have multiple aspects, and some will be highly developed

---

[108] For example, the "Against" team could argue that leaving more criminals alive will cause global warming. Although breathing releases greenhouse gasses, and meeting each criminal's needs generates pollution, the overall increase compared to what is released by all other human activities is infinitesimal. So the advocacy does not uniquely cause all of the bad things associated with global warming. The disadvantage would be "non-unique" to the "For" advocacy.

link scenarios. The clearer the link to the "For" advocacy, the higher the risk that the impacts of the disadvantage will come true. Advocates should be as specific as possible and describe in detail all of the chain of events between the advocacy statement being adopted and the negative outcome of changing the status quo.

Impacts in disadvantages are exactly the same as in advantages: showing that, if the advocacy statement is put into effect, the consequences will be significant. A disadvantage will be a negative drawback, unlike the positive benefit provided by the advantage. The impact story in the "deterrence" disadvantage example is that "More people will commit horrible criminal acts such as murder and rape. Over time, egregious felonies could increase without the death penalty. This will breed a general feeling of lawlessness in the country, and all crimes will increase radically, destroying the social bonds that keep society functioning." When the "Against" side constructs its disadvantage, it should also look to have realistic and likely drawbacks, yet can also include less likely but extremely bad potentialities in its impact story.

A special kind of disadvantage is called an **opportunity-cost** disadvantage. It is a way for the "Against" side to present an alternative action for solving the problems identified by the "For" side. This kind of disadvantage shows that, if the "For" case is adopted, a better way of solving the problems will become more difficult or impossible to implement. For example, if the "For" advocacy were to abolish the death penalty, an opportunity-cost to this plan of action would be that death penalty moratoria would no longer be an option for states or the federal government.[109] However, simply providing another good idea for tackling the problems of the status quo does not show why the "For" advocacy statement is a poor idea; opportunity-cost arguments must be **competitive** with the "For" plan of action. In other words, the "Against" team must show that doing the opportunity-cost *alone* is the best course of action. The "Against" side must show that doing both the "For" advocacy and the "Against" opportunity-cost simultaneously would be less beneficial than doing only the

---

[109] With new DNA testing becoming available, bad public defenders for poor and minority defendants, and questions about the humaneness of lethal injection, some states have decided not to execute anyone until these issues are resolved. Though not ending the death penalty, moratoria do eliminate many of the harms that the "For" team will speak about, while avoiding the problems of a lack of deterrence and justice for victims' families.

251

opportunity-cost. Alternatively, they could argue that both ideas are mutually exclusive and simply could not both be done at the same time, thus forcing a choice between the two. When presenting an opportunity cost, the "Against" speaker needs to be clear about what the option present in the status quo is that would be lost if the "For" advocacy is adopted; this should happen in the uniqueness section of the disadvantage. Though the "Against" team does not need to read a formal counter-advocacy statement, the speaker should still be clear about how the alternative action would work if it were implemented. In the link section, the speaker needs to explain why both the opportunity-cost alternative advocacy and the "For" advocacy statement cannot or should not coexist. Finally, in the impact section, the speaker should explain the benefits of preserving the ability of the alternative action to be pursued, showing that there is a clear opportunity-cost in implementing the "For" advocacy.[110]

REFUTING ADVANTAGES AND DISADVANTAGES

There are many ways to challenge the validity of any given argument. Throughout this text, a variety of different techniques and tactics are presented. The actual arguments used to invalidate advantages and disadvantages (ADV/DA) will vary with every given debate, and will often be subject dependent, but there are a couple of things to consider when formulating responses to the argument structures presented here. How a speaker chooses to challenge any given argument can matter a great deal when the final rebuttals are comparing the likely impacts that will result from the advocacy statement.

Opponents should look to challenge the uniqueness of the ADV/DA. If the problem the argument highlights is unlikely to be caused by or alleviated with the advocacy statement, the chance that the impact will occur is less likely.[111] The "Against" side is generally trying to say that there is not a problem with the status quo, or that the problem has been overstated by the "For" side.

---

[110] If this whole thing is too complex, do not worry: it is not necessary, but rather just one more option for the "Against" team to use if it chooses. This kind of argument often takes competitive debaters many months or even years to really master.

[111] For example, the "Against" side could argue that the criminal justice system is already grossly unfair, so that fixing the death penalty will not solve racial profiling, criminal sentencing disparities, and the disproportionate number of minorities who are locked up. Or the "For" side could argue that life in prison is deterrent enough for potential criminals.

When refuting the uniqueness of a disadvantage, the "For" side is generally saying that the problem is already happening, and that it is thus not uniquely created by the advocacy statement. Challenging uniqueness alone does not disprove the ADV/DA; the impact is still relevant to the debate, but the chance that the advocacy statement will fix or cause the problem has been mitigated.

Attacking the link of a given position is a strong way to defeat it. As most link stories are a chain of related actions, participants should look for a weak link to break and show that it is unlikely that the impact will occur. The "For" side could say that "the deterrence disadvantage does not link to our case because the death penalty is already applied inconsistently, and most people who commit crimes do not expect to be caught." Speakers can even "turn" the link argument: "With less money wasted on endless appeals, more money could be focused on preventing and solving other crimes, so people will think it more likely that they will be caught." The "Against" team could suggest that "some people will think the death penalty was wrongly taken away and take matters into their own hands, which could turn into racial violence," thus "turning" the advantage.

When attacking the impact of an argument, speakers can also look to poke a hole in the logic of the impact scenario of a given ADV/DA. Often the logic may be convoluted, as the impact is stretched and exaggerated. One or more internal explanations may not be made clearly enough. Pointing out leaps in logic can be a quick way to mitigate an impact. It is also possible to **turn** an impact, suggesting that the ADV/DA does not identify a negative consequence but rather a positive one. For example, an "Against" speaker could argue that a particular plan of action would require too much government spending, yet a "For" speaker might respond by saying that during times of recession and high unemployment government spending is necessary to create jobs. It is important to note that **link turns** and **impact turns** should not be used at the same time on the same ADV/DA. The link turn says that the problem identified by the advantage is caused by, rather than solved by, the "For" case. The impact turn says the problem pointed out in the disadvantage is not a bad thing, but a good thing. Put those two ideas together and there is a **double turn**.[112]

---

[112] A "For" double turn on the "deterrence" disadvantage. "The link to the disadvantage is turned because the 'For' advocacy statement will save money and lead to a more effective use of police

253

Responding to an opportunity-cost disadvantage is a little more tricky. The "For" side should first and foremost make sure that the alternative action is competitive with its advocacy statement. The "For" speakers should explain why both their advocacy statement and the opportunity-cost position could happen at the same time. If it is possible to "do both" at the same time, then there is no opportunity-cost of doing the "For" advocacy. The "For" speakers should also explain why the alternative action presented in the opportunity-cost disadvantage is not as good as the "For" advocacy, that it will not solve all of the problems in the status quo, and that the "For" case will still be more beneficial. The "For" speakers can even present disadvantages to the opportunity-cost's alternative action in exactly the same way the "Against" presented disadvantages to the "For" side's advocacy statement.

Do not worry if all this structural argument refutation stuff is not super clear to you. Even people with several years of debate experience mix up some of this material. The ideas presented here are simply descriptions and names of some of the kinds of arguments that people will naturally make. Argumentative structure is simply a way of looking at how arguments interact with each other. The more easily a speaker can see the connections, the easier it is to come up with responses to any given argument. However, do not stop trying just because it is complex; present the best arguments that come to your mind, and maybe after the debate, think about how they related to the structures presented here.

PREPARATION

TEAMMATES

Compared to the panel debates, the largest difference in policy debates is the expectation that within partnerships teammates will work closely together to prepare for and engage in the debate. Partners should be ready to work together while constructing the arguments that they will use in the debate, and also be ready to divide up some of the workload. Though preliminary research might be conducted independently, once speakers are familiar with the topic, research

---

deterring crime." This statement would not go well with a "For" impact turn of the same disadvantage: "Controlling people though deterrence is too much social control; a police state will only breed more violence; people should be nice to one another out of love for humanity."

efforts should be closely coordinated so that participants function as a team and cover as much of the topic as possible without duplicating their efforts. Teammates should make sure to meet and prepare the ideas they plan to use in each debate. Before a debate starts, both people on the "For" side should have a clear idea of what the advocacy statement will be, as well as the advantages that will be used. Both "Against" teammates should know what disadvantages will be presented, as well as having an idea about what responses will be used to refute common "For" arguments. A well-coordinated team will be able to respond to the particulars of an individual debate more flexibly, and they will be more likely to have a fun and educational debate. Everyone has her or his own strengths and weakness; teammates who work together will be able to maximize their respective strengths and minimize their weaknesses.

RESEARCH

Just like panel debates, policy debate requires a great deal of preparation. Unlike panel debates, participants debate both sides of the topic in policy debates, and thus must be able to argue from both sides of the topic. Switching sides and preparing with the knowledge that they will have to cover the opposite side of the topic will help participants understand the terrain of the issue better. By knowing the arguments that could be used against their positions, advocates can better tailor their arguments to be successful in the debate. In researching, speakers should first cast a wide net and get familiar with the topic. It is important for participants to have a holistic understanding of the topic before they begin to narrow their focus and develop their specific arguments.

After some basic research, speakers should work with their partners to pursue specific ideas within the topic that they think will provide the best arguments for each side of the debate. The topics in policy debate reference issues that are very complex, and there will be many different proposals in the research literature about what the best approach to a given problem may be. There will also be a plethora of different attacks made on changing the way that government policy deals with the issue. No debate can cover all parts of the topic, so speakers have freedom in looking for the parts of the issue on which to focus. In this second phase of research, participants develop their advocacy statement and look for the best advantages to support their plans of action.

There will always be many advantages to choose from, so speakers need to be thoughtful in selecting which advantages they will purse with in-depth research in crafting their "For" case. In the second phase of research, participants should narrow down the arguments they will use on the "Against" side of the topic; like the "For" speakers, they will have several options to choose from, and they need to exercise their best judgment in selecting the arguments that they anticipate using in their debates.

In competitive debate leagues that use a policy debate format, research is never-ending throughout the competitive season. Debaters are constantly refining their arguments, augmenting the ideas they use with the arguments they hear from fellow competitors that they find compelling. Though students using this text will not be debating for an entire season, they should still do a little supplemental research in between debates, especially if they see classmates use an argument that they find particularly interesting and useful.

SPEAKER DUTIES

Many of the duties of each speaker in a policy debate are similar to the duties of speakers in panel debates, with some modification and redistribution between the speeches. Many of the new ideas and all of the new argument structures for policy debates have already been presented, so this section, which provides instructions for each speech, is less thorough than the explanations presented for the panel debates. It should not be assumed that there is less need for fulfilling the duties of every speech; rather participants need to understand the roles presented here and incorporate the material already presented.

FIRST "FOR" CONSTRUCTIVE

The first "For" constructive speech needs to lay out the "For" case. The speaker needs to frame the topic, provide definitions, background information, the criteria for the debate, and the advocacy statement. It is important that speakers sign post throughout their speeches. When providing definitions, speakers should make sure that they have clearly explained why their team has chosen to define the topic in a particular way. In policy debates there will be multiple advocacy statements available to the "For" team to choose from, and using definitions to narrow the debate will help to show why the team picked the particular position it advocates. Some of the information that would be provided in the background section of a first "For" speech in a panel debate is covered in the uniqueness section of the advantages used in the policy debate. Speakers should spend a little less time developing their background section, and focus on explaining any information that is necessary to understand the advocacy statement that their team uses. It is still very important that the background present some of the problems of the status quo; speakers just want to avoid redundancy when they present their advantages. The information presented in the advantages should be specific to the advantage, whereas the information provided in the background should cover the breadth of the topic. The criteria should be clearly presented and should segue into the advocacy statement. The "For" team's advocacy statement is the focus of the debate, and it must be clearly presented; speakers may want to repeat it once or twice so that everyone in the debate is clear on what the "For" team is proposing.

After framing the topic, the first "For" speaker needs to present the advantages that will accrue from adopting the advocacy statement. Advantages are the primary way that the "For" team shows why its advocacy is a good idea, and that the topic should be supported, so a significant amount of time should be devoted to explaining them. Speakers should anticipate spending three to three and a half minutes developing their advantages, and they should have two or three advantages. As with the panel debates, having either too many or too few advantages in the first speech should be avoided. Finally the speaker should conclude the speech and emphasize the importance of the benefits gained from the advantages supporting the advocacy statement and thus the topic. If possible, the first speaker should anticipate some of the likely arguments that their opponent will bring up and offer pre-emptive responses.

FIRST "AGAINST" CONSTRUCTIVE

The first "Against" constructive speaker has duties in the policy debate format that are similar to the duties of the same speech in the panel debates: the speaker must clash with the "For" case, attacking the advantages and background arguments, and present major opposition arguments via disadvantages. Policy debate focuses on the details of creating and implementing a new policy, with the benefits and drawbacks discussed in greater specificity. The topics are highly contested issues within society, so there is often a great deal of highly developed specific argumentation for participants to research and present in their speeches. With this level of detail, participants should focus on exploring the arguments that are brought up in the first speeches for each team, and refrain from adding large new arguments into the debate later. Thus it is very important that the first "Against" speaker present the vast majority of the big arguments that the "Against" side will use in the debate in his or her speech, so that those arguments have time to become highly developed through the course of a debate. Where panel debates are more about breadth of argumentation, policy debates are a bit more focused on the depth of the issue.

Speakers should provide a quick introduction to their speech, highlighting a thematic reason why the "For" case, and thus the topic, should be rejected. The "Against" speaker will provide clash and disadvantages in his or her speech. Depending on what the "For" speaker argues, the "Against" speaker may feel that presenting disadvantages first is beneficial, especially if one or more of the disadvantages will be part of how the speaker clashes with the "For" case. In other debates, the first "Against" speaker will find that refuting the "For" case first will be the most logical order for her or his speech. The "Against" speaker has a great deal of freedom in deciding how to best use their speech time, and, depending on how the advantages and disadvantages in the debate interact, the allocation of time in this speech can vary widely from debate to debate.

When providing clash and refuting the "For" case, the speaker should address how the debate was framed. As in the panel debates, if the speaker feels that the debate has been framed unfairly, or unclearly, he or she should provide some brief analysis of their objection, but then also move on and engage the arguments that have been presented. Each advantage offered in the "For" case is potentially an independent reason why the advocacy statement will provide more benefits than harms, so it is important that the first "Against" speaker clash with each advantage. Often the majority of the first "Against" constructive is devoted to developing the disadvantages the "Against" side will use to show that the "For" advocacy statement causes more harm than benefit. The speaker should try to present as much of the "Against" case as possible in this speech; the second "Against" constructive will focus more on filling in any missing pieces to the "Against" arguments as opposed to providing new material for the debate. Finally, a conclusion will help the "Against" team tie its arguments together.

SECOND "FOR" CONSTRUCTIVE

There are two basic functions of the second "For" constructive speech: to defend and advance the "For" case, and to respond to the "Against" disadvantages. Similar to the panel debates, after the first two speeches, the organization that is best for each subsequent speech is dependent on what has already been presented in the debate. The second "For" constructive speaker should use her or his judgment on how to best organize the speech. After a brief introduction, the speaker should clearly roadmap and explain whether he or she will first cover the "For" case, or the "Against" disadvantages. Unlike the panel debate, the speaker rarely presents new advantages; rather the speaker looks to more fully develop the benefits of the advocacy statement that the "For" side has already introduced into the debate. That said, the speech is a constructive speech, and speakers should feel free to present new arguments and ideas into the debate, but only if the situation calls for it. Clear sign posting throughout the speech is necessary so that the debate stays organized. Speakers should have prepared for and be ready to respond to the common arguments that the first "Against" speaker presented. While researching the topic before the debate, it is important for the speaker to brainstorm ideas for responses to the common arguments that support the opposing side of the topic, and have specific notes prepared to respond to those common arguments. Speakers should be flexible in integrating their prepared arguments with the ideas that come into their heads during the debate.

When advancing their team's case, the second "For" speaker should delve deeper into the reasons why the advantages from the adoption of the advocacy statement show that a change to the status quo will be beneficial and why the topic should be supported. Additional examples or comparisons to past actions are valuable as explanatory tools for this speech. Historical and present-day examples are powerful arguments in that they provide empirical evidence that the advocacy statement will work, or that the arguments the "Against" side presents are unlikely to occur. The second "For" speaker should look for places where the first "Against" speaker failed to provide strong refutation against the "For" side's advantages, emphasizing any points that have been conceded.

It is very important that the second "For" speaker cover the disadvantages offered by the "Against" side. Each disadvantage could potentially provide an independent reason why the "For" advocacy statement should be rejected, so leaving one of these arguments unaddressed is very dangerous. A speaker does not have to attack all of the points in a disadvantage, but should rather look for a few weak links in the chain of logic that is presented. Allocation of time in this speech can vary widely, depending on the debate, and it can be difficult for a speaker to effectively answer all of the disadvantages presented, so the speaker must make wise choices about where they spend their time. The speaker should conclude the speech strongly, perhaps offering some impact comparison to show why the advocacy statement will be more beneficial than harmful.

SECOND "AGAINST" CONSTRUCTIVE

The two basic functions of the second "For" constructive speech are similar for the second "Against" constructive, but again the outlook of the advocate is different. The speaker must defend and advance the disadvantages presented by the previous "Against" speaker, and continue the attack against the "For" case. It is unusual for the speaker to present new disadvantages in this speech, but as it is a constructive speech, new arguments, ideas, and examples are strongly encouraged. Organizationally the speech can be developed with the speaker's best judgment, but a clear roadmap in the beginning of the speech and good use of sign posts throughout the speech are critical for keeping the overall debate organized, as they keep the ideas in the debate clear for all participants. In preparing for the debate, the speaker can think about what the common responses to his or her team's disadvantages might be, and prepare responses.

Though covering the entirety of the debate that has occurred before the second "Against" constructive speech is important, the speaker can begin to think strategically. The "Against" burden in the debate is to disprove the "For" case, and by this point in the debate not all of the attacks the first "Against" constructive made will be equally useful in demonstrating that the "For" advocacy statement is a bad idea. Therefore, this speaker should focus time on the arguments he or she feels are working best for the team. Because this speech is the last opportunity for the "Against" team to provide new arguments in the debate, the speaker must make sure that all vitally important ideas have been addressed. Finally, the speaker should conclude the speech, and, as with the second "For" constructive, utilizing some of the impact comparison ideas can be a very powerful way of finishing the speech.

FIRST "FOR" REBUTTAL

The job of this speaker is often considered one of the more difficult jobs in this debate format, as the speaker has fewer minutes to respond to the last "Against" speaker. The first "For" rebuttal begins the process of slimming down the overall content of the debate. Although the speaker needs to address all of the major arguments in the debate, time constraints mean that some of the less significant ideas can be left unaddressed. The speaker must extend the advantages of the "For" case, and also continue the second "For" speaker's defense against the disadvantages. Though the speech is a rebuttal speech and should not have new arguments in it, the speaker can present new arguments if they are in response to ideas that were first presented in the second "Against" constructive. As the speaker has a great deal to accomplish in this speech, and as the nature of the arguments is very dependent on how the debate has progressed, the organization of this speech is again up to the best judgment of the speaker, but it is probably easiest to address all of the arguments concerning the "For" case together, and all of the disadvantages together.

The speech should begin with a very brief introduction highlighting the single most important reason to support the topic. The speaker should clearly roadmap the order in which he or she will address the arguments in the debate, and sign post clearly throughout the speech. Often at this point in the debate, there are a variety of issues being addressed and it can be quite complicated, so the more clear the "For" rebuttalist is in presenting his or her arguments, the more likely it is that the speaker's points will be viewed as persuasive.

Impact comparison is the new feature of this speech. Although some impact comparison may have occurred in the preceding two speeches, it is a vital action in the first "For" rebuttal, and in all subsequent speeches. As the speaker advances their case, they should be comparing the impacts of the advantages to the disadvantages and showing why they are more significant. While continuing the attack against the disadvantages, the speaker should continue to use impact comparison to show that the "For" advocacy will provide more benefits than harms. In concluding, the first "For" rebuttalist should reference the criteria, showing that when everything is taken into consideration, the "For" side will be an improvement to the status quo, and thus that the topic should be supported.

FIRST "AGAINST" REBUTTAL

To continue the back and forth nature of the debate, the duties for the first "Against" rebuttal are similar to those of the first "For" rebuttal. Again, the speaker's perspective relative to the topic is the major distinguishing feature. Though the second "Against" constructive could be strategic in allocating the team's speaking time to maximize the points that the "Against" team feels it is winning, the first "Against" rebuttal speech is where the "Against" team really focuses in on its major arguments against the "For" side. Organization of the speech is left up to the speaker, but clear roadmapping in the beginning of the speech and signposts when the speaker moves from one argument to the next are vital in keeping the debate organized. Finally, the speaker should keep in mind the time pressure that was placed on the first "For" rebuttal, and look for places where the previous speaker was unable to cover all of the "Against" arguments.

It is important for the speaker to show that there are several reasons why the "For" advocacy should not be adopted, but one primary reason should be highlighted in the introduction and conclusion. In between opening and closing the speech, the speaker should be looking to utilize the impact comparison ideas to show that the "For" advocacy causes more harms than benefits. The speaker should especially look for a way to include the criteria of the debate in her or his speech, to show that the "For" side has failed to meet these burdens.

SECOND "FOR" REBUTTAL

The last speech for the "For" side must really focus on why the advocacy statement should be adopted, thus showing why the topic should be supported. To do this, the speaker has two goals: first to show that more good than harm will come from implementing the advocacy statement, and second, to show that the negatives consequences presented by the "Against" side are overstated and insufficient to show that a rejection of the topic is warranted. At this point in the debate it is often good for a speaker to take a step back and look at the big picture of the debate. Before this speech, more than before any other "For" speech, it is a good idea to take some preparation time to think about what arguments need to be covered. The speech should break somewhat from the organization of the past debate, and focus on a few of the most important arguments. Up until this point in the debate, each speech directly answers many of the points made in the previous speech, but here the speaker may want to shake things up a little bit. It is still important to roadmap and sign-post so that people can track the arguments the speaker is referencing, but the speaker should feel free to move between arguments more fluidly. The speaker does not need to cover everything that has been said about a given argument—there were six previous speeches to do that—but should rather highlight the most important messages from each major issue in the debate.

The most important thing for the speaker to do is to reinforce thoroughly all of the benefits presented in the "For" case that will happen if the "For" advocacy statement is adopted. Impact comparison is vital, and often a speaker will present two differing future worldviews. In one future, the speaker describes how the advocacy statement will solve all of the problems of the status quo, and why the risks presented by the disadvantages will not materialize. In the second future world, the speaker shows how bad things will get, how the status quo will continue to deteriorate, and how people will continue to suffer if the advocacy statement is not adopted.

It is also important to be preemptive and to suggest why the likely arguments from the second "Against" rebuttal are not compelling enough to reject the topic. The more that a speaker can emphasize the weaknesses in the "Against" team's arguments, the more difficult the job will be for the final "Against" speaker. Remember that this is the last speech in the debate for the "For" side, so any point that might be important needs to be made in this speech; it is unwise to rely on the memories of your audience to recall a point that a speaker feels is important, but does not bring into this speech. A powerful conclusion will leave a lasting impression in all of the debate participants' minds, and also make it more difficult for the "Against" speaker to begin their speech.

SECOND "AGAINST" REBUTTAL

In a close debate, the difference in determining whether the topic should be supported or rejected is often the quality of the second "Against" rebuttal—the last speech in the debate. The function of the speech is very similar to that of the second "For" rebuttal, but the speaker does not want to follow the lead of the last "For" speech. It is important for the speaker to reshape the debate and try to make the audience of the debate forget all about what the "For" rebuttal just presented. To reshape the debate, the speaker should focus on a few of their most significant arguments to show why the advocacy statement, if adopted, will cause more harm than good. As in the second "For" rebuttal, this speaker should open with a strong introduction and provide a comprehensive conclusion. After a strong opening, the organization is up to the speaker, as long as the speaker clearly roadmaps and provides signposts during the speech.

The speaker should begin the speech with the main overriding reason why the topic should not be supported. After the powerful conclusion of the "For" side, it is important that the speaker change the climate of the debate quickly to favor their own side. The "Against" speaker is still defending the status quo as not being as bad as the "For" side made it out to be, but should concentrate mostly on how bad things will become if the advocacy statement is adopted. Impact comparison is the overriding function of the speech, and the speaker should be using those ideas throughout.

JUDGING AND SUMMARY

Policy debates should be fun and educational. The whole point of the debate format is to give participants a chance to role-play how the government works and how public policy gets crafted. In competitive debates, the judge typically decides who "wins" and "loses" based on the net-benefits of the advocacy statement. If more good will come from a change, the "For" side wins; if more harms will come from a change, the "Against" side wins. Participants should gain an understanding of the sophisticated argument techniques that separate a "heated argument" from an "educational debate." Working with a partner, an advocate will gain a better appreciation for how different people approach different issues and express their ideas. By the end of the policy debates, people should feel prepared to enter into the real world and express their ideas and opinions with conviction. There are innumerable issues that need to be addressed in our society today, and almost everyone has an issue that he or she feels close to; policy debates should help people see how to effect change regarding the issues about which they feel most strongly.

CHAPTER 15

ARGUMENTATIVE WRITING

Argumentative writing is no simple task. As with virtually any craft, writing is a rather diverse enterprise offering vastly different methods and techniques to choose from for any given task. Just as there are a myriad of successful verbal argumentative techniques and styles, practitioners of exposition have great individual freedom in constructing their persuasive texts. Each writing project must be approached individually, with care paid in tailoring the final product to the specific needs of the given objective of the piece. While there are broad themes between successful examples of different types and styles of writing, every specific writing form has its own particular instruments and mechanisms that are necessary for a high-quality end product. Writing for argumentative purposes is no different, and practitioners must be conscious of the goals of their project, and the tools that are best adapted for those specific needs. The first part of this chapter will address some fairly general elements and conventions of effective writing, with the more specific elements of argumentative writing coming in the latter portion. However, even general writing guidelines are quite relevant, as a paper that is difficult to read due to errors in grammar, punctuation, syntax, etc., also make the author's argument difficult to follow and thus less persuasive. In argumentative writing, you want your reader paying attention to your arguments, not your misspelled words and poor grammar.

EASY MISTAKES[113]

Some basic usage concepts should be universal throughout different writing styles and bear some consideration. This section goes through some of the easy mistakes that are commonly made during the writing process. Yes, many are very basic, but readers would be surprised how frequently they are present. Some potential explanations are: the overreliance on the auto-correct feature on most word processing programs that may not always be right; students are too busy/lazy to be careful while writing or proofreading; some people made it though their primary and secondary schooling without learning these fundamental skills; writing is not easy and mistakes get made. Your authors feel that is it probably a combination of the above causes; nonetheless, a quick refresher may be helpful.

GENERAL STYLE ISSUES

Effective writers will develop a style in their usage of language that is individually unique. It is important that writers include their own voice in their writing and personalize their texts. However, there are some general style guidelines that are common in most examples of successful writing. For many this information will simply be a review, but for some, the particular items mentioned here will be new. The style recommendations provided here are not as hard and fast as typical grammar recommendations, but writers who wish to

---

[113] Sources consulted for the creation of the following section:

- drgrammar.org, a project of the University of Northern Iowa, http://www.drgrammar.org/faqs/. A fantastic resource that should be pursued for more helpful hints

- Oxford American Dictionary

deviate should have a specific reason for doing so. If you are already an accomplished writer you will be able to recognize when your specific writing style trumps general recommendations.

SENTENCE STRUCTURE AND SYNTAX

Every word in a given sentence should have its own purpose, and each sentence in a paragraph should accomplish a unique task. Effective writers examine the construction of each sentence and look to make sure that their idea is presented as clearly as possible. The most common problems with undergraduate sentences are syntax issues; sentences that are not completely incorrect, but could be expressed more cogently. Effective writers look for ways of expressing the thought of a given sentence in a simpler but more concrete manner. It is important that the sentence is fluid and precise, it is not sufficient to simply express an idea; rather there should be no way to be more specific or clear in the explanation of the idea. One of the more common reasons that the syntax of a given sentence needs work is that one or more words in the sentence are not the best word choices.

The computer is perhaps partially to blame here for poor word choice, but it is also a desire to impress that can result in inappropriate vocabulary. The word that is best for any given task is the most specific word, not the biggest, fanciest, rarest, or most impressive. Students often rely on the thesaurus function of the word processing program that they use and will select the words that are more complex or unique. The problem is that the thesaurus program is not aware of the context of your writing, and will not make sure that the connotation of the new word fits into the sentence appropriately. Specifically, if the computer suggests a word and you do not independently know what the word means, simply do not use the suggested word. Thesauruses can be very valuable while writing as a brain-storming tool, but it is vital that the writer is making informed choices when using one.

Two kinds of mistakes that are easy to recognize while proofreading a paper but difficult to see while writing are sentence fragments and run-on sentences. There are many different ways of explaining how to identify these two common mistakes; what is important is that writers have an understanding of these problems, not necessarily that they memorize rules. Sentence fragments or incomplete sentences usually are dependent clauses that have been separated from the main clause with a period. Often the easiest way to correct sentence fragments is to combine the fragment with the last sentence using a comma or semicolon. Conversely, run-on sentences most often attempt to combine two related but subtly different ideas. Too many commas or "ands" are often the sign of a run-on sentence. These types of sentences are usually fixed by breaking the sentence into two, with each individual idea expressed as its own sentence. Occasionally the run-on sentences can be corrected utilizing a semicolon or even a colon.

The best writers use a variety of sentence structures and mix them throughout a given piece of writing. Papers that contain only simple sentences will have a monotonous rhythm. Papers with only complicated sentences will be difficult to read, as each idea is tied to several others in each sentence. Writers should look for ways of breaking up the pattern of sentences that they have in their written product, mixing long and short, simple and complex sentences to achieve a smooth voice and flow in their writing.

PUNCTUATION AND PARTS OF SPEECH

Semicolon and colon usage is often tricky for some writers. Semicolons should be used when a writer is combining two closely related independent clauses. Colons are used before a list of ideas in a sentence. When a concept is introduced and several examples will be presented in support of the concept, colons can be useful to separate the concept from the list of supporting examples or ideas.

Writers should be careful while using prepositions and pronouns so that the concept that they are referencing is clear to the reader. Prepositions connect nouns, pronouns, and phrases. Many paragraphs and some sentences contain several different nouns, pronouns, and verbs, and prepositions can be confusing when two or more ideas that they are linking are not explicit. Pronouns can be a great source of ambiguity and confusion in writing, as they are used as a shortcut replacing a noun or noun phrase. Effective pronoun use makes writing smoother as it provides an author a way to avoid repeating ideas that have already been expressed. However, they need to be used with care; there should be no question as to which noun the pronoun is referencing. If a pronoun could be taken to represent more than one noun, the sentence probably needs to be changed so that the reference is clearly representing only one noun, or the pronoun should be eliminated and the original noun reintroduced for clarity.

FORMALITY

Even undergraduate papers are an academic enterprise and should be treated as such. The writing style should be formal. While few undergraduate papers are intended for publication, the level of formality necessary for professional publication should be a goal of every paper you write while in college. Writers should assume that their audience is reasonably well-educated and open to persuasion on your chosen topic. Your paper is not a conversation with a friend, nor even a conversation with your instructor, but rather a presentation of considered and refined ideas. While editing, writers should avoid a conversational tone and shift their paper into a more refined voice. At the same time, writers should not produce material that is not within their natural language inventory, but rather strive to write at the very highest level within their capabilities.

Colloquial expressions should be avoided in most applications—creative or dramatic writing being obvious exceptions. Colloquial expressions are words and phrases that are commonly used in informal conversation that rely on a reader's understanding of the cultural space the writer inhabits. Such expressions are rarely understood according to some universal consensus, and the writer runs the possible risk of their reader misunderstanding the phrase's intended meaning. Slang or popular expressions are the most common forms of colloquialism that appear in undergraduate writing, as well as terms or phrases that are unique to a regional dialect, such as the classic example of the different names that carbonated beverages have across the United States: "coke" in the south, regardless of brand or type of beverage; "pop" in the Midwest; "soda" in the Northeast and California; and a mix of "pop" and "soda" in the Pacific Northwest. A paper produced in any given part of the English world should easily be understood by anyone from a different English tradition. Finally, you might use and make up abbreviations when text-messaging a friend with your phone; a formal paper is obviously not the appropriate place for this.

TENSE SHIFTS

Verb tenses indicate when in time the idea or action occurred. In almost all applications, the tense of the verbs in a paragraph should remain the same. This rule is complicated by the many different tenses in English and can be violated in some specific applications when the writer is providing an example from the past and speaks of it in the present. Generally, however, switching verb tenses within a paragraph should be avoided. When tenses shift, subject-verb agreement in the sentence can become confused, and many pronouns and prepositions become unclear. Tense shifts tend to make the time sequencing of ideas in the sentence difficult or impossible to follow. For example, "John has a great job he does well, but the boss fired him and he is depressed." In the demonstration sentence when John is fired is confusing, and who is depressed is also confused. Tense shifts are most easily detected and remedied with careful proofreading.

PROOFREADING

The life of a college student is busy with many different diversions pulling on the attention of students and competing with academic work for their time. Students also recognize that most undergraduate papers are generally only read by two people, the author and the grader. With these two dynamics present, far too many undergraduates skimp on or even skip proofreading efforts. However, proofreading is perhaps the easiest way for writers to improve their papers and, as a direct result, the grades that they earn with them. Proofreading should ideally be done at some distance from the actual writing of the paper; authors should leave themselves time to pursue another activity before they revisit their papers. This down-time is important as it is often hard to spot some of the simplest mistakes when one has just finished writing. It is preferable if authors can "sleep on it" before proofreading, but even a couple hours' break will give the writer a fresh perspective on the paper and increase the likelihood that both simple mistakes, like typos, and more significant overall structural issues will be recognized.

It is also highly recommended that authors read their papers out loud while proofreading. When you are simply reading with your internal voice, your brain is more likely to gloss over small mistakes subconsciously. The brain is a miraculous and powerful tool that can have a mind of its own. Reading aloud forces the whole brain to engage. Reading and speaking takes more effort and involves more internal thought processes than simply reading, increasing the likelihood that mistakes are caught. Reading aloud helps writers detect concerns with the flow of the paper, such as when they have started too many sentences with the same words or when they have used the same word too frequently. A varied vocabulary in a piece of writing helps to improve the flow of ideas and makes the author appear to have a better command of their topic.

Word processing programs are fantastic tools that help authors avoid simple mistakes and produce better written projects, but there are a few things students should be aware of about these programs while they proofread. Many programs will auto-correct as the author writes; very common grammatical mistakes and misspelled words are fixed on the fly. However, the computer is not always right, and careful proofreading is the only way to correct these inappropriate corrections. Sometimes when the red line appears under a word and a person selects a replacement word from the pop-up choices, they will select the wrong word or have their mouse cursor slip. Either way, these mistakes can be difficult to see and are more easily caught with some distance of time from the writing of a paper and by reading aloud. Beyond simply misspelled words, the grammar auto-correct of many word processing programs is not always accurate. Grammar is complex and not all rules are universal. Students should certainly review any sentence highlighted by a grammar auto-correct function, but not necessarily follow the recommendations of the computer automatically if they feel that their original wording was preferable. The computer is far better at recognizing a mistake than providing a good correction; often writers will change sentences that were highlighted, but not necessarily in the way that the computer recommends.

STYLE IN ARGUMENTATIVE WRITING

The previous section provided recommendations that should work for any kind of writing; the next section will be more specific for argumentative writing. However, the advice offered in the following section is often applicable to other forms of writing as well and an author should look for ways of including the following recommendations in the other forms of writing in which they engage. Our overarching advice is to look for ways to make your writing more efficient; ideas should be expressed clearly and completely in the most direct way possible. Every word in a sentence, every sentence in a paragraph, and every paragraph in a paper should have a specific and unique purpose.

PARSIMONY

Many of you have probably heard the phrase, "less is more"; **parsimony** is perhaps the word best suited to describe this philosophy. Argumentative writing should express each idea efficiently with every word having a purpose and every sentence expressing a complete idea that uniquely contributes to the overall explanation of the concepts being addressed. A related word is "brevity," expressing much in few words. Authors should look to eliminate extra words in their writing without losing any meaning. In much undergraduate writing the author is reaching to puff up the overall length of the paper. Unfortunately this often makes a paper redundant, with the same concept explained several times yet without any new information presented. Reinforcing a concept by repeating it is not necessarily bad, just that each time an idea is revisited it should be presented with some additional information to strengthen the reader's comprehension of the idea.

PASSIVE WRITING[114]

Verb use is often difficult to master, and one way that poor verb use is easily identified in writing is passive verb forms. The passive voice most frequently occurs when the object of the sentence is made into the subject. For example "the lazy dog was jumped by the swift brown fox" as opposed to "the swift brown fox jumped over the lazy dog." In the above example the dog should be the object of the sentence and the subject should be the fox. Generally the use of the verb "to be" (is, are, was, were, most forms of "be" or "been") combined with a past participle will create the passive voice. A past participle is the verb tense that usually ends in "ed." Not all uses of passive voice are inappropriate, but in argumentative writing the more active the tone of the writing the more firm and persuasive it will be. Using the active voice creates more excitement in writing, projects a greater sense of confidence, and helps avoid unnecessary words.

While not necessarily tense shifts, beginning sentences with "But" or "And" can confuse the meaning of a sentence or paragraph. The general rule is that sentences should never start with these words, but in certain limited applications it can be appropriate. The risk is that a sentence starting with a conjunction will be a sentence fragment or run-on. However, English usage is changing, and the use of conjunctions to begin sentences is becoming more accepted. Authors should simply be careful when they have a sentence start with one of these words, and be sure that the reference that they are making to the past sentence is clear and cannot be understood in multiple (and confusing) ways.

QUOTATIONS

While the use of quotations in an argumentative paper is obviously quite useful, even necessary, in proving your point, many undergraduate students view

---

114 The following resource was consulted in the writing of this section and provides an excellent resource to further explore the difference between passive and active writing. http://www.unc.edu/depts/wcweb/handouts/passivevoice.html

quotations as a magic solution to stretch a paper into the length required for an assignment. We will be clear; an intelligent reader will easily spot this technique. Quotations should be used in argumentative writing, but only for a couple of primary reasons. Firstly, quotations are necessary when a writer is providing evidence that is not general knowledge and that is outside of the writer's knowledge. In this instance, it is important to give credit to the original source by properly citing the information conveyed. Secondly quotations should be used when a writer cannot express an idea as eloquently as their source author did. Far too often large and repetitive quotations are used to bulk up a paper, when the bulk that needs to be added is analysis and reasoning unique to the paper that can be supplied only by its writer. Quotations should be incorporated smoothly into the writing, and introduced if there is some context that is necessary to understand the snippet of outside writing that is included. When analysis of a quotation is undertaken, authors should be careful that they are not simply repeating the information provided in the quotation, but instead providing further content and assessment, and firmly anchoring the quotation to the rest of the material in the paper.

Block quotations should be used with extreme care. Different style guides have different formats for block quotations but generally if a quotation is four or more lines long it should be presented in a block quotation format. Long quotations that are not identified as block quotations can easily confuse a reader as they will often be written with a different style than the writer's own language and will create awkwardness. From a presentation perspective, block quotations are nice because they visually break-up what would otherwise be very long paragraphs.

PARAGRAPHS

The final style issue that should be addressed for argumentative writing is the length and purpose of paragraphs. Paragraphs should be the full explanation of a single major idea. In argumentative writing, each paragraph usually serves as a single, significant argument, and it must be introduced, supported, and concluded. In order to accomplish all three goals a paragraph must be at least four to five separate sentences: one sentence to introduce; at least two sentences to explain, analyze, reason, or otherwise support the idea; and a concluding sentence that also provides some linkage to the next paragraph. Conversely, effective writers also avoid paragraphs that are too long. Since a paragraph is ideally the expression of a single large idea, the most common example of paragraphs that are too long combine two or more major ideas into a single paragraph. In some applications the above comments about paragraph length can be ignored, but only when the writer has a very specific purpose.

STRUCTURE OF IDEAS IN ARGUMENTATIVE WRITING

PERSONAL PRONOUNS

Saying "I believe" is the most common use of a personal pronoun in argumentative writing. While we do not suggest that personal pronouns should never be included in argumentative writing, they are rarely necessary. Often personal pronouns lead a writer into using a passive voice. Direct phrasing is encouraged in argumentative writing, and including personal pronouns only distances the ideas being expressed. The ideas included in exposition should generally be universal ideas not dependent on the reader agreeing because the specific author holds them. The reader should be persuaded by the logic of the arguments, not because of who holds the opinion. When a writer is asked to give an opinion, direct phrasing should be used. Instead of "I believe global climate change is bad because it will impinge on the ability of all life to continue to live in its current habitat." Rather, while presenting such an opinion a writer should directly phrase their ideas, "Global climate change is bad because . . . ."

ANECDOTAL EVIDENCE

One specific use of personal pronouns is the inclusion of personal anecdotal examples, "my friend once had this happen to her..." While there is little consensus amongst practitioners of persuasive writing concerning the utility of personal stories, it is perhaps a useful general guideline to avoid them, or at least not to become overly reliant upon them. Most argumentative papers should be aimed at a universal audience, and the supporting evidence should not be dependent on individual context. Personal stories are true in a limited sense, and the experience of a person the author is familiar with may not be demonstrative of the experiences of the "average person." Writers are often tempted to substitute analysis that completely supports a given principle with a general anecdote "this bad thing happened to a person in Missouri; therefore we need to drastically change the law for everyone." The writer could further their point more completely by describing the general issues that could result in problems for people, rather than assuming that the one example they provide is universal. Such generalizations run a very high risk of being fallacious in nature.

However, this general rule can reasonably be violated in some specific contexts. When the anecdotal example is the only practical application of the idea being discussed in a paper, it will probably add valuable evidence without the risk of being an outlier example. The academic community has recently begun to more thoroughly examine the use of narratives in argumentative writing. From the academic perspective a narrative is a fairly specific concept; for practical purposes it is the inclusion of a literal dictation of another person's experience or the direct retelling of an experience of the writer's. Narratives can be very powerful as they can explain the individual consequences of a given idea, but should most likely be used only when they provide greater clarification to an idea that could not be provided in another way. Narratives should almost never be the only example of a phenomenon, but rather should used as a supporting example of a widely occurring circumstance.

QUESTIONS

Questions, even rhetorical ones, should be avoided in argumentative papers unless the writer is skilled at using them. Questions are a passive way of expressing an idea and most questions can be eliminated with a simple rephrasing of the question into a statement or observation. Occasionally a question that exists in the world outside of the paper can be presented and analyzed in an argumentative paper, but often these can be included without directly asking a question of the reader, for example, "society is faced with a decision, should nuclear weapons be eliminated?" could be presented "the utility of nuclear weapons in the world today had been questioned, with many advocates believing that they should be eliminated." Most questions in undergraduate writing are literally asking the reader a question; this is dangerous, as the writer has no control over the perceptions of the reader. Rhetorical questions are not really questions, but rather a way of presenting an argument. They are questions that are asked, not because the writer is unsure of the answer, but rather because the writer hopes that by being forced to answer the question in their head, the reader will have a realization concerning the point imbedded in the question. In the context of the spoken word, where there is an exchange of ideas and multiple opportunities to present and explain information, rhetorical questions can be strategically used to highlight the ramifications from holding a particular opinion. In writing, however, there is no back and forth, no opportunity for further analysis or explanation. A writer lacks the context typically provided by a verbal exchange to frame their question; they do not know how their reader will react. In spoken argument, the advocate can better predict how the target of their question will react. When people read argumentative papers they may be inflexible; if the author is unsure of how the reader will react, then the special utility of a rhetorical question is lost. The reader may simply disagree, and then the argument has lost its persuasive appeal. In very specific circumstances, skilled writers can use rhetorical questions effectively, but until other writing techniques are mastered, for most undergraduates, all questions should be avoided.

PAPER STRUCTURE IN ARGUMENTATIVE WRITING

Most of the papers written by undergraduates are responsive to a specific assignment that has constraints on length. Writers should carefully take the limitations imposed by the assignment into consideration, purposefully selecting the ideas that are necessary for fulfilling the objectives of the assignment. For any given paper there are many potential points that could be included, but writers need to realize that not all of the material that could go into a paper should be included. Writers must remember to fully develop all the points that their papers address, and be conscious of the room that they have available to develop their content.

CLARITY IN STRUCTURE

The strongest argumentative papers are clearly structured; with the way that they are composed, and the ideas presented, reinforcing the overall conclusions being drawn. Generally the paper and its topic must be introduced. In the first paragraph or two the writer should demonstrate how they will cover the content required by the assignment and introduce the topic they will be exploring. Within introducing the paper, any contextual information that is necessary to understand how the topic is relevant to the assignment should be presented. With space for analysis at a premium, introductions should be efficient and not occupy more of the overall length of the paper than is necessary. Argumentative papers should also include a clear thesis statement in their introduction. Usually a thesis should be contained in a single sentence, but for some assignments the writer is asked to demonstrate several different things and in this circumstance more than one sentence may be appropriate. The thesis component should be a statement, or statements, of how the writer will demonstrate the required components of the assignment, and should be as clear and specific as possible. Introductions that also provide an explanation of the overall structure of the paper are usually the strongest.

After introducing the topic and offering a thesis statement, the writer should devote the vast majority of the remaining space to the "body" of the paper. The organization of the body should have been highlighted in the introduction and it is important that the writer conforms to the structure that they present. Each idea in the body section of the paper should be fully explored in an individual paragraph. By the end of the body section, the conclusion that the writer drew in their thesis section should ideally be supported in multiple different ways. While supporting the conclusions they are drawing, the writer should recall the material developed in this book concerning the use of evidence and reasoning. The application of evidence and reasoning is slightly different in spoken argument when compared to written argument, but the methods and techniques that are useful in either endeavor are applicable in both forms of argument.

The final overall structural piece in argumentative writing is a strong conclusion. The conclusion is the final opportunity for the writer to hammer home their points. The conclusion serves two purposes: to remind the reader how the thesis has been proved, and to reinforce the structure of the paper. The first task is the more important one and writers should look to highlight the content of their paper in a way that combines all of the points discussed into an overarching conclusion. Simple redundancy should be avoided, with the ideas recapped in a slightly new way. The second task of the conclusion is still very important. The macro internal structure of the paper should be modeled in a micro way. The beginning of the conclusion should reflect the introduction and the writer should connect and refresh all of the major ideas presented in the body of the paper in order. The last sentence or two should provide the ultimate conclusion of the paper and should be a representation of the thesis statement/s.

TOULMIN MODEL IN ARGUMENTATIVE WRITING

As previously mentioned in this text, Stephen Toulmin developed his model of an argument with exposition in mind. Writing is a time-consuming process that should not be rushed; authors should leave themselves time to be considerate in the construction of their texts. The Toulmin Model may not be the best model of an argument in the specific confines of a debate, but for argumentative writing it is invaluable. Writers who intentionally monitor their advocacy with regard to the Toulmin Model will find their end product more complete and persuasive. While proofreading their argumentative paper, writers should verify that each major argument that they present conforms to the Toulmin Model and that the paper as a whole addresses all parts of the model.

The Toulmin Model can be applied to the individual arguments that make up a paper and also to the entirety of the paper. To refresh the model, the three parts of an argument that are vital are claim, grounds, and warrant. The claim should be presented clearly, as it is the point that the argument is attempting to prove. The grounds are the pieces of evidence (data, facts, reasoning) that are used to support the claim. The warrant/s show why the grounds prove the claim true, often supplementing the rationale provided. All arguments within the paper, and the entire paper itself, should have all three elements. Writers should construct their outlines with these principles in mind and check their work throughout the writing process to verify that they are presenting fully developed arguments.

Your authors feel that the second triad of concepts in the Toulmin Model is critical for crafting the best argumentative papers. Providing backing, qualifier/s, and reservation/s strengthen a paper by providing that answers to the most common objections that could be raised against the paper. Backing further supports the warrant provided; in the context of a paper, it is the additional examples, facts, or analysis that solidifies the reasoning used to support the claim. The qualifier indicates the limits of the argument's applicability, making the author appear more credible as they recognize the boundaries of their argument. Reservations bring up the likely points of dispute that could be raised against the argument that is presented. A paper is a static artifact, it is not amended or added to while it is being read, so strong writers will bring up and dismiss the points that an opponent to their position might make to counter their arguments.

The Toulmin Model is complex and not all writers will be able to easily use it to improve their writing. Your authors suggest that you try, but learning to write well is a process that demands practice, so do not worry if you are having trouble applying the entire model to your writing. Just make an effort and reflect on how you can incorporate the model into your future writing if you get stuck.

CONCLUSION

In most regards, the advice offered in this chapter should be understood as being flexible. The diversity of ways of effectively approaching writing is far larger than the number of possible approaches to spoken argumentation. If writers have a specific reason to diverge from any of the above recommendations they should thoughtfully pursue their own paths. It is often said that, "once a writer understands the rules, they are ready to break them." There is likely some truth to this saying, but the critical part is in the first half of the sentence, not the latter half. The development of strong writing skills takes time, and successful writers have practiced a great deal. Perhaps the most important lesson for effective writing is to spend an appropriate amount of time in the process; do not rush it. A corollary to this bit of advice: every word, sentence, and paragraph should be thoughtfully considered and chosen with care. Care while planning, executing, and proofing any given paper will undoubtedly strengthen the final product.

GLOSSARY

Active Listening: A method of responding that elicits additional information and emotions from a speaker.

Administrative Orbiting: Occurs when a problem is acknowledged as existing, but no serious action is taken.

Advantage: The name of the "For" sides contentions in policy debate. Advantages should the benefits that would be accrued if the "For" advocacy statement is passed. The argument structure has three parts: uniqueness, link, and impact.

Advocacy Statement: The action or belief the "For" team will defend throughout the debate; it must be stable. It is a single set of words that clearly explain how the "For" team thinks the problems highlighted by the topic should be solved.

Against: The debate team that is opposing the statement that is being debated. Also known as "negative", "opposition", or "challenger"

Analogical Reasoning: More simply known as "extrapolation" this type of reasoning is a strategy which assists thinkers in matching similar patterns of data from one area to those in another.

Analogy: To make a comparison between two cases and infer that what is true of one case is also true of the other; a type of reasoning.

Analogy, Figurative: A comparison between two or more items that are of different types, classes, or categories. Children are like birds, they need freedom to fly.

Analogy, Literal: A comparison between two or more items of the same type or category. Literal analogies often provide useful proof as the point of comparison is similar.

Anecdotal: Evidence or examples based on or consisting of observations made by the advocate which may or may not be representative of common phenomenon.

Argument: 1) A heated exchange where people are yelling at one another.
2) A reasoned discussion.
3) A point or idea presented in a discussion to convince another.

Argument Structures: Different ways of organizing ideas into one or more complex arguments. Often information can be presented in a predetermined way so that the totality of the argument being made is more significant.

Assertion: A claim, proposition or idea that is communicated with the desire to convince others of a given belief or truth.

Assertive: The extent to which an individual attempts to achieve his or her own personal goals and interests, potentially subjugating what might be best for "the group". The term can be contrasted to cooperative when considered under dominant conflict management styles.

Autocratic Leadership: May occur when a conflict, particularly one viewed as a crisis with the need for an immediate response, gives rise to a strong, decisive leader thought to be more capable of responding to the conflict than relying on a slower and perhaps less-qualified response of democratic participation.

Backing: Provides additional support, analysis, and credentials for the reasoning behind the warrant (Toulmin Model).

Body Language: The complex set of gestures and movements that humans consciously and unconsciously display during communication activities.

Burnout: Occurs when an individual is overworked, and may actually result in a net decrease of productivity in the long run.

Case: The points that the first "For" speaker advances in support of their side of the topic. The speakers teammates will continue to support and defend the "case" throughout the debate.

Categorization: A process by which a person classifies ideas as belong to a particular group due to the presence of certain attributes which are characteristic of that group; it tends to speed up the thinking process. A matching skill.

Causal Reasoning: Also known as "cause and effect", causal reasoning is used to indicate that a certain force (the cause) is directly responsible for something else (an effect).

Causation: When one variable has a direct effect on another variable or "causes it"; different from correlation.

Character Assassination: An attempt to discredit someone's credibility or reputation.

Claim: The basic premise that the advocate is asking his or her audience to accept (Toulmin and Common models).

Closed Body Position: A general way of situating a person's body where the person is closed and not accepting communication. Often arms are crossed, facial expressions may be hostile, and the person generally appears inattentive.

Coercion: The use of physical force, or alternatively the threat of such force. Normally used in decision making by an external actor interested in shaping the outcome of the decision.

Cognition: Comprises human self-awareness and the ability to rationalize the information provided by the senses to logically and predictably interact with the physical and nonphysical worlds.

Colloquial Expressions: Words and phrases that are commonly used in informal writing and spoken words that rely on a reader's understanding of the cultural space the author comes from.

Common Argument Model: The argument model that is simpler than the Toulmin Model and easier to use in live debates. The model suggests that arguments have three parts: Claim, Warrant, and Impact; and is sometimes called a "Complete Argument".

Conflict: A situation and or an emotion which exists whenever incompatible activities or agendas occur. It can originate internally within a single person (**intrapersonal**), externally between two or more people (**interpersonal**), within a single group (**intragroup**), or between two or more groups (**intergroup**).

Conflict, Behavioral: Conflict in which one group or individual does or says something that may be deemed unacceptable or objectionable by another individual or group.

Conflict, Cognitive: Transpires when one group or individual holds opinions and beliefs that are inconsistent with those of another group; often seen in the case of debates over political or religious issues, where opposing groups hold competing values.

Conflict, False: Are differences that are substantively irrelevant to maintaining a healthy relationship or work environment for both individuals or groups.

Conflict, Goal-oriented: Occurs when one group or individual desires a different set of outcomes than another, and can concern material and immaterial matters.

Conflict, True: Is something that would tend to escalate and result in greater negative consequences if not resolved.

Conflict Management, Accommodating: A person's willingness to meet the needs of others even at the expense of his or her own individual interests.

Conflict Management, Avoiding: A tendency toward avoiding conflict could be the result of either denial—simply refusing to acknowledge that conflict exists in the first place, or suppression—while not fully denying its presence a person downplays a conflict's importance and goes to extra effort in order to steer clear of it whenever possible.

Conflict Management, Collaborating: Views conflict itself is seen as being neither good nor bad in and of itself, but is seen rather as merely a symptom of the underlying tension in a relationship that should be treated accordingly.

Conflict Management, Competing: Views the differences between individual people that are seen as the central and most important issue in the conflict.

Conflict Management, Compromising: Holds the view that differences between people should be resolved in a manner that prioritizes the common good rather than individual advancement.

Consensus: A procedure for determining what is best for the group as a whole. The decision is rarely the first preference of any individual member, and many may not even like the final result, however the decision is made through consultation and all parties can accept it.

Constructive Cognition: Either the creation of entirely new thought patterns and associations or perhaps considerably restructuring existing ones. The process can involve both problem-solving and exposition.

Constructive Speech: A speech in the beginning part of a debate where speakers are adding new ideas and arguments into the debate for consideration. Advocates are constructing their arguments in support of or in opposition to the topic.

Contention: A grouping of many smaller points that all support one larger idea or argument. An organizational argument structure used by the "For" side in a debate.

Cooperative: Refers to the degree which an individual attempts to satisfy the concerns of others. The term can be contrasted to assertive when considered under dominant conflict management styles.

Correlation: When variables change together. Just because the variables change together, causation has not been determined, correlation could be the result of an outside factor.

Counter-case: The points that independently support the "Against" sides ground underneath the topic. While not directly clashing with the "For" case the counter-case will often include points that show why the overall topic should be rejected.

Counter-contention: Just like a contention for the "For" side, a counter-contention is the name of the argument structure used by the "Against" side to group many supporting points into one large and comprehensive argument.

Covert: Action or expression that occurs indirectly or with the purpose and or means obscured.

Clash: Also known as "The Burden of Rejoinder". Each side of a debate has an obligation to respond to and counter the arguments that their opponents have advanced. Clash is a word used to describe this process.

Credentials: Qualifications of expertise offered in support of testimony style evidence presented by an advocate.

Criteria: Also known as a criterion. The decision making tool used in a debate. The criteria is a filter that suggests which kinds of arguments should be prioritized when the topic is being considered. Similar to a rubric, or metric, or weighting mechanism.

Cross-examination: The specific name of the question period in policy debates. The name is a reference to the question period in United States courts where attorneys can question the whiteness of their opponent.

Culturally-specific Decision Making: Utilizing cultural practices to shape the decisions that people make. There is great diversity among cultures on the globe, so too is there an accompanying variety in the decision-making techniques that are practiced in those cultures.

Data Conflicts: Occur when people lack the necessary information to make accurate decisions.

Debate: A form of argument that has strict rules of conduct, follows a structured format, and uses sophisticated arguing techniques.

Debate Community: All of the members and former members of competitive debate leagues. While not a monolithic entity, people still feel a strong connection to the group.

Decision-making: The act or process of reaching a judgment or conclusion.

Decoding: The process a listener goes though while translating and processing observed communication, the second step a listener goes through.

Deductive Reasoning: The relative opposite of causal reasoning, deduction is the application of a general principal to a specific instance. Also known as reasoning from generalities.

Definitions: In argument, clear demarcation and clarification of terms and ideas can be important, and definitions can clarify the context of terms to be used in communication. Part of providing evidence for an assertion is to clarify what exactly is being supported.

Deliberation: The careful, thorough, and intentional consideration of competing arguments.

Deliberation Process: Typically involves consultation with others in order to more fully consider and explore the numerous perspectives and interpretations of evidence brought forward to support competing positions.

Dialogue: An open-ended exploration of ideas, with very few rules. Group members must suspend previous assumptions, treat each participant equally, and facilitators are common to keep the conversation smooth.

Diaphragm: The muscle (more accurately the band of muscles) that separates the lungs from the digestive tract, and it is critical for respiration.

Disadvantage: An unintended consequence will show that significant problems not currently happening will occur if the "For" side's advocacy statement is adopted. In the policy debate format, the argument structure is even more specific containing three points: uniqueness, link, and impact.

Discussion: The presentation of thoughts and ideas in a group situation where everyone analyzes and dissects them from his or her own particular point of view. The most common form of argument and decision-making that people engage in.

Distortion: A factor that affects listening, Distortion is a mental defense mechanism when a person's mind changes a message that he or she might find distasteful into something more pleasant or acceptable.

Division of Ground: In a debate there must be at least two reasonably balanced opposing sides to the topic with plausibly defensible arguments on either side of the question.

Dominant Conflict Management: Most people have developed preferred ways of dealing with conflict. These preferences coalesce over time to become an individual's dominant conflict management style.

Double Turn: When two or more arguments advanced by a speaker clash with each other creating a contradiction in the ideas being presented.

Due Process Inaction: Also known as bureaucratic inaction, is an effort to force the less powerful party to give up prematurely by using procedures for addressing a grievance that are so time-consuming, complicated, expensive, or risky, that the procedures wear down the opponent in the conflict.

Effect-to-cause Reasoning: A type of reasoning by sign where an effect or observable outcome is examined and potential causes analyzed, like when a doctor looks at swollen glands.

Elaboration: When a listener must actually supply some of the necessary information for themselves to process an idea being communicated. Elaboration is the process of inferring information which was not explicitly stated.

Encoding: The process a speaker will go through while translating his or her intention into specific words and phrases, the second step a speaker goes through while communicating.

Ethos: One of Aristotle's levels of proof. "Of good character," ethos refers to the level of credibility a person has with her or his audience.

Evaluation of Logic: Is a process of checking newly received information against an individual's existing internal system of logic, whether innate or learned.

Evidence: The support, provided for an assertion or claim. Can take many forms: facts, data, quotations, examples, statistics, esteemed opinion, rational justification, etc.

Examples: A way of providing evidence in support of an assertion or claim, examples are the presentation of a similar situation or occurrences to be used as demonstration of the likely outcome of a contested situation.

Exit Response: Entails either a physical or psychological withdrawal from a conflict situation.

Exposition: The practice of creating new information in order to more effectively express an idea or position. In the context of writing: expressing and explaining a concept or idea with the attempt to convince or clarify the material for the audience.

Expositional Rhetoric: Is that discourse which explains or describes a concept more fully in order to enhance its persuasive effect.

Expressing: When a person literally verbalizes their communication, the final step a speaker undergoes while communicating. After expression the speaker often becomes a listener.

External Distraction: A factor that affects listening. Any external event that can grab a listener's attention and shift it from the communication he or she was previously engaged in.

Fallacy: A flawed form of reasoning or logic and an argument which uses flawed reasoning or logic is said to be fallacious. It is quite possible that the reasoning will initially seem to be valid, but upon further reflection is found not to be.

291

Fiat: A Latin phrase literally meaning "let it be done" and often used in reference to a sovereign's will or the will of a political leader. In policy debate it is an assumption that participants debate the outcome of a proposed advocacy statement, not if it is likely to be adopted by the status quo.

Flow: The way that people take notes in competitive debate. The flow is a visual map of the arguments made by all participants in a debate, and serves as an organizational tool. Sometimes called flow sheets.

For: The debate team that is in support of the statement that is being debated. Also known as "affirmative", "proposition", "the government", or the "proponent".

Formal Logic: The study of logic focused heavily on formal elements of reasoning, such as the evaluation of syllogisms, the use of model and proof theories, Venn diagrams and Boolean indicators, and a host of other fairly methods.

Frame: The process where one side (usually the "For" side) explains what the topic means and how they will proceed to demonstrate that their side is the correct side of the topic. May also be called framing.

Framer/s: The person or people who craft the topic for a debate.

Ground: A phrase used by debaters to describe the spectrum of available arguments for each side of the topic.

Grounds: The information that is used to support the Claim – often evidence or data – used in the Toulmin Model.

Group Cohesion: A common response to conflict wherein external threats cause a group to set aside their internal differences and become more cooperative.

Hearing: Inactively or reflexively absorbing noise. A physiological process, but not a psychological one.

Hierarchal Conclusion: A "top-down" decision made by an authority figure with the power to dictate an outcome.

Impact, argument model: The last part of the common argument model, this point suggests that if the statement is true that it is also significant, it answers the "so what".

Impact, policy debate: Is the big benefit at the end of the day from solving the problem the "For" team's advantage covers. It is also the really bad thing that will occur according to the "Against" team's disadvantage.

Inductive Reasoning: The examination of a series of particulars (examples) in order to form a general conclusion. Also knows as reasoning through induction.

Informal Logic: Focuses on such things as basic reasoning, the discovery of fallacies, and critical thinking. It is a way to question and analyze arguments for their relative levels of validity. Informal logic is most often used when engaging in argumentation theory and analyzing rhetoric and discourse.

Intention: The idea a speaker wishes to get across to the listener when she or he communicates, the first step a speaker goes through while communicating.

Internal Distraction: A factor that affects listening. Any number of thoughts or conditions, which lead to a person's mind wandering.

Interpersonal Decisions: Decisions that are made with at least one or more other person involved in the process.

Interpretation: The third step a listener undergoes in communication. The decoded communication is analyzed and situated with any other knowledge the listener has concerning the context of the communication.

Interviews: Also known as personal observation, interviews can be offered up as evidence by an advocate.

Intrapersonal Argument: A factor that affects listening. Another reaction to controversial messages, or to just a statement with which we personally disagree, is to anticipate the conclusion or goal of the message before actually hearing it and to begin a discussion of the issue inside our own heads.

Intrapersonal Decisions: Decisions that take place internally or without the involvement of another person.

Irreversibility: A tool for impact comparison that suggests that problems that can never be reversed or fixed should be considered as the most important.

Jargon: Specialized vocabulary used in specific communities. Often jargon is a shortcut or simplification used to communicate complex ideas that members of the community are already acquainted with.

Judicial Ambiguity: Is a conflict that emerges when it is unclear exactly where responsibility for an issue or a certain action lies.

Link: The second part of an advantage or disadvantage that connects the advocacy statement to the impact. Why the proposed advocacy will fix or cause a problem (depending on if the argument is used for an advantage or disadvantage).

Listening: Actively absorbing auditory communication directed at oneself. A physiological and psychological process.

Logical Fallacy: Any one of the many different patterns of flawed reasoning Greek and Roman philosophers identified and categorized.

Logos: Rational and analytical support offered for a claim, such as statistics, scientific data, definitions, etc. One of Aristotle's levels of proof.

Loyalty Response: Involves the continued maintenance of a personal or professional relationship, despite the presence of challenging differences.

Magnitude: A tool for impact comparison that suggests that the size of a problem should make it more or less significant compared to other potential impacts. The largest potential benefits or problems should be viewed as the most significant.

Majority-rule Conclusion: A decision made through a voting mechanism where participants are able to express their preferences, and the most common preference is accepted.

Matching Skills: Enable a person to determine how newly received information and concepts are either similar to or different than those concepts and data which are already stored in long-term memory.

Mirror Neurons: Neurons present in primates and most likely in humans that fire in conjunction with the neurons that control physical actions. These neurons also fire when an animal witnesses the physical actions of another animal potentially forming the base for mimicry and empathy.

Mnemonic: A memory technique which uses a system of acronyms, rhymes, unusual phrases, and other means to help in the recall of specific data such as facts and figures or perhaps historical sequences.

Monotone: The quality of a speaker's delivery when few if any changes are made to the quality of the sound being produced. Speaking in a flat, even, and boring manner.

Narratives: The inclusion of a story or example that highlights an individual experience.

Neglect Response: Involves a basic denial of conflict. It is an inactive response form that simply ignores whatever the problem may be in the hope that it will somehow go away on its own.

Net-benefits: A common criteria used in policy debates. The criteria suggests that all the potential benefits and drawbacks of a given advocacy statement be compared, and if there is an overall (net) benefit from adopting a change then the team proposing the change should win.

Neutrality: While listening, keeping an open mind is important so that messages are not prejudged. Speakers will suppress or alter communication if they feel it will be reacted to harshly.

Non Causa Pro Causa: The specific Latin name for a Correlation vs. Causation logical fallacy, when one event is suggested as the cause of another when the two events only occurred in proximity.

Non Sequitur: Latin for "the conclusion does not follow" The support offered for a given conclusion is irrelevant.

Objectivity: Although it must be recognized that total and complete impartiality at all times is virtually impossible for any human being possessing even minimal cognitive function, this does not mean we should not question a source's biases and subjectivity

Observation: The first step when listening to communication, collecting the communication.

Open Body Position: A general way of situating a person's body where the person is open and ready for communication, arms are open, the face and eyes are visible and the person is ready to listen.

Open-ended Question: One way to actively listen is to ask a question which allows a speaker to elaborate or provide more detail concerning a specific idea.

Opportunity-cost: A type of disadvantage that suggests that pursuing the "For" advocacy will make it less likely or impossible for a better solution to be pursued latter. Also called an alternative action, or a counter plan, the idea can be presented with a counter advocacy statement so that exactly what opportunity is lost can be debate.

Overt: Action or expression that occurs directly or with the purpose and or means transparent.

Panel Debate: A format of competitive debate that focuses on bringing together a diverse set of experts to share their ideas on a topic and critique the ideas of their associates. Usually there are 5 or 6 participants, but the format can be expanded to accommodate more or less participants.

Parsimony: The idea that less is best. In terms of writing, expressing an idea parsimoniously would entail accurately describing a thought in as few words as possible.

Pathos: One of Aristotle's levels of proof. Pathos is the use of an audience's emotions, such as sympathy, fear, or romance, in an effort to motivate their beliefs and/or behaviors.

Personal Space: The area close to a person that people feel is theirs to be used exclusively. Also know as a personal "bubble", when violated people feel crowded and uncomfortable.

Pitch: Is where a sound made during communication falls on the tonal register, commonly expressed as how high or low (deep) the sounds being made are.

Preparation Time: A limited amount of time within the policy debate structure for teammates to consult each other and get ready for their next speech. The preparation happens in the middle of the debate between speeches.

Policy Debate: A debate format that is centered on public policy analysis. Commonly used in high school and college competitive debate league, teams of two people debate a topic preset for the whole year.

Probability: A tool for impact comparison that suggests that the most likely impacts should be considered as the most important impacts. The certain risk of a bad thing is more significant that the teeny tiny risk of a really bad thing.

Problem-solving: The process of discovering new information and/or developing a strategy to achieve a desired outcome or to overcome a particular challenge.

Proof:
1) The establishment of a claim's validity through the use of evidence and/or reasoning; the objective demonstration of factual truth.
2) Not necessarily based upon a clinically objective verification, but rather on the much more subjective consideration of persuading an audience in terms of their beliefs or behaviors.

Qualifier: Explains when the argument is applicable, and recognizes the relative strength of a given argument (Toulmin Model).

Quarrel: A hostile dispute or altercation between two or more people; a fight.

Random Decision Making: Also referred to as uncontrolled decision making. These decisions involve little or no reasoning, but are rather left up to mere chance.

Reasoning: The capacity for logical, rational, and critical thought; to use sound judgment in drawing inferences or conclusions.

Rebuttal Speech: A speech in toward the end of a debate where advocates are refining the arguments that have already been presented. Speakers refrain from bringing up new ideas, and instead respond to and develop the points their side and their opponents have raised in the debate.

Reflection: A way to actively listen also known as paraphrasing. A listener can summarize what a speaker has communicated and check with the speaker to see if they have understood the speaker correctly.

Refutation: To argue against or counter points made by an opponent. Responding to and dismissing the ideas your opponent has advanced.

Reservation: Also called "The Rebuttal" by some. Reservations suggest that arguments are not universally true, but rather should be applied to the situations that they fit (Toulmin Model).

Response: The final action a listener undergoes during communication. The listener becomes the speaker and follows through the same three steps.

Rhetorical Questions: A statement that is phrased as a question where the answer is already presupposed by the framer of the question. Not inquisitive, but rather a way of making an argumentative point.

Roadmap: A statement at the beginning of a debate speech that identifies the order that the speaker will address major ideas within the debate. Used to help participants organize their "Flows".

Round: One individual debate. At competitive debate tournaments, many rounds are held culminating in the "final round".

Selective Exposure: A factor that affects listening; people tend to seek out that discourse with which they agree and avoid that with which they do not.

Sign: A type of reasoning were one infers a relationship or correlation between two variables, where the absence or presence of one variable indicates the absence or presence of the other, "If we can see smoke, there is fire".

Signposting: Labels speakers used to show which argument in the debate they are referring to during their speech. Signposts are quick organizational comments provided throughout a speech so that all observers are on the same page.

SPAR: Spontaneous argumentation and refutation. A short debate format with two participants speaking twice each.

Spiritual Decision Making: Also referred to as mystical decision making. Decisions where a person turns to an outside metaphysical source for help some form of spiritual guidance for assistance.

Stage-fright: The feeling that most people have when addressing an audience. For some the feeling can be so overwhelming as to make delivering vocally for an audience an impossibility.

Statistics: The numerical expression of knowledge useful for providing a quantitative and potentially "objective" justification for claims.

Status Inconsistencies: Are based on relative degrees of authority and power, and they may result in conflict under such situations as a manager who takes extra time off and arrives to work late.

Status Quo: Latin for "state in which". For debate it is a term to describe the way things are now, the current reality of things, or what the situation is like before an advocacy would go into effect.

Storage and Retrieval Skills: Enable a person to transfer information both to and from long-term memory. While focusing on the information being evaluated, the thinker associates it with information that is already in long-term memory.

Tabula Rasa: Latin for "Blank Slate" the idea that all past knowledge of the world is held out of a debate judges mind so that they can concentrate on the points and ideas made in the debate by the debaters.

Testimony: The process of quoting or paraphrasing the words of another person or group.

Timeframe: A tool for impact comparison that suggests that the timeliness of impacts should be considered first.

To Argue: To engage in an exchange of ideas centered on a common subject matter.

Topic: The idea or phrase that is debated. Also known as "the motion", "the resolution" or "the matter at hand".

Topic Education: The knowledge that participants in a debate hopefully gain about the topic being debated. Often topic education is a critical factor in how topics are chosen and why people continue in competitive debate.

Toulmin, Stephen: Author of The Uses of Argument published in 1958.

Toulmin Argument Model: The Argument model which contains: Claim, Grounds, Warrant, Backing, Qualifier, Reservation.

Turn: A kind of argument that can be used by both the "For" side and the "Against" side. An opponent's argument is accepted as partially true, then the speaker shows that as a result of the argument being "true" their side is actually supported. The argument can be further specified as a "link" turn or as an "impact" turn depending on which particular kind of argument an advocate is accepting from their opponent.

Two Ships Passing in the Night: A colloquial debate expression that references a debate where there is little or no clash. In other words that participants of the debate present ideas supporting their side of the topic, but the interaction of those arguments and points is never made explicitly.

Two-way Exchange: For communication to occur, ideas must be both expressed and received.

Uniqueness: The first part of an advantage or disadvantage, the point describes the status quo and sets up why the advocacy statement will uniquely affect the way that things are in either a positive manner (for and advantage) or a negative manner (for a disadvantage).

Visual Imagery: A storage and retrieval skill where a person creates a visual representation for the information which is to be remembered, or alternatively, may recall an existing visual image to be used in testing new information.

Voice Response: Happens when an individual directly challenges the issue at hand by openly vocalizing his or her feelings.

Warrant: 1) The principle(s) and/or provision(s) that show that the grounds provided are appropriate proof for the claim being presented (Toulmin Model).
2) The "Why" or "Because" of an argument. The reasoning and analysis that supports the claim and links it to the impact in the Common Argument Model.

INDEX

WORKSHEETS

WORKSHEET #1: TOULMIN MODEL

This worksheet should help you develop an argument using the Toulmin argument model. In the spaces below, come up with your own argument and provide each part called for. You do not need to be extensive; a sentence, two or three should suffice.

CLAIM: the premise of the argument, what you are trying to prove 'true' or have accepted by the receiver of your argument.
Example: "The sky is blue."

GROUNDS: the evidence or data used to support the claim, part of the "because".
Example: "Humans perceive the sky as blue because of the way that light is absorbed and reflected by molecules in the atmosphere."

WARRANT: the reasoning connecting the claim to the grounds, why the grounds explain the claim.
Example: "Scientists have measured the different absorption properties of the dust and gasses in the atmosphere and have also measured how the brain interprets different wavelengths of light as colors. The wavelength of light that is most absorbed and then reflected is the blue wavelength."

BACKING: additional support for the warrant used and why it is appropriate.
<u>Example:</u> "Scientists are best able to study and analyze why natural phenomenon occur and explain the physical reasons behind observations."

QUALIFIER: limits to the claim, or the conditions when the claim is "true".
<u>Example:</u> "Sometimes the sky appears to be grey, yellow, orange, red or a color other than blue. This is not the average color of the sky, but rather occasions when other atmospheric conditions intervene with the usual appearance of the sky."

RESERVATION/S: presenting and then answering potential counter points that receivers of the argument may bring up.
<u>Example:</u> "Some might say that the sky is usually grey around the Puget Sound, but those are clouds in the sky, not the sky itself. Others might say that the sky is blue because God made it that way, while this might be true, science provides a more detailed and empirically verified explanation as to why it is blue."

WORKSHEET #2: COMMON MODEL

This worksheet should help you develop an argument using the Common argument model. In the spaces below, come up with your own argument provide each part that is called for. You do not need to be extensive; a sentence, two or three should suffice.

CLAIM: the premise of the argument, what you are trying to "prove".
Example: "The sky is blue."

WARRANT: the evidence, facts, reasoning and analysis that supports the claim, the "because" or "why".
Example: "Humans see the sky as blue because of the way that light interacts with the atmosphere and is absorbed and reflected. The blue part of the electromagnetic spectrum is most interactive with the atmosphere and thus lends the color blue to the sky's appearance. Scientists have done many simple and fancy experiments to empirically prove this true."

IMPACT: the "so what", why if the claim is true it is significant or important.
Example: "Since the sky is blue, airplanes should not be painted blue so that pilots are better able to see other aircraft and avoid midair collisions that could kill many people."

WORKSHEET #3: ASSUMPTIONS AND BIASES

Instructions:

Read the story then answer the questions below. Discuss the answers with your group.

The Story

A businessman had just turned off the lights in the store when a man appeared and demanded money. The owner opened a cash register. The contents of the cash register were scooped up, and the man sped away. A police officer was promptly notified.

Indicate whether you think the following statements are:

T – True   **F** – False   **?** – Uncertain

	T	F	?
1. A man appeared after the owner had turned off his store lights.	☐	☐	☐
2. The robber was a man.	☐	☐	☐
3. The man did not demand money.	☐	☐	☐
4. The man who opened the cash register was the owner.	☐	☐	☐
5. The storeowner scooped up the contents of the cash register and ran away.	☐	☐	☐
6. Someone opened a cash register.	☐	☐	☐
7. After the man who demanded the money scooped up the contents of the cash register, he ran away.	☐	☐	☐
8. The cash register contained money, but the story does not state how much.	☐	☐	☐
9. The robber demanded money of the owner.	☐	☐	☐
10. The owner was middle-aged and of Asian ancestry.	☐	☐	☐
11. The robber was a young, unemployed "drifter".	☐	☐	☐
12. The police officer was a man.	☐	☐	☐
13. The following events took place: a man demanded money, a cash register was opened, its contents were scooped up, and the man ran out of the store.	☐	☐	☐

Offer a brief (2-3 sentence) answer to each of the following questions:
1. What is an assumption and why do we make them?

2. Are assumptions a positive or a negative thing?

3. What are biases and where do they come from?

4. Why do we hold on to our biases?

5. What are the negative consequences of holding on to our biases?

6. What are the positive consequences of holding on to our biases?

7. What are some biases that you have?

8. How do your biases affect your life?

9. Do you want to change any of your biases? If yes, how would you go about doing so?

WORKSHEET #4: FALLACY MATCHING

Match the most appropriate type of fallacy to each of the statements below:

1. Hasty generalization   2.Appeal to popularity   3. Post hoc, ergo proctor hoc

4. False dichotomy   5. Complex cause   6. Coercion

7. Ad hominem   8. Begging the question   9. Straw person

10. Slippery slope   11. Appeal to fear   12. Deductive fallacy

13. Appeal to tradition   14. Tu quoque   15. Red herring

__ Patriotic Americans will support the flag burning amendment.

__ We know God exists since the Bible says so, and the Bible is the word of God.

__ I asked my friends what they thought of the new budget restraints and they all

     thought it was a good idea, so it must be a popular decision.

__ Because illegal immigration from Mexico has increased significantly over the past

     two decades, we now have millions of people on welfare.

__ You can't accept anything Bill O'Reilly says—he's just a hyper-conservative nut job.

__ You had better agree with the new company policy if you expect to keep your job.

__ Polls show that the republicans will win the election in California, so you might as

     well vote for them.

__ Drunk drivers kill many innocent children each year therefore random police

     roadblocks to check driver licenses are needed.

__ If the UN wants the US to pay its dues, it had better approve the resolution on Iran.

__ I saw several cars almost hit pedestrians today on campus so there must be a

     problem with the drivers on campus.

__ All compassionate Americans will agree that we must reevaluate the death penalty.

__ America: love it or leave it.

__ If we pass laws against fully automatic weapons, it won't be long before we pass laws on all weapons, and then we will begin to restrict other rights, and finally we

will end up living in a communist state.

__ We should not believe President Clinton when he claims not to have had sexual

relations with Monica Lewinsky. After all, he's a liar.

__ Your Australian friend stole money from my wallet. It just goes to show you that

Australians are thieves.

__ By leaving your oven on overnight you are contributing to global warming.

__ If the factory were polluting the river then we would see an increase in fish deaths.

Fish deaths actually have increased, so the factory is polluting the river.

Name: _____

Date: _____

WORKSHEET #5: ARTICLE ANALYSIS

Answer the questions below for any article of your choosing on a controversial topic.

Source/Title:

_____

1. **Motivation**: What are the author's main reasons for writing the article?

2. **Purpose**: What is the main purpose or intention of the article?

3. **Focus**: What is the key issue or question the article addresses?

4. **Concepts**: What are the primary conceptual elements presented in the article?

5. **Assumptions**: Does the article make any assumptions or assertions that are taken for granted rather than explained?

6. **Data**: What are the main bits of information used to support the author's claims?

7. **Sources**: Where is the information in the article coming from?

8. **Consequences**: What consequences are likely to follow if the ideas and concepts in the article are accepted/rejected?

Name: _____

Date: _____

WORKSHEET #6: BODY LANGUAGE

Complete the following questions utilizing both your text and the website listed below.

1) Name three ways that physiology affects the way humans process communication:

2) Why can standing while speaking improve a person's delivery?

3) What are mirror neurons and why are they important?

4) Go to www.changingminds.org, and direct your attention to the section on body language. What are two things you did with your body to maximize your communication in your debates?

5) Find three parts of the body that the website analyzes and consider your most recent in-class debate. How could you have maximized your communication utilizing your body differently?

6) The process of socialization teaches most people all sorts of body language, often without being directly addressed. Humans will pick up on the mannerisms of others that are most effective. What have you picked up?

7) Try practicing the things you learned from changingminds.org by engaging yourself in a SPAR debate in your bathroom mirror (to avoid embarrassment make sure to lock the door and do this at a time when your roommates are not home).

CPSIA information can be obtained
at www.ICGtesting.com
Printed in the USA
LVOW02s0943180716

496547LV00007B/24/P

9 781615 492664